Odyssey of Terror

Best wishes always...

Capt. Wm. R. Haas

Ed Blair

Memphis Tenn.
Aug 22. 1977

ODYSSEY OF TERROR

Ed Blair
with Captain William R. Haas

Broadman Press
Nashville, Tennessee

4279-08

ISBN: 0-8054-7908-2

Dewey Decimal Classification: 364.1

Subject Heading: HIJACKING OF AIRPLANES

Library of Congress Catalog Card Number: 77-072886

Printed in the United States of America

Dedication

To the men and women
who fly the world's airliners

The name of the passenger who was a Delta Airlines stewardess has been changed to protect her right to privacy.

Acknowledgment

Numerous people made valuable contributions to this book. However, one person in particular, a writer, former journalist and television colleague Carol Ippolito, provided indispensable assistance and inspiration, for which the author is extremely grateful.

Preface

This is a story that emerges in detail after more than three years of research and interviews. Its revelation finally lifts a veil of secrecy formerly imposed, mainly by airline Captain William R. Haas, in the public interest. The commercial air carrier for which the captain is a veteran pilot continues to maintain its official position of silence five years after the incident occurred.

It is a story about an air piracy—the most death-defying, prolonged, and bizarre hijacking to have ever taken place in the annals of United States aviation history. A dramatic adventure that involved hundreds of people at the time, it subsequently affected millions of others.

Ranging the gamut of human emotions, from outlandish and sometimes macabre humor to stark terror, it is also a chronicle of raw courage on the part of Captain Haas, whose devotion to the principles of the airman's creed was most exemplary throughout.

As a direct outgrowth of this piracy, Cuba ended a long-standing practice of affording sanctuary for criminals who engaged in skyjackings. Following close on the heels of this incident were other long-overdue developments that brought to air travelers a high degree of protection against the likelihood of being hijacked. Security measures that are commonplace today at the nation's major air terminals and stringent new antihijack legislation were adopted soon after this odyssey took place.

The men, women, and children of this incident were pushed to the limits of their mental and physical endurance by their three armed and depraved captors. For thirty hours the hostages and crew were forced on a crisscross journey that took them over the eastern United States, Canada, Cuba, and the Atlantic Ocean. The ending of the ordeal can only be described as a truly astounding miracle. People throughout the world watched and prayed while the unfolding drama involved the White House, the Atomic Energy Commission, the Federal Aviation Administration, the Royal Canadian Mounted Police, the Federal Bureau of Investigation, countless local law-enforcement agencies, the United States Navy and Navy Reserve, the Coast Guard, and the United States Air Force.

Of great significance is the fact that this skyjacking became the turning point and stemmed the tide against successful armed United States air piracies.

The United States Justice Department officially impounded recorded ground-to-air communications with the hijacked aircraft. This action was taken when the author made a formal request for the tapes under provisions of the Freedom of Information Act. Government attorneys representing the Department of Transportation withheld the tapes, contending that public disclosure might jeopardize the rights of the hijackers to a "fair trial or an impartial adjudication."

However, the air-to-ground communications included within the text are authentic. They were obtained by the author from various other sources in the United States and Canada.

Every effort has been made to present this story to the reader without revealing specific security information or measures whose disclosure might tend to be detrimental to the air-traveling public or the airline flight personnel.

ED BLAIR

Atlanta, Georgia

Contents

Odyssey of Terror

1
Takeover

With each step Alvin Fortson leaned heavily on his walking cane as he moved along the concourse of Memphis International Airport terminal. He was a frail, elderly gentleman from Arkansas, and the walk to the distant departure gate of Southern Airways Flight 49 seemed long to him. A granddaughter, Bertie Mae Blassingame, had driven Fortson to Memphis from his home at Trumann. She walked with him to the gate where they could say goodbye.

Nearing the designated departure point, Fortson realized the futility of resisting any longer. He had pleaded with his family to let him make his usual bus ride to Haines City, Florida, where he could spend the winter and fish with his son, Calvin. They wouldn't approve. The length of the trip, combined with his failing health, might prove too strenuous for a man of his advanced years.

Fortson had never been on an aircraft during his eighty-three years. He had not contemplated such an adventure at this stage of his life. Until the idea of flying to Florida came up, he had looked forward to the pleasant prospects of viewing the countryside once again from the window of a moving bus. Besides, the ground conveyance was more nearly suited to his life-style. Aboard a bus he would find his kind of people—the kind with whom he could talk. As a former row cropper, he would feel uncomfortable among people who could afford to jet here and there. At least those were the arguments he had used in opposing the flight.

Entering the gate area, he was more convinced than ever that flying was out of his character. Fortson asked his

granddaughter about a group of about sixty people, men
and women, who were wearing funny-looking hats and
waving red and white triangular pennants. She explained
that they were football fans going to Birmingham. The next
day's game pitted Alabama against Louisiana State University in a battle that would decide the Southeastern Conference championship.

Fortson concluded they had to be rich to be able to fly to
a football game!

It would be another fifteen minutes before boarding
time. The old man and his granddaughter sat down in one
of the scooped-out plastic chairs. He had never sat in such a
chair and couldn't decide whether it was comfortable.
Neither could he understand why the chairs were linked
together. Surely no one would want to steal one. He hoped
the seats aboard the aircraft were more comfortable. The
airline should know about his straw-bottomed chair. They'd
be sure to like it better.

In addition to the football revelers there would be seventeen other passengers boarding Flight 49 at Memphis for
various destinations—Birmingham, Montgomery, Orlando, and finally Miami.

Sixty-six-year-old Mary Melton, a retired schoolteacher
and grandmother from Jonesboro, Arkansas, was traveling
to Montgomery to spend the upcoming Thanksgiving holi-
days with a daughter, Elizabeth, and her family.

Marge Brennan, pretty, blonde mother of seven, was en
route to Montgomery. With her was a fourteen-year-old
son, Patrick. They were going to attend the Southeastern
Charity Benefit Horse Show. Marge's husband, Bill, was
already riding in the show; and their four-year-old stallion,
Delight's Easter Gold, was expected to capture the coveted
blue ribbon in his class. The Brennans lived in a fashion-
able Memphis suburb, Germantown.

Banker Jack Eley was returning to his home in
Montgomery from a business trip to St. Louis.

Ecie Welch, Jr., had been in Tennessee making arrangements to move his family from Montgomery.

Vivien Didien and her two-year-old son, Keith, were going to Orlando to visit Mrs. Didien's hospitalized father.

Navy recruits Ira Lee Echols, David J. Forward, and Derrek O. Isaac were Orlando-bound.

Memphis steel company executive Robert S. McDonald had business to conduct in Montgomery.

Auburn agronomy professor Gale Buchanan was returning home from a meeting of educators in Memphis. He and his wife were to entertain dinner guests later in the evening.

Dick Senft, a restaurant chain executive, was en route to his Orlando home from a Memphis business conference.

Refrigeration plant manager Luther Waller had been to Wisconsin on business and would be glad to get back to his family in Montgomery.

Rounding out the passenger list would be sales representative John Witucki of South Bend, Indiana, and Taylor Bryant of Selma, Alabama.

The airliner would be carrying a full load of seventy-five people from Memphis.

While the passengers waited to board, Flight 49's captain, William R. Haas, chatted with his first officer, Harold Johnson, and flight attendants Donna Holman and Karen Ellis, in a nearby crew lounge. They waited for the servicing of their DC-9 to be completed out on the ramp. The tail section of the airliner displayed the fleet numbers 904.

Haas had arrived two hours ahead of the scheduled flight-departure time. A man of impeccable grooming, the captain got a shoeshine and a haircut. Then he picked up copies of the company's latest revisions to its Flight Operations Manual, inserting them in their proper places among the pages of the thick book. A stickler for detail, he demanded the same conscientious performance from others on his flight crew.

Up at 6:30 on that morning of November 10, 1972, Haas had spent most of the day with his wife, Ann, their two-year-old daughter, Betsy, and four-year-old son, John, and a visiting brother, Ed, shopping for acoustical ceiling tile in

Memphis. The material was needed for their 1834 Victorian house, known as Twin Gables. The Haases were restoring their home at historic La Grange, fifty miles east of Memphis. They occupied the dwelling while doing much of the renovating themselves, as time and money permitted.

Advised that the DC-9 was serviced and ready for boarding, Captain Haas told his crew, "Let's go—we've got some time to make up."

They walked the short distance across the concrete stand to the parked jetliner. All went aboard except for the first officer, who conducted the required visual inspection of the aircraft.

Passengers were released at the gate and began mounting the steps to be checked aboard.

Alvin Fortson and his daughter exchanged good-byes, and the elderly man took his place in line.

Once all were aboard and seated, the front loading steps were retracted and the cabin door was closed and secured.

While the plane was taxiing away from the ramp toward the assigned takeoff runway, Donna spoke into the microphone, extending the customary "Welcome Aboard," reminding the passengers to observe the "No Smoking" and "Fasten Seat Belt" signs, demonstrating use of the emergency oxygen masks, and announcing the expected arrival time of 7:00 P.M. at the first stop in Birmingham.

Sleek and swift, the blue and white twin-engine jet lifted off of the runway. The twinkling lights of the city merged rapidly into a soft glow and disappeared as the aircraft climbed steeply on its bulletlike trajectory while banking off on a southeasterly course.

Somebody among the partisan football fans shouted, "Go Alabama—we're number 1." A deafening chorus of yells echoed from the crowd.

Jack Eley reached overhead and turned on his reading light. He opened the cover of a new paperback about college football.

Mary Melton thought of her husband, who was at a deer

camp in South Arkansas. She hoped he would have a good hunt. Undismayed by her horoscope, which said it was not a good month for her to travel, she relaxed in her third-row seat on the left.

Alvin Fortson was discovering the exhilarating sensation that comes with one's first flight. The view from the window was like none his eyes had ever beheld. A gleam of purple sunset reflected off of the wing. He marveled at the aircraft's interior: the comfortable high-backed seats with their multicolored upholstery, the plush carpet, the fold-down eating trays, the bewildering set of buttons and vents above his head. He thought flying wasn't so bad after all. And there was certainly more whooping and hollering than he had ever encountered on a bus.

In Birmingham, Frank Morkill, a forty-eight-year-old management consultant with Miami-based Donahue, Groover, and Associates, glanced at his watch. Having been in an all-day conference with a client, Frank had been forced to cancel flight reservations for an earlier departure. Now he would have to make a hurried drive to the airport to be on time for Flight 49. It would be his last chance to make a planned Friday-night rendezvous with his wife, Nancy, and their three daughters. They had driven from their Miami home to Orlando, where the family would take in a weekend at Disney World.

Morkill was one of thirteen passengers holding reservations to board the flight on the second stop of its southward journey.

Marcia Timbers thanked her mother for the ride to the airport. A vivacious twenty-two-year-old brown-haired native of nearby Homewood, Alabama, she was going to Miami to begin her work week as a flight attendant with Delta Airlines. Miami was her home base, and she had a flight to work out of the Florida city at three o'clock the next morning.

Also converging at Birmingham Municipal Airport was financier Arthur Tonsmière, Jr., a resident of Mobile. He had been in Birmingham on business and was returning to Montgomery, where he would join his wife, Elaine, at the horse show.

Alex Halberstadt, management engineer for a large new hotel under construction in Birmingham, was eager to spend the weekend with his wife Dottie at their home in Key Biscayne.

Bruce Barnes, a businessman from California, awaited the arrival of Flight 49, which would take him to Miami for a connecting flight to San Juan, Puerto Rico.

Frank Robinson of St. Petersburg, Jerry Menke of Orlando, and Richard J. Wanklyn of Miami sat together in the terminal building's cocktail lounge. They had formed a partnership for the distribution of a water purification device manufactured in Birmingham. They were returning to their respective homes.

Charlotte Watts, a ticket agent with Eastern Airlines, had been in Birmingham for a visit with relatives. She had attempted to fly back to her home in Orlando early that morning, but there had been no space available. Her luggage had gone on the earlier flight.

Fred Cherney, one of Miss Watts' fellow employees, also was returning to Orlando. They were riding on pass privileges and would find space available on Flight 49. As a matter of fact, there would be forty-five empty seats out of Birmingham.

All of the Flight 49 passengers—with the exception of Morkill and three others—had checked in at the Southern Airways ticket counter.

Aboard the inbound aircraft, Donna and Karen were busy picking up food trays and cocktail glasses. Captain Haas had begun his descent from cruise altitude as the forty-minute first leg of the flight neared its intermediate destination. First Officer Johnson would take the controls for the next leg as the two crewmen alternated to relieve the stress and fatigue that accompanies the piloting of high-speed jets.

Frank Morkill had his usual Friday-night upset stomach as he strode through the terminal lobby to the Southern ticket counter. He had to have his ticket revalidated. *Have I made it in time?* he wondered. Morkill stood behind a big black man who was leaning over the ticket counter and talking to the agent. Another black man was purchasing a ticket at the adjacent position. Morkill's business involved extensive traveling. He made it a practice to observe people. The man in front of him rested his weight on a cane. *Probably a wounded veteran,* Frank thought. Then his brain numbed with fright as he overheard a question put to the black man by the ticket agent.

"Emphatically no," the man answered.

Frank dismissed the question from his mind. He had likely misunderstood the agent, a result of his Friday-night jitters. He was relieved to hear the agent tell the man that the flight to Montgomery would be twenty minutes late in arriving at Birmingham. That would give him time to exchange his ticket and obtain something for his stomach distress.

Flight 49 eased onto the runway at 6:50 P.M.

After its rollout, Captain Haas maneuvered the aircraft down a taxiway toward the terminal facility. It would be on the ground only long enough to deplane the Birmingham passengers, take on food and other provisions, and board the new load of passengers.

As the football fans disembarked, Captain Haas wished he were going to the big game to root for his favorite team, Alabama's Crimson Tide. He was an admirer of running back Johnny Musso. By the time Saturday night's game would be played at Legion Field, the captain hoped to be back at home to enjoy the action on nationwide television.

The fans filed rapidly down the steps and across the concrete apron, then proceeded through the terminal to the baggage area. Their spirit was contagious as they marched along with their festooned hats and pennants.

Frank Morkill reached the departure-gate lounge in time

to see the procession, but his eyes were drawn to something else. Another black man, one he hadn't seen before, sat among the small group of waiting passengers. He, too, carried a shiny walking cane—just like the one he had seen a few minutes before. Shaking his head in disbelief, he concluded it was a mere coincidence.

A muscular, gray-haired man of medium build, Morkill was a Peruvian by birth. He traveled with a Canadian passport, having once lived in Canada and served a stint in the Canadian Army during World War II. His square-jawed good looks would have enabled him to play the role of a Bond-like character in the movies. His speech combined an excellent command of the English language with a fluency in Spanish. Frank would have been equally at home in any part of the Western Hemisphere. He had spent many years in his native Peru, where his father had been an explorer and a developer of the country's earliest system of railroads. Morkill had been in and out of numerous tight situations in South and Central America, where politics frequently ignited into bloody coups and revolutions. He had met and married Nancy in Peru. Studying at McGill University in Montreal provided his educational background, while he obtained his business acumen by working in the United States. He bought a home and settled his family in Miami.

When Flight 49 was announced ready for boarding, Morkill was first through the gate. Climbing the steps to the cabin, he held his briefcase and raincoat in one hand and the boarding pass in the other. Donna took the pass, and Frank selected an aisle seat just behind the galley, in the forward section of the cabin. Placing the attaché case in the center seat, he stowed the raincoat in an overhead bin. He took a current-events magazine from the case, which he then stashed under his seat. Before sitting down he turned around to face the rear and stretched his body to relieve the tension. That was when he noticed Alvin Fortson with his walking cane propped against the window. Morkill slumped into his seat and began to read as others came aboard.

Mary Melton moved over from her aisle seat to the one by the window. Despite her frequent travels, she had never before landed in Birmingham; and she wanted to catch a glimpse of the terminal building.

Tonsmiere selected a seat in front of her and began thumbing through some papers in his briefcase.

Marcia Timbers took a seat further back and continued reading the book she had brought along for the trip.

Luther Waller seated himself by the window on the row behind Morkill.

Charlotte Watts and Fred Cherney sat in a triple-seater across from Mrs. Melton.

One of the black men with a cane walked toward the rear to a seat on the aisle. He was followed by another black male, carrying a raincoat, who sat on the aisle opposite him.

Richard Wanklyn sat forward in the cabin while his partners, Robinson and Menke, occupied a two-seater on the left of the cabin in the rear.

Alex Halberstadt took a seat midway of the cabin and began making notes from an article he was reading on how to organize one's time.

Last to board was the other black with a cane. He sat in an aisle seat next to Watts and Cherney.

Donna informed Captain Haas that the flight was ready for departure.

Winter's early darkness spread over Birmingham as the DC-9 engines whined to a start. Haas put up the paperback (about corruption in the Canadian Parliament) that had absorbed him while he was awaiting the loading of passengers.

Donna gave the passenger briefing over the public-address system while Karen walked down the aisle, checking seat belts and articles stowed under seats. Nothing appeared unusual.

The jetliner taxied to the end of the runway, revved up its powerful engines, and took off, its blinking navigational lights disappearing into the evening sky.

Less than five minutes after departing, the airliner raced along through a clear November night sky toward the next destination. The leg to Montgomery was about ninety miles. The plane was speeding along at better than seven miles a minute; the brief flight would take only fifteen minutes.

The leg was made easy for the two flight attendants by its brief duration. There would be no cocktail service, so there was little stirring about in the cabin.

Forward in the cockpit there was no time for Captain Haas and his copilot to relax, although the captain had phoned Donna in the galley and ordered a cup of coffee.

Fifty-five miles from Montgomery, Johnson throttled back and was just beginning the gradual descent from the eleven-thousand-foot apogee of the flight. Both Haas and Johnson, veteran commercial pilots, brought to their jobs a high degree of professionalism.

Letting down from altitude continued while the airmen scanned the starlit sky for other aircraft and marked off items on their checklist.

An unusual commotion was originating from behind the bulkhead of Johnson's right seat. Haas dismissed the rattling noise as Donna fumbling for the key that would unlock the metal bifold door separating the flight deck from the passenger compartment. The captain reached up to an overhead control panel to readjust the cabin pressurization. Suddenly, his upraised arm and the darkened flight deck were bathed with light streaming in from the cabin. Haas turned to glance over his right shoulder in the direction of the door. It was standing wide open and knocked loose from its ceiling track.

Donna was shoved into view, a large black arm encircling her neck and lifting her off of the floor. Another black arm thrust forward, slamming the chromium-plated barrel of a .38 caliber Smith and Wesson pistol against Haas' cheek.

Both arms were the extensions of a silhouetted figure that shouted:

"HEAD NORTH, CAPTAIN—THIS IS A HIJACK-ING."

For an instant Haas gave his brain an opportunity to absorb the scene and sort out his options. He wanted to reach for the crash axe and bring it down across the gunman's skull, but the miniature cannon pressing against his flesh eliminated that and all other options.

Nearly choked by her captor, Donna gasped, "It's for real—Billy Bob—he's not kidding."

The captain thought that had to be the understatement of the year. His eyes followed the length of the gun barrel and lifted to the hijacker's face.

Capitulating, Haas told the gunman, "You've got it."

He hadn't taken his hand down from the overhead panel. As he spoke, his fingers flipped on the "No Smoking" and "Fasten Seat Belt" signs. With the dexterity of a concert pianist, he continued with the in-range checklist procedure—hydraulic pumps in high position, speed book checked for landing speed.

Meanwhile, a traffic controller in Atlanta observed a signal on his radar screen that he had hoped he would never see. It indicated Southern 49 had been hijacked.

Haas and Johnson exchanged confused looks as if asking each other, *A hijacking headed north?* The two pilots didn't permit themselves any additional mental speculation.

Reinforcing his demand, the gunman said, "Look, man—you'd better do what I say. There are ten of us on board armed with grenades, pistols, and machine guns."

Haas appealed to the gunman, "Just be calm—don't hurt anybody—let's avoid any kind of panic. We'll do whatever you want."

The captain remembered that this was not even his trip. He had been called off of the reserve list to fill in for another captain who had to adjust his flight time for the month. *Here I am being held captive and ordered around by a gang of terrorists,* he thought. He wondered if the hijacker exaggerated the number of his accomplices, but he didn't beg the question. At least for the time being, he was willing to believe there was a Sherman tank rolling down the aisle toward the flight deck.

Haas realized from the excited shouts coming from the passenger compartment that there were other participants in the takeover. They were barking orders to the stunned and frightened hostages.

Frank Morkill had witnessed the violent capture of the flight attendant. He had looked up just as a big black man, the one who had stood in line in front of him at the ticket counter, grabbed Donna and kicked in the cockpit door. The instant it happened he told himself, *This is it—just as surely as God makes little green apples.* Why hadn't he followed up on his premonition? Why hadn't he asked airport authorities to search the man for weapons before he was allowed to board at Birmingham? Well, he was in another tight situation; and perhaps this one would be the tightest of them all.

Armed with a pistol in one hand and a grenade in the other, another black man crouched and swiveled through the aisle, commanding, "Don't nobody move—we're not gonna harm you as long as you do what we say."

Near the rear of the cabin, another grenade-and-pistol-wielding black echoed the order.

Petite flight attendant Ellis was sitting on her jump seat at the rear of the cabin. Not wearing her glasses, she thought her vision was playing tricks on her. The scene was one of frozen unreality. Unfastening her seat belt, she started to get up and go forward to tell those men she would have to report them for having weapons on board.

Suddenly, her vision came into sharp focus as one of the hijackers whirled around. Sticking a pistol in her face, he dragged her from the jump seat and shoved the attendant midway up the aisle, where she was slammed into a passenger seat. For several moments she sat trembling.

Before she realized what she was doing, she turned to the gunman standing behind her. In a shrill voice she said, "Hi—I'm Karen Ellis. What's your name?"

The impulsive introduction was met by an icy, silent stare from the man she concluded had to be the meanest in the world.

First Officer Johnson had responded to the cockpit gunman's first command by swinging the aircraft about on a new heading. A quick glance at the fuel indicators told Haas that the aircraft was too low on fuel for any long-range flying. Anticipating that the gunman could be convinced of the necessity for a refueling stop, Johnson was proceeding back in the direction of Birmingham. He expected that there would likely be a confrontation between the hijackers and lawmen once the plane was on the ground.

Birmingham flight controllers, monitoring the flight path of the airliner, were mystified to discover that the aircraft was not on a course usually taken by pirates. Immediately they used hot-line telephones to relay the news to the FBI in Washington and a special hijacking command post of the Federal Aviation Administration. Simultaneously, word was flashed to the jetliner's operation base at Southern Airways in Atlanta.

Startled officials on the ground went into action. The Birmingham departure controller, James Graydon, advised the Atlanta control center of Flight 49's position forty miles southeast of Birmingham. Atlanta center reported, "OK—we're watching him."

For the next five minutes a direct radio link between the Atlanta and Birmingham centers buzzed with conversation.

"It's Southern 49 going back to Birmingham for fuel."

"For what?"

"For fuel . . ."

"OK—I understand."

"And you got the inbound and you're watching it?"

"Yeah—we're watching it. It's actual—huh?"

"I don't know what it is . . ."

"OK—we're watching it . . ."

Birmingham Approach Control brought the airline's local operations agent in on developments.

"Southern—this is Harbison up in Approach Control."

"Yeah?" awaited the operations agent.

"Your Southern 49 that took off here is on the way back."

"Aw, shoot."

The Approach controller added, "We think he's been hijacked. We don't know. We haven't talked to him yet. We don't know what the situation is. He's thirty miles south. The center says he's coming back for fuel."

"Thank you," said the agent.

Meanwhile, the gunmen commanding Flight 49's cabin were carrying out a well-planned control of passengers.

"Take your clothes off," one of them shouted.

Marge Brennan reached for the zipper on the back of her dress.

Looking at Marge, one of the hijackers waved his pistol from side to side, saying, "We mean for only the men to undress down to their shorts."

A gunman forward in the cabin said, "We're not trying to steal your money. Just put your clothes in the aisle. And you women toss your purses into the aisle."

They were taking no chances that armed sky marshals were aboard.

"If you've got a gun on you, toss it in the aisle or we'll kill you," said one of the gunmen.

Indignantly, male hostages began disrobing.

Jerry Menke turned to Marge, who was seated nearby, and said apologetically, "If you think this is something— keep an eye on Richard up front."

The man he referred to was left standing in only his socks while trying to shield himself behind a headrest cover hastily removed from a seat back.

Frank Morkill had removed his suit coat and shirt when he remembered he had on one of his breezier pair of shorts. The wearing of tattered undergarments had become a constant source of chiding from his wife. But through the years he had found it difficult to break old habits. Jokingly he had rationalized that in event of a disaster, his remains could always be identified by his ragged and torn underwear.

Captain Haas and his copilot were discussing the need for refueling when their captor interrupted.

"You all talk too much. Don't talk to each other," commanded the gunman.

Haas informed the hijacker of the problem.

"Why didn't you refuel at Birmingham?" stormed the gunman.

"We were scheduled for refueling at Montgomery," Haas answered.

Assuming the gunman would buy his arguments, the captain talked while Johnson descended toward Birmingham. Haas called the hijacker's attention to the fuel indicators, explaining that the readings reflected the number of pounds of fuel on board.

"The eight thousand pounds remaining will enable us to fly for only about another half-hour or so," he cautioned.

Thinking the hijacker in agreement for an immediate landing, the letdown continued while Captain Haas maintained radio communications with Approach Control.

"This is Southern 49—we're out of five (five thousand feet) right now on the way to three."

"Southern 49—roger—and continue to descend to twenty-five hundred, and that's left to heading zero-two-zero?"

"Affirmative."

Nineteen minutes had elapsed since the jetliner had departed Birmingham. It was now back to within ten miles of the airport. Approach controller Don Weathers reported, "Southern 49—the measured ceiling—thirty-two hundred broken—visibility six miles with smoke—the broken variable scattered."

There was a brief pause before Weathers issued further instructions.

"Southern 49—turn left heading three-three-zero."

"OK—three-three-zero."

Three minutes later Flight 49 was nine miles out in line

with runway 23. The tower chief, Bill Anderson, took over directions of the flight.

"Southern 49 is cleared to land," said Anderson.

Full flaps were extended on the jetliner. Throttle levers were backed off. Streetlights and automobile headlights zipped by below, and the bright lights of the runway stretched out ahead.

The aircraft was two hundred feet away from touchdown.

Jamming his revolver against the captain's right nostril, the hijacker shouted, "Take this banty-legged thing up. We're not landing here."

Reacting instantly, Haas took over the controls from Johnson. He simultaneously pulled back on the control column and shoved the throttles forward; and the airliner flew over the runway.

Bewildered flight controllers in the tower looked on as the big jetliner disappeared into the night sky. There had not been enough time to assemble a force of lawmen at the Birmingham airport, but the hijackers weren't taking any chances.

Johnson was now handling radio communications with the tower operator.

"OK—Birming—uh—Approach—they just changed their mind about landing in Birmingham—so we'll just go . . ."

Controller Weathers advised the tower chief to disregard Southern 49.

"He's gonna leave the area," he said.

"Leave the area?"

"Yes."

Weathers radioed, "Southern 49—what initial heading do you propose to fly?"

Copilot Johnson replied, "OK—we changed our mind. Uh—stand by there. We'll get you a new course or something."

When the aircraft had cleared local traffic patterns and leveled off again in flight, Captain Haas renewed an urgent appeal for a refueling stop. Quickly naming off several alternatives within the aircraft's fuel-endurance range, the hijacker approved Jackson, Mississippi, about 150 miles to the southwest.

Johnson reported the new destination to ground authorities, who assigned a vectored heading direct to Jackson and instructed, "Southern 49—maintain sixteen thousand feet."

The departure controller extended his customary sign-off, "Good day."

Johnson drawled back, "We'll see y'all."

If all went well, the flight would take about thirty minutes. Flight 49 and its hostages would be on the ground at Jackson shortly after eight o'clock.

At Montgomery, relatives of the seven passengers who were scheduled to disembark there waited. Mary Melton's daughter, Elizabeth, was informed by Southern Airways officials that the flight would be at least an hour delayed. She, her husband, John, and her young son, Craig, decided to visit a nearby restaurant for dinner while they waited.

Undaunted by the gunman's previous display of hostility, flight attendant Karen Ellis asked for and was given permission to go forward and check on Donna's condition. The senior attendant had just been released by the gunman in the cockpit.

"Are you all right?" Karen asked.

Donna assured her she would be if she could just stop shaking.

"I thought he was going to kill me," she said.

Karen asked how it began.

"Well, that big guy came up to me at the galley where I was fixing a cup of coffee for the captain and said someone had fainted in the back of the cabin. I started following him to the rear when he turned and stopped. He held a gun on me and said we were going to the cockpit to tell the captain the plane was being taken over."

Continuing to relate the harrowing experience, Donna

said, "I told him we had to use the telephone to ask the captain's permission to go into the cockpit. And as I reached for the phone he stuck his gun in my ribs, grabbed me around the neck, and took the door key."

"Did he hurt you?" Karen wanted to know.

"Just scared me to death," Donna said.

Karen's presence helped Donna regain her composure. Color returned to her attractive oval face. Her voice was restored to its gentle, melodious qualities. She reached up and smoothed her brown, uncurled hair, which was worn in a ponytail.

"This is terrible, Karen. What are we going to do?" she asked.

With a tone of resignation Karen answered, "I guess we'll have to do what they tell us to do."

Seated where instructed by the hijackers, in the two forward seats on the left of the cabin, the two flight attendants didn't get to continue their conversation.

Young Keith Didien began crying.

Donna asked the bandits for permission to go back and check on the boy.

"Sure—you're the stewardess, aren't you?" was the surprising reply.

Vivien Didien explained to Donna that Keith was crying because he was hungry.

The attendant went back to the hijacker and asked if it would be all right to serve dinner to the youngster.

"That would be a good idea," he said; "serve everybody."

Donna and Karen seized the opportunity to regain control of the cabin.

Karen went to each passenger, asking if he would like to have a cocktail. She was careful to direct her eyes toward the eyes of each of the male passengers to avoid making their near-nakedness more embarrassing. The men welcomed the opportunity to fold down the eating trays over their laps.

The hostages were more at ease once they saw the flight attendants moving about the cabin again. However, one man with a glazed, confused look on his face got out of his seat and stood in the aisle. Karen rushed up to him and ordered him to be seated. A few minutes later he was back on his feet.

"Sit yourself down, sir, before you get shot," she demanded.

"I just want to look for a magazine to read," he retorted.

The man's action was beginning to agitate one of the hijackers.

Seated across from the man was John Witucki, who said to the unruly passenger, "Shut your face, sit down, and keep your mouth shut before you get us killed."

The man sat down.

Guards in the cabin were pleased to have others enforcing their instructions and appeared more relaxed. Karen took advantage of their more benevolent frames of mind by asking the gunmen to put their weapons away.

"They're not necessary. You don't need to be waving them around. We believe you're serious," she advised.

Alex Halberstadt had been less fearful of the gunmen since the hijacking began than had the other passengers. He assumed that they wanted to go to Cuba and that the piracy would end as soon as they arrived at their destination.

Halberstadt asked one of the hijackers to stop and talk with him a minute.

"Yeah—what do you want?" asked the gunman.

"Sit down, please, for just a minute," Alex pleaded.

The bandit sat down in the empty seat by the engineer.

"Now tell me, please, what is this all about," Alex asked.

Without hesitation the hijacker began, "Well—there's a certain big city in this country that's done us a grave injustice. We mean to make them pay for it, and we're gonna get the biggest bundle of money out of 'em you've ever seen."

"Well, look," Alex said, "we haven't done anything to you . . ."

Shaking his head adamantly, the gunman cut him short,

saying, "Naw, man, this ain't no racial thing with you people. We ain't gonna harm nobody on this airplane. You're just our means to an end."

It was clear to Halberstadt from the remark that the hostages would be held by the bandits until some kind of ransom was paid. He didn't pursue the question. Something else concerned him more.

"What I would like to point out," Alex said, "is the potential danger that exists with all of these purses, shoes, and clothing being in the aisle. One of you might trip over something and touch off an explosion with that grenade. Then we'd all be dead."

"Yeah, you're right. You're pretty cool, man," agreed the hijacker.

Getting up out of the seat, the gunman yelled at Karen and Donna. "C'mon, let's get this stuff up out of the aisle. Throw it in the back of the plane where we can search it," he ordered.

They began gathering up the articles.

Mary Melton stopped one of the hijackers to explain that she had a hearing loss and that her glasses contained built-in hearing aids.

"My purse contains a spare set of batteries that I must have," she said.

"Well, pick it up," he said. "I don't want it."

None of the hijackers hinted at who he was, where he was from, or where the final destination of Flight 49 was.

However, the gunman commanding the flight deck made clear the ground rules he demanded once the plane landed for refueling at Jackson.

The engines would be kept running.

No communication between the aircraft and the control tower would be permitted.

And no one would be allowed to approach the aircraft except for a lone fuel attendant.

Flight 49 continued on its course to the southwest.

2
Revenge

Friendly laughter and conversation filled the room at a northwest Atlanta cocktail party. Southern Airways' flight division vice-president, James W. Godwin, stepped out of the room to receive a telephone call from the company's duty dispatcher.

"Say that again," Godwin requested; "it's a bit noisy here."

Shifting the receiver away from the noise, Godwin listened intently. Only sketchy information was available, but the dispatcher reported that one of the Southern airliners had just been hijacked over Alabama. He advised that all key management personnel were being called back on duty.

"Who's the pilot in command of the flight?" Godwin asked.

"Captain Haas out of Memphis," said the dispatcher. "That's where the flight originated."

"Billy Haas, you say?"

"That's right, sir," confirmed the dispatcher.

"OK—I'm on my way," said the executive.

He regretted the hijacking of any flight; but if there had to be the hijacking of a Southern Airways plane, he was glad Haas was in command. With his cool, calm, deliberative temperament, Haas was surely the best-dispositioned captain to deal with such a situation.

Godwin placed the receiver back in its cradle and returned to the adjacent room, where he informed his wife, Yvonne, of the news.

"Honey, I want you to return home, get my flight uniform, pack me a suitcase, and follow me to the airport as quickly as possible," Godwin said.

The eighteen-mile drive to the airline's headquarters building at Hartsfield International seemed longer than usual as Godwin sped south along the interstate. Nervously, he ran his fingers through his neatly trimmed gray hair. His rugged, good-looking face contorted as he recalled the late-afternoon briefing he had attended. The weekend flight operations outlook over the system had been forecast to be normal.

"Normal?" he asked aloud.

At forty-eight, Godwin was five years older than Haas. They had formed a close, lasting friendship and gained mutually high professional respect for each other that went back to 1959, when Haas won a pilot slot with Southern. Godwin was already a captain at that time; then the company fleet consisted only of DC-3s.

During those early years Haas flew as Godwin's copilot. The temperaments of the two men were vastly different, but they both shared a strong passion for flying.

Each had arrived at goals to be airline pilots by differing, but difficult, paths.

The United States Air Corps enlisted Godwin for service during World War II and sent him off on bombing missions over North Africa and the Middle East as a flight engineer-gunner. When the war ended, he invested his savings in a vintage model single-engine Piper cub coupe, which he purchased at Atlanta's original airport, Candler Field. His flight instructor was a book, *Patters of Elementary Flight Maneuvers.* Once he was checked out on the aircraft, Godwin climbed into the cockpit and headed home to Dawson, Georgia, navigating along the highways and railroad tracks.

For the next few years he operated a fixed base and barnstormed around the South in a variety of aircraft, including crop dusters and sprayers which he flew for hire over the boll weevil-infested delta farmlands of Mississippi and Louisiana.

Southern Airways came into existence in the late forties.

Godwin disposed of his seven aircraft and signed on as a station agent at Memphis. Within a short time he was piloting for the fledgling airline.

From the beginning he took a leading role in union activities, and over the years he was an unyielding advocate of air safety. He served as the Airline Pilots' Association central safety chairman for Southern as well as vice-chairman of the Atlanta Safety Committee. In these roles he was often a thorn in the side of the company.

Godwin's eventual elevation to the ranks of management came as a great surprise to his flight-line colleagues, many of whom viewed the promotion as an effort to neutralize his stubborn will.

Haas had developed a yearning to fly at the early age of five. For hours he would sit in his backyard, patiently waiting for the overhead flight of an aircraft. On one late afternoon he raced inside to say, "Mommy—that plane up there is going to crash. It doesn't have enough attitude." (He was referring to its lack of altitude.) The plane did crash, injuring its lone occupant, Haas' cousin.

Not until his early twenties did Billy Bob Haas take his first flying lesson. It was to be the last for a long time. He lacked the financial means to support the deep-seated ambition. Haas had developed another equally compelling ambition. He wanted to marry Ann George, a beautiful flight attendant with Delta Airlines. Ann was already engaged to be married and gave Haas little encouragement. She failed to take into account the determination of her suitor.

Haas was willing to do any kind of work just to be around aircraft and airports. American Airlines provided the opportunity he was seeking. He landed a $280-per-month job as a flight service clerk with the airline. During the next nine years he worked in almost every ground operations capacity available.

Extra money for flight instructions was rarely in his pockets, but when it was Haas added a few more hours to his logbook. At the rate he was going, it would take twenty years for him to qualify as a pilot. The dogged determination that sustained him also won the respect and admiration of a number of pilots who frequented airports in the Memphis area. They encouraged his ambition by giving him lessons at their own expense in their aircraft.

Eventually, Haas was able to borrow $750, with which he purchased a Piper J-3 Cub. This money enabled him to log an average of one hundred hours a month while he worked toward his private and commercial licenses.

On one occasion when he was aloft in the J-3, he exceeded the aircraft's normal operating ceiling by twenty-five hundred feet. An Air Force tanker crossed his path a thousand feet below him. Haas chuckled when the tanker pilot looked up and spotted the smaller aircraft. Seeing the tanker's wing dip, he could picture the pilot's look of disbelief as he did a double take.

Not until Haas had reached the age of thirty did he log 920 hours, enough to qualify for an airline job. But his age now became a barrier. An abundance of younger, more qualified pilots were getting out of the Air Force. The airlines could take their pick from among the ex-military pilots having thousands of hours of flight experience. Haas took time off from his job and sought interviews with the various domestic and foreign air carriers.

Door after door slammed shut in his face.

Getting weary of the pursuit that was leading nowhere, Haas kept reminding himself that he would make it because he *had* to make it. Men of lesser stamina and willpower would have given up.

Then one day his faith in prayers and miracles was confirmed. Southern Airways called him to Atlanta for an interview. He was accepted as a copilot. The job would mean a lower salary; nonetheless, he was jubilant. The end of a struggle against years of adversity represented a great personal victory. It was a triumph as well for his many friends who had rekindled the flames of his ambition when they flickered low.

After four years with Southern, Haas was promoted to

the rank of captain. Godwin penned a brief note of congratulations which read: "I predict you will make the finest captain this airline has ever produced. And justly so— you've made every mistake in the book, at least twice."

Haas treasured the oblique compliment and placed the note among his mementos.

Indeed, Haas had become one of the airline's finest pilots. And on this November night his piloting skill and his cool, calm, deliberative disposition faced the greatest challenge of his thirteen-year commercial-flight career.

Wheeling into the airline parking lot on Virginia Avenue, Godwin began to realize the enormity of the situation. Initially, he speculated that the hijacking would end like most others had. It would be a one-way trip for the pirates and their hostages to Cuba, followed by a return trip for the aircraft and those aboard. Meanwhile, it would be a nuisance and diversion for the airline to deal with as best it could.

Observing that most of the executive parking spaces were filled and that the headquarters office building was ablaze with lights, he was overwhelmed with sudden doubt that this piracy would end as he hoped.

Entering a side door of the building, Godwin raced up a flight of steps to the second level. Long, quick strides took him to the operations center.

Inside the long, rectangular room there was a frenzy of activity.

Telephones jangled. Teletypes clattered. Loudspeakers carried the voices of Southern Airways pilots reporting their in-flight positions along the system. The progress was marked by green strips of cardboard by each flight number. Flight 49's progress had been posted as far as Birmingham.

The normal complement of dispatchers, assistants, and communications clerks had been joined by management personnel from security, sales, customer services, maintenance, engineering, and public relations. Grave and worried looks were on their faces as they attempted to piece together fragments of the hijacking reports.

FBI agents from the Atlanta field office arrived just as security chief Joe Davis began an update on developments.

"Flight 49—en route from Memphis to Miami—was hijacked during the Birmingham-to-Montgomery leg at approximately 7:15 tonight," he reported. "The aircraft, with its thirty passengers and four crew members, has been commandeered by an unknown number of pirates and diverted to Jackson, Mississippi, presumably for refueling," he added.

Davis informed those assembled that attempts were underway to communicate a request to the hijackers to permit the airliner to fly to Atlanta and to free the hostages.

"If they consent, we will provide them with another DC-9 and a crew to fly them anywhere they want to go within the airline's capability," he concluded.

The vice-president and associate general manager, George Gross, ended the briefing by suggesting that executive personnel report to their respective duty stations to remain on standby pending receipt of additional information.

Godwin left the room and crossed the corridor to his office. Picking up the telephone on his desk, he dialed the number that would connect him with the Haas home in Tennessee.

Ann was in the kitchen warming a bottle of milk for Betsy, who was with Johnny and their Uncle Ed in the sitting room.

Stepping across the kitchen, Ann picked up the receiver on the phone's second ring. The voice on the other end of the line said, "Annie—this is Jim." She recognized Godwin's resonant tones, although they were softer than usual.

"Hi, Jim—how are you?" she asked in the soft, caressing speech that betrayed her Mississippi origins.

Jim hesitated and stuttered for a moment. Searching for a delicate way of breaking the news, he could find none.

"Annie—ole Billy Bob's been hijacked," he blurted.

She laughed and said, "Aw—you're kidding."

"No—I'm not kidding," he assured.

"Oh—you are—you must be kidding," she said hopefully.

"No—it's serious now," Godwin insisted.

She knew Jim too well. He wouldn't kid around about
such matters anyway.

Finally accepting the news as being genuine, she asked,
"Well—what do you want me to do?"

"Nothing right now," he said. "We have very little information to give you at this time except that the aircraft
should be on the ground right now in Jackson, Mississippi,
for refueling."

Godwin promised he would keep her advised as often as
new information became available.

When the conversation ended, Ann walked through the
large dining room and down the long entry hall to the
sitting room. It was not until she broke the news to Ed that
a sickening fear churned within her, a realization that she
might never see Billy Bob alive again.

The incredible, tense journey that began in the skies
over Alabama had actually had its genesis many months
earlier in the city of Detroit.

A series of rape and assault cases commanded the attention of the Detroit police. Nine cases that remained un-
solved involved descriptions of the same two men. But
police were unable to fit the descriptions to the right suspects.

Among the victims were young, old, black, and white.

Eventually, police hauled in twenty-five-year-old Henry
D. Jackson and twenty-seven-year-old Lewis Moore.

During a police line-up the victims identified the two
men as their assailants.

Steadfastly denying the charges, the accused pair
claimed that a previous incident at Anderson's Gardens
rendered them seriously incapacitated.

According to a police report, in 1971 one Brenda Wade
told another patron, while in Anderson's Bar, that she was

being held against her will by Jackson and Moore. She asked that police be summoned.

Although police arrested Jackson as soon as they arrived at the Third Avenue establishment, Moore ran. He was pursued and apprehended.

The report on the incident stated that Moore "purposefully and viciously kicked one of the officers and had to be forcibly restrained."

Miss Wade never appeared to sign a complaint against the pair.

Jackson and Moore began wearing neck braces afterward. They carried shiny walking canes and new attaché cases everywhere they went.

Robert M. Cohn was retained by the two men to represent them in a four-million-dollar police brutality suit they filed against the city. Before accepting the case, Cohn argued with his clients that "we have no proof of any injuries" and that it was their word against that of the police. But the two men were adamant. In the suit, Jackson and Moore claimed that they were punched repeatedly by police officers in the squad car that took them to jail. Police replied that they used no more force than was necessary.

The Anderson's Garden incident was just another in a series of setbacks the pair had encountered. They had been the joint owners of a Detroit restaurant named Lou and Smooth's Soul Palace. It had folded.

Patrons of the restaurant considered Jackson to be weird. He told them of his belief that he had been a former biblical character in another life and that God told him that he should "smite those who raised a hand against me." He called himself "Reverend."

While the police brutality suit was pending, Jackson and Moore developed a belief that there was a conspiracy plot against them by unknown authorities.

On one occasion the two men appeared before the Detroit City Council. Showing President Mel Ravitz a message composed with letters cut out of newspaper ads, they said police had sent the messages as threats against their

families. Each claimed his wife had moved out because of
the threats.

They pleaded to Ravitz, "Sir—for the sake of the people
of Detroit—your family, as well as mine—we pray for
help."

Jackson and Moore may have had real fears. Calls to their
attorney were made from phone booths in the belief that
their home telephone lines were tapped. Letters they
wrote were scattered among relatives and acquaintances in
different cities. It was a precaution they believed necessary
in case of police raids.

Insisting that their police brutality suit was not a matter
of race, they maintained instead that they wanted the four
million dollars—if not for themselves, then to be applied to
improving the police of Detroit so racism would end.

Jackson and Moore's complaint was never considered
seriously by city officials. In an effort to forego litigation
expense, the two men were offered a token settlement of
twenty-five dollars. The offer blew their minds.

They were incensed even more when police booked
them on the rape and assault charges. Policewoman
Joanetta Greer dogged the case until the suspects were
apprehended. In their minds, Jackson and Moore believed
Greer had trumped up the charges.

Their arrest took place on October 13, 1972.

Municipal Judge Joseph A. Gillis set a low bond of five
hundred dollars because neither of the accused had previous records. A hearing date of October 30 was set.

Ironically, according to Civil Aeronautics Board records,
Gillis had been "selected out" by the government's hijacker
profile in 1971. The profile system was based upon studies
of the characteristics of previous hijackers. Gillis was
selected out while boarding a Detroit to Tampa flight. He
had to undergo a search for which he lodged a complaint
with the CAB.

Policewoman Greer sought to have Jackson and Moore
returned to jail on a third charge, but failed in the attempt.

Detroit police would not get a chance to prosecute the

pair. Vowing they would have their revenge, Jackson and Moore decided to skip bond and leave the city.

In reconstructing events that followed, as nearly as possible, we see that the two men stole an automobile and drove from Detroit to Oak Ridge, Tennessee. There they rendezvoused with Moore's half-brother, Melvin Charles Curd. The twenty-two-year-old younger brother preferred to be called by his mother's last name, Cale. A fugitive himself, Cale had recently escaped from a minimum security imprisonment at Tennessee State Prison at Nashville. He had been sentenced to serve a five-year term for grand larceny. His conviction stemmed from the theft of four hundred dollars from a department-store cash register in Oliver Springs, Tennessee.

Cale had had several other scrapes with the law. He had been picked up once and accused of stealing some sardines from a food market. And he had been shot once during a Detroit robbery.

Returning from the Michigan city, Cale sought to live with his father, William V. Curd, Sr., at Knoxville. The elder Curd was a construction worker with the local Housing Authority. Cale's father became disgusted with young Mel because of his failure to seek employment. He told him to hit the road.

For a brief time, Cale served in the Army and then entered the Job Corps. He also got married and had two children.

During the short period of service in the Army, Cale underwent psychiatric examination. Writing to his wife, Mary Ann, about the examination, he said, "They sent me to a head specialist. Ha—there's nothing wrong."

Writing on another occasion, he stated, "If your family is together and the kids are in good health, and you are happy, this to me is the greatest gift the Lord could possibly give any young man."

Cale had it easy while serving his time in prison. The minimum security arrangement enabled him to attend classes at Tennessee State University.

Much of his time was spent in the school library, where his attention was drawn to numerous newspaper clippings about previous hijackings. Photocopies of the clippings filled his notebook bearing the university emblem.

After his escape and subsequent get-together with Jackson and Moore, the trio gave careful study to the material Cale had accumulated. They underscored what they considered to be the "do's" and "don'ts" of hijacking. The collection of clipping copies became their textbook on the subject.

Cale suffered from severe intestinal problems. Poor health had convinced him that life was not worthwhile. When the embittered Jackson and Moore arrived, Cale was ready to participate in any scheme they could devise.

For several days, the trio drove around the South visiting various big cities served by the airlines. They slept in their stolen station wagon, which provided cramped quarters at best. Jackson and Moore were of the approximate same height and weight, five feet ten inches and 170 pounds. Cale was slightly smaller.

At each city visited, they stopped at the airport to observe security precautions. During their travels they maintained a spartan existence, mostly eating bread and sandwich meats. Among them they had little money. What they did have was used to purchase gasoline, pep pills, and food.

Ultimately, Jackson, Moore, and Cale settled on Birmingham Municipal Airport as the facility having the least amount of security. At Birmingham, they were convinced, there existed the best possibility of clearing security with a small arsenal of weapons.

On Thursday night, November 9, 1972, they took the initial step in their plan. Armed with a .22 caliber "Saturday Night Special" they held up and robbed a Birmingham convenience store. The total loot taken was less than two hundred dollars. But they relieved the store operator of a 9mm Luger automatic pistol and a .38 caliber Smith and Wesson revolver. To this collection of weapons they added three hand grenades obtained from an Army salvage store.

Witnesses claim to have seen the trio in and around the airport terminal building throughout the day on Friday, November 10. In any event, the trio moved to implement the next step in their plan at 6:30 P.M., Eastern Standard Time.

Jackson, Moore, and Cale abandoned the stolen automobile bearing Michigan license plate PSK-450 in the airport parking lot. They left behind the parking-lot claim check, a book from the Tennessee State University library, a Michigan waterfowl hunting guide, road maps, a Southern Airways flight schedule, and a ticket for airline trip insurance.

Entering the terminal building, they split up, Cale going to the Southern Airways ticket counter. Jackson would follow a few minutes later.

Two counter attendants were on duty.

Cale approached the position manned by agent Larry S. McCammon and asked if Southern had a flight to Montgomery. McCammon advised Cale that the next flight to Montgomery was scheduled for departure at 6:55 P.M.— that it was due to arrive shortly from Memphis and would be departing a few minutes late.

Cale inquired further if he could obtain two seats on the flight. Informed that he could, Cale gave his name and that of Moore's for ticketing purposes. Cale had a camera and case hanging on a strap from his neck and a set of binoculars in his hands. He placed the binoculars on the counter and removed a wallet from his pocket, from which he took forty dollars and paid for the two tickets. McCammon asked for some identification. Cale produced a Social Security card and a Tennessee State University identification card bearing his photograph. McCammon examined the documents and handed them, along with the tickets, to Cale. The ticket agent then informed Cale that he and his carry-on articles would be checked at departure gate number 1 with a metal detector. Cale was wearing only a shirt, trousers, and shoes and replied, "All I got is this," holding up his camera and binoculars. Cale left the ticket counter and joined up again with Moore. Together, they went to the gatehouse waiting area.

At the same time Cale was purchasing tickets for himself and Moore, Henry Jackson was securing his ticket from Robert D. Morrison at the adjacent counter. Neither Jackson nor Cale acknowledged the presence of the other. Jackson was wearing a mod-type shirt and trousers and a long brown leather coat with a fur-trimmed collar. As a disguise, he carried a walking cane and smoked a pipe. He sported a mustache, goatee, and Afro hairstyle. Jackson paid twenty dollars in cash for his ticket. After fumbling around in his wallet, he produced a Michigan driver's license for identification purposes.

Before handing Jackson his ticket, Morrison asked, "Do you have any luggage or carry-on baggage?"

"No," Jackson replied.

"Do you have any objections to a magnetometer test?" he was asked.

"Emphatically no," he answered.

At the boarding area, Cale and Moore occupied seats nearest the check-in point. They gave no outward indications of nervousness. When the flight was announced ready for boarding, they took up positions third and fourth in line.

As Moore approached the clearance point, he held out both arms in order to be checked.

"I don't have anything on me," he offered.

Attired in shirt and trousers, Moore carried a combination raincoat and overcoat which he held at arms' length away from the agent. The coat was not given an examination, and Moore was cleared to board.

Cale moved up to undergo screening.

A lens protruded from the camera carrying case which hung from a strap around his neck, thus was not suspect. The binocular case he carried was opened and visually inspected by McCammon without removing the binoculars. After undergoing screening, Moore was cleared to board and proceeded out the gate.

Seventeen through passengers from Memphis sat in their seats on the jetliner.

It was with a certain sense of relief that Moore and Cale climbed the passenger steps. Although each cleared the gate, they had conformed to the "hijacker profile" of likely suspects then in circulation by the Federal Aviation Agency. But they had succeeded in foiling the unsophisticated security precautions.

Upon entering the aircraft, Moore selected seat 12*a*. Cale sat down in 13*c*, one row back and on the aisle.

Other passengers boarding at Birmingham proceeded to the aircraft. Among the last to board was a black woman, Charlotte Watts. Miss Watts had been engaged in small talk by Jackson while she waited in the gatehouse. They had stood aside from other passengers. Miss Watts broke off the conversation and walked to the aircraft.

After all other passengers had gone through the door leading to the ramp, Jackson approached agent McCammon.

"Is this the flight to Montgomery?" he asked.

McCammon told him it was. Walking with the aid of his cane, Jackson went through the door to board.

The agent followed Jackson and the remaining passengers up the steps of the aircraft, went on board to exchange necessary paperwork with the flight attendants, confirmed that thirteen passengers had boarded, then left the aircraft and closed the door.

3
Ransom Demand

Charles Binkley monitored the gauges on the side of his fuel tender. Within a few minutes the refueling of Flight 49 would be completed, and he would be glad. Never before had he been required to service a hijacked airliner. Thompson Field at Jackson, Mississippi, was not a likely stopover for air pirates.

Binkley went about his job with dispatch. The pumper was running at top speed, pouring 250 gallons per minute into the wing tanks. The operation would take twelve minutes from start to finish.

Parked on runway 15 left, halfway down the eight-thousand-foot strip, the DC-9 was off limits to everyone except the twenty-five-year-old fuel attendant. Both engines of the aircraft continued to run. The landing lights remained on, as did the bright exterior lights mounted on the fuselage of the jetliner.

A caricatured face on the aircraft's nose cone smiled down at Binkley, who smirked at the message emblazoned in black on the yellow radome. "Have a nice day," it suggested. Trying not to be obvious about it, he let his eyes drift up toward the cockpit, where he could see two black gunmen standing guard over the flight crew. One of them trained a pair of binoculars on the terminal building a quarter of a mile away.

FBI agents in the darkened control tower stared back, sighting through high-powered night-viewing telescopes.

Radio silence between the tower and aircraft was broken only once.

"Southern 49—can you give any information?" inquired the tower operator.

"Negative," Harold Johnson responded tersely.

Immediately after the fuel tanks were loaded, one of the hijackers said, "Leave."

Captain Haas replied, "There is not enough runway ahead—we'll have to go to one end or the other."

"Get outa here," repeated the gunman.

"A takeoff from here would be impossible," Haas said. "We wouldn't even clear the trees at the end of the runway."

Reluctantly, the hijacker accepted the warning and permitted a turnaround of the aircraft. Haas maneuvered the craft back toward the southeast end of the runway.

A thousand feet later the gunman held a grenade to Haas' head. "Turn around and take off," he commanded.

The Captain continued to inch forward, gaining as much extra runway as he could. Talking as he rolled, Haas said, "We need to know where we're going."

"We'll take care of that later," said the gunman. "For now, either turn around and take off or there won't be any need to know where we're going. We'll blow this thing up right here."

Haas would push his luck no further. He had reached the six-thousand-foot marker, which gave him a safer runway length.

Dispensing with customary procedure requesting takeoff clearance, Johnson radioed the ground controller.

"Southern 49 is ready for departure," he advised.

"Roger," came the reply.

Positioning the nose wheel on the white center line, Haas braked to a halt. His right hand eased the throttles forward. Brakes were released, and the airliner began its roll, quickly gaining a speed of 150 miles per hour and taking off to the northwest.

The copilot entered a notation under the takeoff heading on his log sheet: It was 8:35 P.M. Johnson had regained his composure and was doing his usual meticulous job of record-keeping. Earlier, Haas had asked him if he were being methodical; and Johnson had replied that he couldn't even remember what he was supposed to be doing.

Tension among the hijackers had run high while on the ground at Jackson. Wisely, Captain Haas and his first officer had sat silently, awaiting further instructions from their captors. But the hijackers had been too busy with surveillance to tip their hands.

The suspense was soon lifted as the climb back to altitude progressed. The big, burly black male who had been in command of the flight deck from the beginning broke his silence.

"Take it to Detroit," he ordered.

No respect intended, Haas acknowledged his latest instructions with his usual soft-spoken politeness.

"Yes, sir," he said.

Copilot Johnson reacted to the command by pushing the button on his microphone.

"Southern 49 would like a radar vector direct Detroit," he advised traffic controllers.

Instantly, a voice responded with the requested new heading.

At the same time, Haas recognized the voice of a Southern Airways captain on stopover at Tupelo, Mississippi, who was transmitting on the company radio network.

"Where are those crazy guys going to want to go next?" the voice inquired.

Haas reached over and shut off the company receiver, fearing similar remarks could land the crew in deeper trouble.

Insufficient time had prevented the serving of dinner to the passengers before the arrival at Jackson. Donna and Karen now began delivering trays of hot food to the hostages, most of whom had lost their appetites because of the excitement.

Dick Senft was pleasantly surprised to see that the menu consisted of steak, potatoes, and a salad. He wouldn't have to eat fried chicken after all.

Mary Melton worried over the concern of her awaiting relatives in Montgomery, as did the others who were now overdue in the Alabama city. Her daughter, Elizabeth, had phoned Southern Airways from the restaurant, only to be informed that there would be a delay of indefinite duration. She, her husband, and her son then went home, where they would telephone the airline every forty-five minutes. Mrs. Melton was not concerned about herself. She considered she had lived a full and good life.

Nancy Morkill and her three daughters, along with wives Allyson Senft and Linda Menke and relatives of Robinson, Watts, Cherney, and Fortson also awaited the jetliner's arrival at Orlando. They were not aware of the hijacking. Although the flight was overdue by now in the Florida city as well, the status report beside "Flight 49" at the Southern ticket counter read simply "Delayed."

Lateness was also a problem with members of the Detroit police force. Officers had gone to the home of Lou Moore earlier in the evening to pick him up for jumping bail on the rape and assault charges. They were unaware that their fugitive was now a hijacker headed for the Michigan city. They would be hearing from him shortly.

It occurred to Frank Morkill that he was sitting in a vulnerable position at the front of the cabin near the door. At some point, he feared, he might be caught in a hail of bullets, should police on the ground attempt to storm the aircraft. After carefully rehearsing the words in his mind, he stopped Moore, who exposed a silver tooth in the front of his mouth when he talked.

"Listen," Morkill explained, "I have a heart condition."

He wasn't lying entirely. He was scared to death and his heart was about to pound out of his chest.

Continuing, he told the gunman, "Because of my condition, this excitement could cause me to have a heart attack; and if I were to drop dead it might interfere with your plans."

Morkill was playing a hunch that Moore, like many blacks, wouldn't want a corpse anywhere near him. He could imagine that the suggestion had sent shivers up and down the neck of the hijacker.

Apparently his hunch had paid off. Moore gestured toward the rear of the cabin.

"There's an empty seat by the window back there on the left. Take that one," he said.

Clutching his briefcase, the nervous hostage, attired in his breezy underwear, walked down the aisle to the seat designated.

Other passengers aboard the flight were tiring and becoming increasingly apprehensive. A few had resigned themselves to the futility of worry and tried to sleep. Others sat silently and expressionlessly, contemplating the fate that awaited them at some future minute or hour. They wondered: *Who are these maniacs? What do they want? Where are they taking us?*

Marge Brennan fingered the rosary that hung from a chain around her neck. A devout Catholic, she was proud of her large family. She would often tell new acquaintances she had seven children—all by the same man. She prayed the family would not be too worried about her and Patrick.

Alex Halberstadt continued to make notations on his legal pad. For some reason he just wanted to write a letter to his wife—not that he didn't think he would ever see her again. But he had the time to record his thoughts. Alex wrote that he thoroughly appreciated her role in their lives and that in the future he would try to not let their time spent together be minimized by other events.

Forward in the cockpit, Captain Haas had decided to implement a fuel conservation measure. He had established 250 knots as his top cruising speed and would maintain that limitation unless it were detected and changed by the hijackers.

Although the gunman commanding the cockpit had boasted that there were ten armed terrorists on board, only three different ones had put in appearances on the flight deck. They had begun a system of alternating guards up front. The reason soon became evident. They had found an attraction in the galley's supply of liquor. Karen was kept busy refilling their glasses with screwdrivers, a combination of vodka and orange juice.

Wanting to improve communications between the flight crew and the pirates, Haas asked the bandit who had originally taken over the flight deck, "What do we call you—Hijacker 1, Hijacker 2, and Hijacker 3?"

The gunman's tension was giving way to the effects of the alcohol.

"No, man," he said, "call me Henry."

Pointing in the direction of Moore, who was standing in the cockpit entrance, he said, "Call him Lou."

Moore smiled as the introduction was made, revealing the glistening silver tooth in the front of his mouth.

"What about the others?" Haas queried.

"He's called Mel" was an apparent reference to Cale.

Haas and Johnson concluded from the exchange that there were only three gunmen aboard, not ten, as had been claimed.

"What's your name?" Jackson asked the captain.

"Bill—Bill Haas," he answered.

Nodding toward the copilot, Jackson asked, "And his?"

"Harold Johnson," Haas informed. "He's the mayor of a small town in Arkansas."

"Yeah?" Jackson said, obviously impressed. "What town is His Honor from?"

"College City," Haas replied. "That's the home of Southern Baptist College, which he attended."

Johnson was the town's mayor in addition to being an airline pilot. He had taken the oath of office in 1971 while piloting his own private aircraft over the city. His wife, Janie, was also a pilot. They had often discussed the possibility of his being hijacked, but Harold always laughed it off as something that wouldn't happen.

With the lines of communication open, Haas hoped to establish a liaison with one of the bandits who would act as spokesman at all times for the trio. It had become obvious that the three pirates shared a single purpose, but he wasn't sure there was complete agreement on how it was to be achieved. He feared he or Harold might get caught in a cross fire of conflicting orders.

Before the subject could be raised, the pecking order was revealed to him. Jackson had stepped just outside the cockpit to the galley to help himself to a miniature bottle of whisky. When he returned he was wearing the captain's uniform jacket and silver-braided cap, which he had removed from a coat closet. The cap sat loosely atop his Afro. Laughing, Silvertooth went to the closet, where he appropriated Harold's jacket and cap. Insolently, he strutted the aisle of the cabin, displaying his newly found symbols of authority. The sight provided a rare moment of comic relief, giving the hostages a hope that the hijackers were not as hostile as they had appeared to be.

Taking advantage of what seemed like a calmer atmosphere aboard, Captain Haas leaned around to his right, where he could see Donna standing in the galley.

"What's going on back there, Donna—are the passengers all right?" he asked.

"Yes, sir," she reported. "They just don't have on any clothes."

"You mean the ladies are undressed?" he asked.

"No, sir—just the men—they are in their underwear," she advised.

"Look—Henry, this is unnecessary," Haas said. "There's no need to humiliate those people like that. Let them put their clothes on."

"Well—I guess it'd be OK," he agreed.

"Hey—Lou," Jackson called to Moore, "let 'em dress."

For the next ten minutes Donna and Karen retrieved various articles of clothing from the pile in the rear of the cabin. Going up and down the aisle, they held up shirts, jackets, trousers, and ties for the men to identify and reclaim.

When they were all dressed again, Moore instructed the men to check their pockets and make sure nothing was missing.

After doing so, the hostages found everything in order.

Captain Haas didn't like what he was seeing on the

radarscope as the flight continued on its course for Detroit. A big weather front was closing in on the vicinity, with low-hanging cloud formations producing heavy rain and fog.

Radio transmissions from Detroit indicated that the frontal approach would shut down the airport by the time Flight 49 arrived there.

Haas was getting worried. Apparently the hijackers had a specific reason for wanting to fly to Detroit, and their plans no doubt called for a landing there. They had been drinking constantly during the two hours since leaving Mississippi. At times they had been calm and friendly, but they were armed and dangerous. Haas was concerned about how they would react when they learned that the weather was playing havoc with their plans.

Jackson kept a leery watch on Haas as the captain studied the radarscope.

"Cut that thing off so they can't track us," said the gunman.

Radar aboard an aircraft receives signals. It does not transmit to the ground. But the hijacker didn't know that. Haas protested the order.

"Henry—there's no way we can be tracked by having the radar on," he assured.

"Cut it off," Jackson insisted.

Haas did as instructed.

A few seconds later the aircraft was buffeted by severe turbulence. Jackson had to reach out to the walls of the cockpit passageway to brace himself.

"What was *that?*" he demanded.

"Well—you made me cut off the radar, and I couldn't see where I was going," Haas explained. "I plowed right into a severe cloud buildup."

"Cut that thing back on," said the hijacker.

Haas switched on the radar.

Jackson leaned forward for a closer look at the green scope.

Deciding the time was right to break the bad news, Haas

said, "Look, Henry—the whole area around Detroit and to the west of the city is experiencing extremely bad weather that's producing heavy rain and fog."

"Yeah—that's typical this time of year," he commented.

"Well—we heard a report a few minutes ago that the air traffic into Detroit is being diverted and the airport closed," the captain said.

"We came up here to set these people straight, and that's what we mean to do," Jackson said.

Angered, he was beginning to raise his voice again.

Moore stuck his head in the cockpit.

"What's happening, Smooth?" Lou inquired.

"Bad weather ahead," he answered.

"That don't change anything," Moore said.

Captain Haas looked over at Henry and suggested that if they had planned to land at Detroit, they had better forget that.

"No way, man; we are going to set this thing down right where we planned," he said.

"If we try that, do you know what will happen?" Haas asked.

Jackson returned a stoic look. He didn't want to know.

Haas said, "Remember that turbulence we hit a few minutes ago? We are at 3,500 feet, and we got caught by a minor bit of turbulence back there. If we were to try to descend through the stuff that's below us, the wings on this ole bird would shake off in less than five minutes."

"Use the radar, man—you said you could miss the clouds with that thing on," he argued.

Patiently, Haas tried to explain it was not that simple.

"The weather below us is solid. Radar won't enable us to find holes that aren't there," the captain said.

Jackson's brow was covered with tiny beads of perspiration. Removing the captain's hat, he slammed it to the cockpit floor and stomped his foot. He mopped his forehead with the sleeve of the uniform jacket. Facing his second major stumbling block since the takeover, the hijacker didn't know what to do. Haas had been convincing, and he didn't want a bigger dose of the turbulence than he had already experienced. Besides, his head was aching, and his stomach was knotted up.

"We are over Detroit," Haas reported. "What do we do?"

"You sure there ain't no way to land this thing?" Jackson asked.

"Listen to the radio, Henry. Do you hear any air traffic into or out of Detroit?" inquired the captain.

Jackson listened. There was no inbound or outbound traffic.

Jackson and Moore held a whispered conversation. When it ended, Henry told Haas to get a radio hookup between the aircraft and three Detroit city officials, who were named.

"Henry, I can't do the flying, operate the radio, and remember the names of those people," he replied.

Enraged, Jackson shouted, "Get those guys on the radio. We'll show them they can't push us around anymore."

Turning to Johnson, Haas said, "Harold—just give him the microphone and let him talk direct to the people on the ground."

Johnson pointed to a microphone, which hung in its mounting bracket on the bulkhead behind the copilot's seat.

"Just pick that up and press the button to talk. Release it to listen," Johnson said.

Jackson picked up the mike and pressed the button.

"Listen down there," he began. "This is Henry Jackson, and I've got me a planeload of passengers up here. If you don't want them killed, you do what I say."

Ground authorities at the Detroit airport waited for an indication from the hijacker that he was finished with his statement.

Jackson came back on the radio, saying, "You got it."

A traffic controller spoke into a pencil-thin microphone that was a part of the headset he wore.

"Yes, sir—what is it we can do for you?" he asked.

"We want to talk to Mayor Gribbs, Police Chief Nichols,

and the D.A., Cahalan," Jackson said.

"We'll do our best to accommodate you," said the controller, "if we can locate them."

Then he asked if there were any further instructions.

"We want them to know that we are going to hold these passengers and this aircraft until they get us ten million dollars and ten parachutes," Jackson advised.

As an afterthought he signed off with, "You got it."

"You want the mayor, the police chief, and the district attorney on the radio, and you want them to be informed of your demands for ten million dollars and ten parachutes," the controller repeated.

"That's roger," said Jackson.

"How would delivery be made?" inquired the controller.

"Just get it up—we'll let you know about that later," the hijacker said.

FBI agents who had arrived in the Air Traffic Control center received the information from the hijacked airliner.

One of the agents picked up a telephone and dialed a number.

Mayor Roman Gribbs answered the phone.

"Mr. Mayor, this is the FBI," the agent identified himself. "We are calling to relay a message transmitted from aboard a hijacked Southern Airways DC-9. The person who spoke from the airliner identified himself to the controller as one Henry Jackson."

"Yes—go ahead," said the mayor.

"They are holding the hostages aboard the airliner for a ransom demand of ten million dollars," said the agent.

"Are you kidding?" asked the mayor. "What would they be wanting with that kind of money?"

"I don't know, sir," replied the caller, "but presumably the money is demanded of the city of Detroit."

"They must be crazy," Gribbs observed.

"We are standing by at the airport to render whatever further assistance might be possible," the agent offered.

"Yes, thank you," concluded Gribbs.

Clearly the mayor faced a dilemma of gigantic proportions. But the ransom demand was not a problem for him alone. Even if he were inclined to, he could not cough up ten million dollars to the hijackers. He shared responsibility of the demand with the city's governing body. And the city council was not likely to accede to the demand by parting with tax funds entrusted to the Board.

Nonetheless, the demand had been made; and it called for some kind of action.

Mayor Gribbs issued a call for an emergency meeting of the council. It would be held as soon as its members could be assembled.

Simultaneously with the FBI's relaying of the demand to Mayor Gribbs, the Bureau passed the demand on to officials of the airline in Atlanta.

The initial shock over the amount was difficult to withstand.

Why just ten million? Why not twenty, fifty, or a hundred million? The company was so strapped financially that any amount was unrealistic. For the first time in four years, the airline was expecting to make a profit. That prospect appeared lost now because the burden of meeting the hijackers' demands likely would rest on the small regional carrier.

General manager Graydon Hall, associate general manager Gross, and other top brass held a hurried conference on the problem.

Aboard Flight 49, which was circling over Detroit while awaiting a reply from city officials below, word of the demand filtered back among the passengers from a hostage who had been seated in the front of the cabin and had overheard the conversation between Jackson and traffic controllers.

Frank Morkill took a hand-off of the information from the hostage in front of him. He thought, *We have really had it now.* Glancing at Bob McDonald, who was seated across the aisle, Frank held up ten fingers and mouthed the words "ten million." McDonald drew his index finger across his throat in a slashing motion.

The phone on the kitchen wall next to a window rang at the Haas home in La Grange.

Ann answered.

It was Jim Godwin making his fourth call of the evening.

"Annie, we have just received word that the hijackers are demanding ten million dollars and ten parachutes as ransom for the hostages," he advised.

"Jim—this is Friday. Where can you get ten million dollars at this time of the night?" she asked forlornly. She knew Southern Airways didn't have ten million dollars in cash to begin with.

Jim didn't want to build up false hopes, but he tried to give her some assurance.

"If that's what they want, Ann, we'll get it somehow," he said.

Godwin realized she knew he was lying. The robbery of every convenience store in the country at 10:30 on a Friday night wouldn't yield a haul of ten million dollars.

"Don't worry, Ann; we'll get it some way," said Godwin.

He reminded Ann that Southern had given its flight personnel extensive training in methods of dealing with hijackers.

Godwin wanted to know if anyone were with her other than Ed and the children. She told him that her parents, Lealon and Vivian George, had arrived from Booneville, Mississippi, and that her next-door neighbor, Betty Walley, was there, too. The children had been sent to bed an hour earlier.

Godwin promised to call again as soon as possible.

There was little communication between air-traffic controllers and the hijacked DC-9 as the airliner continued to circle overhead.

The silence was broken occasionally by controllers advising that the ransom demand had been relayed to the mayor. They reported also on the fast-moving weather

front and inquired about the fuel state of the jetliner. Fuel
was not a critical matter at the time, but would become a
problem in another hour. Henry Jackson had been up all
day. He had had little sleep the night before. Having been
the principal guard in the cockpit since the takeover,
Jackson had been on his feet for almost four hours.

Exchanging places with silver-toothed Moore, Jackson
went to the cabin and took the seat he had originally
occupied beside Charlotte Watts. Looking in her purse, he
kidded her.

"You ain't got a gun in there, have you, baby?"

She didn't.

He let his head fall over on her shoulder and went to
sleep, the gun and grenade held in his hands.

Captain Haas waited for action by authorities on the
ground. He felt more at ease with Jackson out of the
cockpit, although Moore's temper had not been tested. He
hoped there would be no need to test the gunman.

Unconsciously, Haas had begun to softly whistle a tune
written about the city over which he was flying. The lyrics
of the song ran through his mind as he whistled, and he
came to the words about "that ole cotton field back home."

Separating his property from that of his neighbor, John
Walley, back in La Grange, was a six-acre cotton field. He
wondered if he would ever see that field again.

Haas had dreamed of living in La Grange for most of his
adult life. Born in nearby Jackson, he had lingered around
the small town every chance he got. For him, La Grange
and its surroundings held a special fascination. It was a
place filled with history and yet a place where time seemed
to stand still. Being there was like going back a hundred
years in history; and Haas liked that. He was a history buff.

Known in times past as "La Belle Village," the hamlet
now had a population of 150 but still exhibited the remains
of a life-style that had ceased. It had once been a center of
culture and refinement, and its citizens had extended hospitality and courteous entertainment.

The War Between the States left the village and its countryside ravaged. Not all of its former glory was destroyed, however. Beautiful antebellum homes with large and spacious grounds are in perfect repair.

La Grange served first as a trading post for the Indians, who were its earliest inhabitants. They called it "Cluster of Pines." It became the red man's center of commerce long before there were many other settlements in West Tennessee. Eventually, the Indian settlement gave way to the "progress" that came with the arrival of the white man.

La Grange thrived in its new role as a center of commerce for the influx of early pioneering families who moved in from North Carolina and Virginia.

Ideally situated, the town stood on a three-hundred-foot bluff overlooking the Wolf River and commanded a view to the south of twenty-five miles or more.

By 1874 "La Belle Village" became a part of the newly formed Fayette County, which was named in honor of the Marquis de Lafayette. The Marquis had recently visited the South, and it was appropriate that the county's oldest settlement should be named La Grange after Lafayette's ancestral home in France.

The year 1828 saw the town's population at 240. It had sixty houses, four stores, two taverns, and twelve mechanics. Cotton was the king of commerce. As a thriving cotton market, La Grange surpassed Memphis as the dominant town in the southwestern part of the state.

Memphis, still an infant, was a rough, rowdy river town and not the place where cultured people from Virginia and North Carolina would settle.

One of the first men attracted to La Grange was Maj. Charles Michie, a veteran of the War of 1812. His military services had earned a land warrant for him. He personally set about the task of supervising the building of his mansion, named Woodlawn. Marking each piece of timber that went into the house, putting a deep hatchet cut on every inferior piece, Major Michie built a mansion that still stands less than a half-mile east of the Haas home on

Tennessee Highway 57.

Among other newcomers was Mary Gloster, a widow who had come to live with the family of her son-in-law, John Anderson. They found everything that they wanted—wealth and attractive, cultured people. But there was no church. Mrs. Gloster would change that. Filling a water jug with peach brandy for fortification, she and her son-in-law rode horseback over two hundred miles of wilderness to Franklin, Tennessee. There she prevailed upon her godson, Episcopal priest James Hervey Otey, to help establish an Episcopal church in La Grange. She offered to donate the land. Her slaves would make the bricks and hew the timber for the building. She got results. Immanuel Church was organized in 1832 to become the oldest Episcopal church in West Tennessee.

The church was established during the year when Lucy Holcombe was born. Lucy spent her girlhood in La Grange, living in a house that still stands. While a young woman, she met and married Francis W. Pickens, a young congressman from South Carolina. Their marriage in 1858 took place shortly before the congressman accepted the post of United States Minister to Russia. They became close friends of Czar Alexander II, and their daughter was born in the royal family's winter palace and became the godchild of the Czar and Czarina.

When the Pickenses returned to the country, Francis served as the governor of the Confederate State of South Carolina. Lucy became known as the "Queen of the Confederacy," her portrait first being placed on the Confederate one-dollar note of June 2, 1861, and later on three different one-hundred-dollar Confederate notes. Lucy Pickens was the only woman so honored by the Confederate States of America.

The idyllic life to which residents of La Grange had become accustomed disappeared on June 13, 1862. That was the day dreaded Yankee troops moved in from Memphis to occupy the town.

Well connected by rail, it was a natural outpost which

afforded a view for miles into Confederate Mississippi. The full fury of the Civil War was not unleashed on La Grange. Most of the townsmen who would have defended against the invaders were away fighting when the Union soldiers arrived.

But the occupiers brought a vulgar desolation to the town in the form of burned fences, trampled gardens, and the appropriation of private and public structures for the trappings of war.

Woodlawn, the home of Major Michie, became the West Tennessee headquarters for General William T. Sherman. When Sherman moved southward with his advancing armies, the mansion, with its nine huge rooms, each having a fireplace and fourteen-foot ceilings, was converted into an emergency hospital.

Immanuel Church served as both a hospital and barracks. The pews were torn out to make coffins for the dead Union soldiers.

By late 1863 only five of fifty plantations along the road from La Grange to Holly Springs, Mississippi, were still occupied. The fields lay uncultivated and in waste as a new enemy struck—hunger and starvation.

La Belle Village never recovered from the natural consequences of war and strife. Valiantly, the few old families who were left tried to restore the town to its antebellum glory. But it was not to be. Gone were the strong-bodied young, many of whom had fallen in battle. Gone, too, were the beautiful lawns, filled with evergreens and rare shrubs. Gone were the plank walks edged on either side with sweet violets. Gone was an era that would never return.

More than half a century passed before a new generation would come to the rescue of La Grange.

Memories of Major Michie, Mary Gloster, Lucy Holcombe Pickens, and others linger on.

However, new names have come into prominence: Cowan, Griffin, Walley, Baker, McNamee, Beasley, Jones, and Bender, among numerous others.

Largely through the efforts of those families, La Grange

was given a rebirth. Except for a ribbon of asphalt that stretches through the town, one yellow caution light, and an overhead traffic signal installed to control modern conveyances, the town bears a strong resemblance to its earlier quaintness and beauty.

Residents are determined to keep it that way.

Not until the fall of 1970 did Ann and Bill Haas acquire Twin Gables.

The couple was married in July of 1961 in a secret ceremony at Ann's home in Booneville. Secrecy was necessary to protect her job with Delta Airlines, which, at the time, had rules against flight attendants being married.

Complicating matters was a long and bitter pilots' strike against Southern Airways, which saw Haas walking the picket lines. His walrus mustache became a symbol of the protracted walkout. Decals bearing the symbol appeared prominently everywhere as a reminder of the labor dispute.

Ann's salary surpassed the meager strike benefits Haas received. Their combined earnings were barely enough to support themselves. Too, Ann had taken on the job of raising Bill's three sons by a previous marriage—Billy Bob, Jr., Gerry, and Jim.

The strike came to an end in 1962, enabling Ann to quit her job as Haas returned to the Southern flight line.

There was another marriage ceremony as Ann and Bill took their vows publicly during a church ceremony at Booneville. It took place exactly one year from the date of the first one: July 20, 1962. She was twenty-five; he was thirty-three.

During the next few years the Haases lived in New Orleans until Bill was able to build up enough seniority to pick Memphis as his permanent base.

In 1968 Ann and Bill started a new family with the arrival of a baby boy, who was named John Garner Haas.

When time permitted, Bill scouted around the countryside for a new place in which to live. The city was all right, but he wanted his children to grow up hearing the sounds of the whippoorwills and to be able to enjoy the beauty of the natural surroundings found only in the country.

His search eventually led him to Twin Gables. Taking a deep breath of fresh air, he noted that the old house was in bad repair. A great deal of sweat and hard work would be required to make it livable. But that was where he wanted to be, and he promised himself that he would devote his energies to getting the 136-year-old house restored to its once-imposing appearance.

Ann, Bill, and young John moved to La Grange in the summer of 1970. The months that followed saw the rebuilding of the big kitchen with a multitude of cabinets and the addition of modern appliances. Sleeping and sitting areas were given the same priority on the renovation schedule. The long and spacious entrance hall, which had looked like a drab funeral parlor, took on a new look with highly polished wood floors. A sparkling chandelier with ten crystal pendants hung from the plaster medallion on the ceiling. The old and peeling paper on the walls was replaced by a bright new wall covering.

That Thanksgiving brought reasons for giving special thanks for the bountiful blessings that seemed to be showering down on the Haases. The most joyous event had occurred just a few weeks before, on November 5, when Ann gave birth to a blue-eyed girl. The coming of cherubic-faced Betsy had special significance. She was the first girl born into the Haas family in forty years.

Life couldn't have been better. Billy Bob had realized his lifelong ambition—a happy family, peace of mind, and the anonymity of life in the country.

Now, less than two years later, the dream seemed to be on the verge of evaporating. The lives of his passengers and crew weighed heavily on his shoulders. His every decision could spell the difference between life and death. And the anonymity the gentle, quiet-spoken West Tennessean had sought was being stripped away as the world watched and waited for the outcome of this latest hijacking.

Lou Moore shifted uneasily on his feet as he stood guard over Haas and Johnson. He was growing impatient at the lack of response to the hijackers' money demand.

Preparing for the inevitable need for another refueling diversion, Captain Haas informed the gunman that when the instrument panel gauge registered eight thousand pounds, they would be left with only enough fuel for about an additional thirty minutes of flying.

"Tell 'em we're down to six thousand pounds—that'll hurry 'em up," Moore said.

Harold Johnson advised ground authorities that the airliner would have to leave the area for refueling soon.

"What is the status of the money request?" Johnson asked.

"Sir, the last report we had," said the controller, "was that the city council had been called into a special session to consider the matter."

"Roger," said the copilot.

"You tell 'em they better get in a hurry down there, or we'll take this mother right down into the Wayne County courthouse," Moore threatened.

Sensing a part of the problem confronting the city officials, Haas reminded Moore that the banks were all closed and that cash was normally locked away in vaults with timing mechanisms for the weekend.

"They better find a way of getting into one somewhere," said the pirate.

Fred Parham, Southern Airways' station manager in Chicago, drove down a ramp that took him to the lower level parking deck beneath the First National City Bank.

A dozen FBI agents were waiting. They escorted the short, balding airline representative to a ground-level office, where he introduced himself and produced proper identification.

Graydon Hall was standing by on a long-distance telephone hookup to the company's headquarters in Atlanta. Parham spoke briefly with the executive, who then informed the banking official that he recognized his representative's voice.

Parham put his signature on a piece of paper presented by the banker and departed with a heavy suitcase, in the company of the FBI agents.

He entered the second of four unmarked cars that would escort him back to Midway Airport.

Capt. Walter M. Wright and his copilot, Carl Epperson, waited at Midway for Parham's return. Wright had just piloted a passenger flight to Chicago from Memphis. Having been informed of the hijacking of one of Southern's planes, Wright and his crew were told to stand by for a special assignment in connection with delivery of the ransom demand.

"It's a bad night to be goofing around with silly stuff like a hijacking," Wright observed to Epperson.

It was shortly after eleven o'clock when Parham and the force of FBI agents arrived at Midway. They assembled in the airline's operations area. A Southern Airways DC-9, designated 905, stood ready on the ramp just outside.

Captain Wright noted that in addition to the suitcase carried by Parham, a number of agents carried suitcases.

"What's in the bags, gentlemen?" he asked.

He was told that Parham's suitcase contained money and that the bags in the possession of the agents contained collapsible rifles.

"Well, now—I've checked with my union chairman," he said, "and we don't want any shootin' up of any of our aircraft."

The captain told the agents, "You can go aboard with your personal sidearms—but you'll have to leave the other guns behind."

There was no argument. Captain Wright had asserted his command.

Harold Johnson was checking by radio on possible points to which to divert for refueling. After two hours of holding over Detroit, it was becoming necessary to make plans to fly elsewhere. Windsor, Ontario's airport, was below weather minimums for landing. That left only one other point within the near vicinity.

Henry Jackson had been aroused from his sleep by Moore, who informed him of the need to go somewhere for refueling. Jackson got out of his seat and staggered to the cockpit. Charlotte Watts was glad to see him leave her seat. She had been terrified by his presence but afraid to say anything to the gunman. To discourage his return, Miss Watts lowered the armrest between the two seats. Covering herself with a blanket, she curled up in an attempt to sleep.

Jackson picked up the mike mounted on the cockpit bulkhead and spoke to authorities on the ground.

"I don't have any more time—really. Get that money together down there," he insisted.

"Yeah—they're working on it for you. They're doing all they can," came the controller's reply.

"OK—hurry up," he demanded.

Believing the flight crew to be just as sleepy and tired as he was, the hijacker ordered Johnson to tell authorities to add stimulants for the crew to the list of demands. The taking of stimulants by crew members is prohibited. But Johnson was in no position to cite regulations. Speaking into his mike, he did as instructed.

"Would you get something from the airport for the pilot and the crew to keep us awake? When we continue the flight, we have got a long way to go. Get something that will keep us awake and alert."

Then he cautioned, "Be sure you check with the FAA and make sure it's something that won't affect our flying ability."

Captain Haas asked Jackson what city would be suitable to the hijackers for refueling. Windsor was out. They didn't want to go to Montreal. That left Cleveland as the only other nearby destination. Jackson was agreeable.

"Check Cleveland real quick-like, and give us directions," Johnson radioed the controller.

Jackson interrupted with instructions.

Johnson continued, "We need the money, stimulants, and parachutes flown to Cleveland immediately."

"All right, we'll do that—fly the money, parachutes, and stimulants to Cleveland," acknowledged the controller.

"Be advised there should be no one—repeat—no one but one man coming to the aircraft to fuel the plane and to bring the money, the parachutes, and the stimulants," Johnson emphasized. "Only one man, and he is to have on swimming trunks."

"The pilot is advised his instructions will be carried out," replied the controller. "But it will take about one hour and twenty minutes to fly the money and goods to Cleveland."

Henry Jackson didn't like the length of time that would be taken. Knowing that the distance between Detroit and Cleveland was only a hundred miles, he picked up the microphone to protest the delay.

"Hey—well, look—I don't—I don't know what they're putting that stuff on, but they act like they're jivin' down there. You tell somebody that they better do better than an hour and twenty minutes."

Captain Haas had already turned southward, heading for Cleveland.

Pain stabbed with the sharpness of a knife at Alvin Fortson's chest. At first the elderly man fought to disguise his agony, not wanting to be a bother in an already bothersome situation. But the intensity and frequency of the attack was becoming unbearable. The pressure was suffocating, eventually touching off a violent spasm of wheezing and coughing. His hands were becoming cold and clammy. Worn and wrinkled by the unkind passage of years, Fortson's skin paled.

Marge Brennan and Gale Buchanan, seated nearby, looked at each other knowingly. They summoned Mel Cale's attention to the old man's plight. The gunman agreed that Fortson needed aid and went forward to inform Donna of the sick passenger. She hurried to the triple-seater where he sat, removed the armrests, and placed him in a reclining position. Buchanan removed Fortson's boots and began massaging his feet and legs to restore circulation. Marge rubbed the man's arms vigorously. Donna had been trained to render first aid, but not during her six years with the airline had she been confronted with an apparent heart-attack victim. The flight attendant asked Fortson if he carried medication with him. Through the torturously uncontrolled coughing, he managed a reply that he had some nitroglycerine tablets and had taken one.

Donna was permitted to enter the cockpit to advise Captain Haas of the medical emergency.

"All we need now is to have a pregnant woman on board and to have to deliver a baby," he said.

Flipping on the "No Smoking" sign, he told Donna to place the ailing passenger on the aircraft's supply of pure oxygen and to make him as comfortable as he could be under the circumstances.

Gusty winds whipped a misty rain across Hopkins Field at Cleveland, making the pirated aircraft's approach difficult. Looking out the windows, the hostages tried to determine where they were as the jetliner touched down for the second time in five hours. Landing on the main runway, Flight 49 rolled to a stop midway down the strip. Jackson ordered the aircraft to halt at a point where two runways intersected, thus blocking all inbound and outbound traffic. The hijacker instructed the crewmen to keep the engines running while the jetliner was on the ground. Having gained a familiarity with the radio microphone, he warned airport authorities that the aircraft would remain stationary where it was until refueling was accomplished.

Alvin Fortson lay quietly now, his nose and mouth contained by the yellow oxygen mask. Cale held Fortson's left wrist, timing the pulsating rhythm of the old man's heart. The hijacker's grip never found the beating artery for which it searched, but after a minute elapsed he nodded approvingly.

Cale's apparent concern for Fortson prompted Karen to

make an appeal for the release of the sick man, as well as all of the other hostages. He laughed at the suggestion.

She followed the gunman as he walked away.

"I'm serious," she insisted.

Cale didn't know what it was about her, but something made him like her. Maybe it was her unfearing attitude or her forthright manner. Perhaps it was the awkward attempt she had made earlier to be friendly with an obvious foe.

"Please listen to me," she pleaded. "These passengers have done nothing against any of you. They are being victimized unnecessarily. Their families are worried to death. And the sick man could die if he's not taken to a hospital."

Tears welled up in her blue eyes as she continued the plea.

"Let the people off while we're on the ground here. Let them go home. They're just a liability. You can hold me hostage."

"Now, you listen to me," he shot back. "You must be losing your mind. There are probably a hundred snipers around this aircraft right now just waiting for us to get dumb. There ain't no way we're gonna open these doors."

Defeat melted the sweetness of her face. Even her dimpled cheeks lost their rosy glow. She realized it would do no good to say more.

Haas and Johnson waited nervously for the fuel truck. Despite repeated assurances radioed by the tower operator, nothing was moving on the airport. Jackson was growing edgier by the second. He told Johnson to get on the radio and tell those flunkies either to send that fuel truck out immediately or watch as the dead bodies of the hostages were thrown out the windows one by one.

The copilot transmitted the threat.

Regular fuel attendants on duty at the airport balked at going near the hijacked aircraft. An FBI agent was being instructed in the operation of the fuel truck. He would have to perform the operation.

Meanwhile, relief for the crew was being planned.

Captain Godwin sat in his office, listening as George Gross revealed the plan.

"Jim, Mr. Hall just received news from Chicago that a fairly substantial amount of money has been put together."

Knowing that Gross had already formulated details of his plan and was merely seeking concurrence, Godwin asked how the money was to be delivered.

The company third-in-command spelled out his strategy.

It was approaching one o'clock on Saturday morning.

After Gross left his office, Godwin again telephoned Ann Haas at La Grange.

"Annie—I just want to let you know that Graydon Hall will be calling from here on out," he said.

"Well—you need some rest, Jim," she consoled.

"It's not that, Ann. The crew of the hijacked aircraft needs relief more than we do, and we're going to try to give it to them," he explained.

"What do you mean, Jim?" she pressed.

"Well, we have another DC-9 with two fresh crews ready to go. We are going to try to rendezvous with the hijackers in hope of exchanging one DC-9 and crew for Billy Bob's aircraft and the people aboard," he explained.

Ann broke down in tears.

Jim listened as she sobbed into the telephone.

Finally composing herself, she said, "Jim, I don't want any other lives risked." Lips quivering, she said, "Neither would Billy Bob—let him handle the situation."

"Ann, the decision has been made. I must leave now. Mr. Hall will be in touch. Be brave—we'll get out of this thing somehow," he said.

Stepping across the corridor to the operations center, Godwin talked for a few minutes with Captains T. M. "Bubba" Shanahan, Bob Pipkin, and Guy Steele. Accompanied by two FBI agents, the four pilots left the building and proceeded by crew bus to the flight line. Gross and sales vice-president Frank Wheeler would join them shortly.

Four flight attendants would complete the complement

of crew members. Regina Eaton, Barbara Garrison, Sherry Stempel, and Mimi Davenport had been selected from the supervisory stewardess roster for the assignment. Barbara was on weekend supervisor duty. She had not expected to become involved in anything like a hijacking. A statuesque and gorgeous redhead, she was attired in her hot-pants uniform.

Sherry had been accompanied to the company headquarters by her husband, Frank, who was standing outside in the corridor when his wife learned of the assignment. She stepped outside to tell him about the plan for her to be aboard the plane intended for exchange.

His reaction could have been expected.

"You may as well go in there and tell them you're not going—'cause you're not," he said. "You must be crazy, thinking I would let you go."

"Frank, it's not a consideration of ours," she said. "It's my obligation to go. I am the one who trained these girls. If I can't go, how can I expect them to be out there performing the things I taught them to do?"

Beauty and winsome ways made it difficult for Frank to deny any of his wife's requests. But this was one to which he was rigidly opposed.

"Sherry, there's to be no argument about this," he said. "Tell me who to talk with—you are not going."

Mortified at his refusal, Sherry wanted to crawl off into a corner and get lost. *Of all people,* she thought, *not to be able to go on the flight.* She was angry with herself. She was even angrier with Frank, although she appreciated his concern.

Frank went into the operations room and spoke with Gross.

"Sherry has advised me of plans for her to be aboard the exchange plane. The only way she can go is for me to go along to try to protect her," he said.

Gross declined the offer and assured Frank there would be no problem, since there were three other flight attendants able to make the flight.

Sherry watched sadly as Regina, Barbara, and Mimi went out the door, leaving her behind. She would remain on in the operations center, hoping there was something helpful she could do.

A DC-9, bearing fleet numbers 963, was ready for flight when Godwin's crew reached the line. Boarding the aircraft, the FBI agents were briefed on various interior features. They were shown a compartment door behind the captain's cockpit seat. It provided emergency access to the aircraft's electrical and electronic compartment beneath the flight deck. One of the agents maneuvered through the opening and went below. The second agent secreted a half-dozen handguns in various passenger seat pockets and overhead racks in the cabin.

Haas and Johnson were doubtful that they would ever see another fuel truck. Henry Jackson had consumed a dozen miniature bottles of liquor. Reasoning with the gunman had become as impossible as trying to reason with a bear caught in a trap. He stomped, cursed, and demanded. Directing his words to Lou Moore in the cabin, Jackson yelled, "Get your gun ready back there. We're gonna show these people we mean business."

The hostages feared the gunmen would go beserk and start shooting them at any instant. All they could do was hope and pray, and they were doing plenty of praying.

Captain Haas picked up his microphone and, in a slowly measured cadence, attempted to impress upon authorities in control the gravity of the situation aboard.

"We are laying across the razor's edge out here. What happened to the fuel truck you promised—did you send our request to the grievance committee?"

Haas did not hear the reply. The reference to the grievance committee blew Jackson's mind. Its meaning was beyond his comprehension. Thinking the captain had transmitted a veiled request for armed intervention, the hijacker waved his pistol in Haas' face.

Shouting, he warned, "Shut your mouth—you say

exactly what I tell you to say—nothing else—or I'll blow your brains out. Do you understand?"

Haas understood.

He had always considered himself a man with a limited vocabulary that was not likely to provoke anyone. Jackson's explosive reaction had been unexpected. But it convinced him that his captor was totally irrational.

The flashing beacon atop the approaching fuel truck failed to produce a calming effect. During the next twenty minutes the atmosphere aboard was charged with tension.

Word was relayed to the aircraft by radio that the ransom money was being placed aboard a DC-9 in Chicago. It would be flown to Cleveland.

Haas thought Jackson would react favorably to the news. However, the Chicago flight would not be due for another two hours.

"I could *drive* down here from Chicago in two hours," Jackson said. "You tell those people we mean business."

Jackson had become apprehensive over the lengthy stay for refueling. They had been on the ground for almost an hour. The attempt to prolong the stay excited his imagination. Believing authorities were setting a trap, the hijacker spoke with his two accomplices.

Mel Cale had been watching the fuel attendant through a cabin window on the right side of the aircraft. He had spotted what appeared to be seven figures moving toward the plane about a hundred yards away.

He yelled to Jackson and Moore at the front of the cabin, "There are seven snipers moving up on us out there."

Reaching into the cockpit, Jackson picked up the microphone.

"Get those guys back, or we'll throw a grenade at them," he threatened.

From the aircraft the hijackers watched as the figures retreated. They had heard the threat on the portable field radio they carried.

Lou Moore took over again in the cockpit.

"We're gettin' outa here . . ." he said.

"Would you tell us where we're going?" asked Haas.

"What difference does it make?" Moore replied.

"Well—we can't just take to the sky in this overcast without navigational assistance from the ground. We have to climb above the weather and follow compass headings assigned by air traffic controllers."

It was an admitted oversimplification. Moore just scratched his head. He didn't want the crew to know the depths of his ignorance, so he decided to go along with the captain's explanation.

"Tell those people to meet us in Toronto—and they had better show up with the money," he said.

Harold Johnson radioed controllers with news of the new destination as the jetliner began taxiing to its takeoff position at the end of the runway. Flight 49 had been on the ground in Cleveland for exactly one hour.

Captain Haas had considered making an appeal to await the Chicago jet's arrival. But he abandoned the idea in the interest of passenger safety. He was in no position to negotiate a further delay, and the gunmen had apparently formulated their plans.

Controllers guided the airliner on its new course as it climbed out over Cleveland. During the ascent Moore questioned the need for the two pilots to make repeated reference to the standard flight checklist. He wanted to know why they had to have a piece of paper to tell them what to do.

Tired and exasperated, Haas explained that the printed list contained over one hundred essential items: positions of switches, fuel counters, pressurization settings, radio controls, and many others, all of which should be accomplished in a proper sequence.

"This just insures we don't neglect any of the necessary functions during various stages of flight," said the captain. Bringing it down to Moore's level of understanding, Haas added, "It's a little more complex than driving a car. There are too many things to be accomplished to trust our memories."

The flight to Toronto had been airborne for ten minutes when Moore instructed Johnson to get on the radio to ground authorities and to remind them to have ready not only the money, but ten parachutes as well, to be placed on the aircraft when it lands. The copilot was tempted to ask who would be using the ten parachutes. But he was afraid the answer might include the hijackers and members of the flight crew. The thought was too insane to contemplate. Johnson put the question out of his mind.

Haas was perplexed by the request for so many parachutes, too. Allowing himself some mental gymnastics, he speculated that the hijackers would pick up the money in Toronto and that during the next trip aloft they would parachute to their escape somewhere over Canada.

If that were their plan and they went through with it, Haas could picture the scene. The trio would have to drop from the aircraft using the ventral steps located in the tail cone.

Once they popped the silk canopies, there would be a brief moment during which they would realize their doom was sealed.

The high-speed jet thrust would make confetti of the parachutes.

4
The Chase

At Chicago the force of FBI agents boarded Captain Wright's DC-9 to fly the ransom money to the extortionists in Toronto. Their departure for the Canadian city was being held up while they were waiting for the parachutes, which were aboard an inbound military plane.

Streaking through the sky over western North Carolina, Captains Godwin and Pipkin piloted their DC-9 jetliner on a direct course for Toronto.

Gross, Wheeler, the alternate crews of Shanahan, Steele, and the three flight attendants occupied seats in the passenger compartment. They talked over details of the exchange plan. The chase plane was estimating an arrival at its destination around 4:00 A.M. Captain Godwin hoped to land ahead of the hijacked airliner.

Aboard Flight 49, Captain Haas could put off his request no longer.

"Lou—I need to go to the rest room," he announced.

Without hesitation the hijacker said, "Sure—go ahead."

"Well, look," Haas said, "while I'm back there in the cabin, how about me talking to these passengers? It might help avoid a panic later on and prevent somebody from getting hurt."

Moore agreed it would be a good idea.

Haas had not been out of his seat for over eight hours. His stiffened frame uncoiled reluctantly. For a minute he stood in the cockpit, regaining his balance. He did not want to present himself to the passengers with an uneasy footing. Straightening his posture, he proceeded down the aisle to the rear of the cabin, magnetically attracting the eyes of the

hostages to his tall, broad-shouldered figure. It was the first
time the passengers had viewed their captain. His dark,
graying hair and handsome, tanned face conveyed the
maturity of his forty-three years. A neatly trimmed walrus
mustache completed the image of a man of aristocratic
gentry. His German ancestors would have been proud of
the admiring glances he received.

During the return walk up the aisle, Haas stopped to
introduce himself and speak briefly with each passenger.
He apologized for the inconvenience as well as the terrifying conditions to which they were being subjected. Implor-
ing each person to remain calm, he promised that his crew
and the company were doing everything possible to mollify
the hijackers in the interest of bringing the piracy to a safe
conclusion. His unwavering voice and sincerity instilled
confidence. The hostages knew the captain shared their
anxious reservations. But his attempts to raise their spirits
reflected qualities that were reassuring. The kindness and
sympathy he displayed were innate qualities in the man
who held a great measure of their destiny in his hands.

Sandy Didien explained that her two-year-old son,
Keith, was hypertensive and hoped he would continue to
overcome the excitement. Captain Haas told the blond-
haired youngster he had a little girl of the same age. Notic-
ing Keith had lost interest in the coloring book resting on
his lap, Haas took a piece of paper and penciled the outline
of a large, round gourdlike object with irregularly shaped
eyes, nostrils, and mouth. Showing it to the tot, the captain
asked, "Do you know what this is?"

Keith said he did.

"What is it?" the captain prompted.

"Pum—kin . . ."

"That's right," Haas said, "and when you color it for me
it'll look like the one sitting on my front porch in Tennessee."

Haas asked the youngster if he had had a jack-o'-lantern
for Halloween. Keith said he had.

Moving up the aisle, the captain bent over to ask

Fortson how he was feeling.

"All right," murmured the old gentleman.

Before leaving the cabin, Haas told Donna and Karen to do their best to make the passengers comfortable. Stepping back into the cockpit, he turned and said, "Keep those pretty chins up . . ."

They would have hugged his neck and wished him luck, but he stepped out of sight. It was just as well. They would not have wanted the captain to see their tears.

It was 2:00 A.M. when Haas sat down.

"Harold, I'll take over the controls. See if you can find out from Toronto what the situation is on the money."

"Right, sir," Johnson replied.

Keying his mike, the copilot spoke.

"Toronto approach, this is Southern 49 with a request. Are you ready to copy? Could you check with the United States government and see if the money is en route to Toronto?"

"Yes, sir, I'll do the best I can."

The controller radioed instructions to a small private aircraft that had just departed on a flight to Wiarton. Rain and snow blanketed the area. Only two aircraft were aloft in the vicinity. The pilot of the small aircraft inquired about the position of the Southern Airways jet.

"He's holding about fifty miles southwest," advised the controller.

Johnson repeated his request for information regarding the ransom. "This is extremely urgent," he reminded.

"Roger, sir—we are aware of the urgency, and we are checking as of now."

"OK, Toronto—while you're checking, also check with the Canadian government and see if they can help out with things in any way."

Henry Jackson stood in the aisle at the seat of Marcia Timbers. She complained to the hijacker that she was cold. Laying his pistol in her lap, the bandit went to the clothes closet, removed his long leather coat, and gave it to her.

Toronto arrival had received a status report on Captain

Wright's DC-9. Transmitting to Flight 49, the voice said, "Your company has an aircraft departing Chicago in forty minutes with the money on board—destination Toronto."

Confirming receipt of the message, Johnson said, "OK—we have an aircraft departing Chicago in forty minutes with the money."

Lou Moore was displeased with the report.

"I thought you told us that plane was ready to leave Chicago when we were in Cleveland. Now they say they haven't even left yet."

"They're probably trying to locate the parachutes for you, and that's not easy at this time of the night," Haas alibied.

"Yeah—I guess so," Moore remarked.

Officials at Toronto's huge international airport went about the task of efficiently coordinating their actions in the unfolding drama.

Telephoning down to arrival control in the terminal facility, the tower operator inquired, "Is the supervisor down there by his desk?"

"Yes, he is pretty well tied up on the phone. What do you want?"

"I just wanted to talk to him for a minute."

Assuming that the tower operator wanted to know what was going on, the arrival controller gave him an update on the situation.

"The latest we have is that Southern has dispatched another aircraft from Chicago or will have very shortly, within the next forty minutes, with the money on board and the destination Toronto."

"I see; OK."

"And, oh, John!"

"Hello."

"The airport is closed now till further notice—that comes from the shift manager."

"OK," acknowledged the tower personnel.

Copilot Johnson radioed the control center with plans to

continue circling southwest of Toronto.

"Roger, Southern 49."

Karen had become concerned over Henry Jackson's increased drunkenness. And Lou left the cockpit frequently to help himself to the whiskey. His speech had become so incoherent that she had difficulty in understanding him. The diminutive stewardess looked up at Jackson and told him of her concern.

"I'm getting tired of your drinking. It's a threat to the well-being of everybody on this aircraft. You should keep a clear head if you hope to accomplish whatever it is you hope to accomplish."

Jackson reacted patronizingly. He said, "That's great, baby, that you're thinking about us." He reached out and gave her a little pat on the shoulder.

"Let me get you some coffee," she offered.

"Yeah—that'd be fine," he accepted.

Jackson wasn't quite ready to abandon the advantage of the abundant store of liquor. He sneaked another miniature from the supply and relieved Moore of his guard duties in the cockpit.

Haas and Johnson were distressed at his return. But in anticipation of the moment, the captain had saved a surprise for the hijacker. The piracy was now in its ninth hour. Both Jackson and Moore had stood guard while leaning against the cockpit bulkhead. Haas said, "Henry, you must be getting pretty tired by now."

"Yeah, man, this is like that restaurant work me and Lou used to do all day and night. Gets to you."

Indicating the wall at the front of the flight deck passageway, Haas asked, "Why don't you fold down that observer seat and sit for awhile?"

Haas showed him how to unstrap the seat. Once it was in position, Jackson boosted himself up on the chair, thinking Karen and the captain to be two of the most considerate people he had ever met. He was beginning to like them both.

The captain was not trying to aid his known enemy. He

thought the move might help him keep the gunman under better control.

"Look, Henry—about all this money you're demanding. I think you picked the wrong airline. Let me tell you something. Southern's financial condition is among the poorest in the industry. We're a small regional airline, and the company hasn't made a profit in years. We just try to pay the bills and stay in business to serve our customers."

Jackson could understand. Haas had told him honestly about the situation. The hijacker said he was sorry that Southern was caught in the middle.

"We ain't got nothin' against the airline," Jackson assured; "we want Detroit to pay for harassing us the way they have. They picked on Lou and me 'cause we're black. We didn't do those things they accused us of doing."

Haas believed he was probably lying, but accepted his claim of having been mistreated for racial reasons.

Driving home his point, Haas summed up, "Well, you may not have anything against Southern, but what you're doing could close us down. You know those people in Detroit couldn't give you ten million dollars if they wanted to—they don't have the power to give away money belonging to the taxpayers."

"They better cough it up," Jackson warned. "We don't want it from nobody else."

Whatever the source of the ransom money, the hijackers would have to be made to believe it was extracted from the city of Detroit. Most likely it would come from Southern Airways, however.

Karen stepped to the cockpit to advise the captain that the galley was out of coffee.

"We'll try to get some at Toronto," he suggested. Harold wrote it down on his list under "ten million dollars, parachutes, and fuel."

As she turned to leave the flight deck, the stewardess caught a glimpse of the liquor bottle in Henry's hand.

"I thought you agreed to leave the liquor alone," she chided.

Jackson asked, "Do you think you could keep us outa that stuff?"

"I think I can," she replied.

"You really don't like my drinking, huh?"

"No, I don't," she reiterated. "I don't think it's going to do anybody any good."

"Well, if you could keep us outa the booze, go ahead and do it," he urged.

She went to the galley and locked the liquor cabinet.

At the Toronto airport, thirty Royal Canadian Mounted Policemen assembled in the security division office. The tower operator put through another call to the arrival control station.

"Clare—Clare—are you down there, Clare?"

There was no immediate reply. He tried again.

"Are you getting me, Clare?"

"Yeah—go ahead . . ."

"I guess you're back, eh?"

"Yeah."

"Uh, I guess the supervisor is still tied up, is he?"

"Yes, pretty well—I'll have him give you a call as soon as he can."

The tower operator was confronted with a problem.

"I'm starting to get calls now from the press, and I'm wondering what—uh—information—or if I am supposed to give out any info about this."

"No, I would give nothing for starters and work from there; and refer them to this phone number or the airport manager's office."

The red phone on the tower console jangled. It was the hot-line connection to the Royal Canadian Mounted Police. When the brief conversation ended, the operator renewed his discussion with arrival control.

"Uh—who is actually working the hijacked aircraft now? Are you working him, or is somebody else?"

"No—I am."

"Yeah, well, I just received word from the RCMP that they've got a tip from somebody that your frequency is being monitored. What he said was that the—ah—frequency in use right now is being monitored, so you're supposed to watch what's being said."

"OK."

Police officials had taken the precautionary step of alerting the arrival controller to the possibility that the hijackers were listening to all of the radio exchanges.

The DC-9 bearing its cargo of money and FBI personnel was now in flight between Chicago and Toronto. A second DC-9 out of Atlanta was rapidly closing the distance and had established communications with the arrival control center that relayed the information to the tower.

"Got an inbound when you're ready to copy," advised the controller.

"Try it again . . ."

"Have an inbound for you when you're ready to copy . . ."

"Go ahead."

"It's Southern 963 out of Atlanta."

"OK."

"And he'll be landing on runway 5."

"OK."

"That's not the hijacked one. It's—which—the money one?"

Arrival cautioned. "It's not to be released—the fact that this aircraft is inbound."

"I see—OK."

Henry Jackson heard the reference to the inbound jet from Atlanta. It unnerved and aroused the inebriate's suspicion.

"What's going on here—what's that plane coming here for?" he demanded.

Captain Haas didn't know the answer to that question himself. After some fast thinking, he came up with a fast answer that he hoped would satisfy the gunman.

"Look, Henry, they're bringing the money you demanded in ten- and fifteen-dollar denominations from all points on the compass. The more planes you see and hear, the more money you're gonna get," Haas said.

Of course, the answer was implausible. However, it had a ring of truth in it as far as Henry was concerned. He didn't hear any more about the aircraft. Captain Haas switched to another radio frequency.

Fuel aboard Flight 49 was reaching a critical level once again. In a race against time, Haas was uncertain whether the aircraft could remain airborne until the Chicago jet arrived. Arrival controllers worried over the status.

"Southern 49 on arrival?"

"Toronto—this is Southern 49—go ahead."

"Roger—what is your fuel status?"

"We are down to twelve thousand pounds—getting low," said the copilot.

"OK—and on arrival Toronto, what type of fuel will you require?"

Harold Johnson was momentarily distracted by Henry Jackson, who mumbled, "You tell 'em they better get off their duffs down there and get that money together, or we won't be comin' down for fuel."

The question was repeated.

"Southern 49, what type of jet fuel will you require on landing Toronto?"

"JP4," he answered.

"Roger."

The controller picked up the telephone to the tower.

"And I have another inbound for you."

"Hang on for a second," the tower requested. "I've got to answer the RCMP line."

"OK."

First officer Johnson asked arrival control for a weather condition report.

"Yes, sir—measured six hundred overcast, six miles light rain and fog. Wind zero-sixty at ten, the altimeter . . . twenty-nine . . ."

The tower operator cut in.

"Do you have a time on 905, the Chicago inbound?"

Johnson needed additional weather data.

"Your temp and dew point?"

"Forty-one and thirty-nine."

Arrival queried, "Southern 49, you do want the approach information on runway 5, right? I understand you don't have the approach charts . . ."

"OK—give us the information then, please."

"OK—the elevation of the airport is 569 feet; the outer marker on 5R is the Juliette beacon frequency 236 KHZ; the localizer frequency on 5R is 109.1; and the procedure turn altitude is 2500 feet. The localizer heading straight in will be 055."

Johnson noted a discrepancy and asked for clarification.

"OK—and—uh—we cross the outer marker at 2500?"

"No, that was procedure turn altitude. The outer marker altitude is 1770 feet."

Weather conditions would necessitate an instrument-landing approach. The early-morning fog had reduced visibility below minimums. Johnson called for the instrument-landing data.

Arrival reported, "The ILS straight-in-minimum is a decision height of 829 feet . . . that's three hundred and three quarters of a mile."

"OK," Johnson acknowledged, "and what is the missed-approach procedure?"

"Climb to three thousand feet on a track of 076 degrees, the direct to the Oshawa nondirectional beacon, frequency 391 KHZ, and maintain three thousand feet."

"I see; we thank you."

"OK—and one thing more," advised the controller. "I didn't give you the distance from the outer marker to the runway. It's 3.9 nautical miles."

Captain Haas instructed the copilot to determine the progress of the inbound from Chicago. It was now 4:00 A.M. Flight 49 had been in the air for approximately two and a half hours, flying oval holding patterns ten miles long to the southwest of Toronto. Fuel aboard was getting lower and lower. The cabin's overhead lights had been turned off. Some of the hostages slept fitfully. They were mentally and physically exhausted. Adrenalin was the only thing keeping the flight crew alert. Captain Haas hoped the ordeal was nearing its climax. He hoped the hijackers would not sober up enough to lose their nerves and change their minds about parachuting from the aircraft after receiving the money.

Arrival control was busy conveying new information to the tower controller.

"Here is the inbound if you are ready to copy."

"Go ahead," said the tower.

"OK—Southern 905, DC-9 from Midway, is due at 4:28."

"That's Southern Airways, is it?"

"Yes, Sunny Southern . . ."

Arrival relayed the expected time of arrival to the hijacked aircraft. Johnson said, "OK—Arrival, we need the runway length and the DME distance from the VOR to the runway and the radial from the VOR to the runway."

"Yes, sir, the runway length is 9500 feet; and the VOR is located on the airport."

"That's good," Johnson replied. "Is it raining now? Is your runway wet?"

"Yes, it is light rain, sir."

"Thank you."

Arrival continued to coordinate plans with the tower.

"That Southern 963 from Atlanta I gave you—he will be calling himself Douglas 963."

Captain Godwin had advised the controller he would not make reference to Southern in the hope of arriving without the hijackers' knowledge. He knew Captain Haas would recognize his voice on the radio and the numerical call sign. What he did not know was the fact that his presence in the Toronto air space had already been disclosed earlier. As expected, the inbound from Atlanta would beat the Chicago flight in landing. The jetliner was out of eight thousand feet and descending to four thousand. It, too, would be tracked on the arrival controller's radar and guided in for an instrument landing.

"Douglas 963—this is Arrival—we have you in radar contact. Toronto altimeter is 2979. I'll have vectors in about fifteen miles for an ILS 5R straight in."

"Roger, 2979—Douglas 963 level at four."

"963 level four—turn right heading zero-nine-zero to intercept localizer 5R—fly it inbound—maintain four— keep your speed up as long as you wish. I'll give you a check ten miles from the Outer."

"Roger—a zero-nine-zero vector and maintain four. We'll keep our speed up."

From the air the two pilots could see nothing on the ground. Their view was obscured completely by fog and low-hanging clouds. Captain Godwin was at the controls of the three-and-a-half-million-dollar jetliner. Captain Pipkin helped monitor the various instruments while maintaining radio contact with the arrival controller. An instrument landing at an unfamiliar airport would demand the utmost alertness and flying skill on the part of the three inbound crews. The greatest strain would be on the hijacked skipper. He had been at the aircraft's controls almost constantly since the flight originated at Memphis, a period of more than ten hours.

Captain Godwin held the fuel control levers with his right hand, maintaining an airspeed of 240 knots. Descending to three thousand feet, the arrival controller followed the jetliner's path on the radar scope, reporting, "Douglas 963—you are eight miles from the outer marker. You can reduce at your convenience."

The Atlanta flight touched down safely a few minutes later. It was none too soon for the arrival controller. He was beginning to feel the pressure of handling the three inbound craft at the same time.

Harold Johnson radioed for a report on the location and progress of the Chicago inbound. He was informed that the airliner was just slightly west of London, Ontario. It was two minutes ahead of its estimated time of arrival.

The busy controller on the ground sought to establish the next landing sequence.

"Southern 49—are you going to land after your company aircraft or before? I have to know as far as selection of runways for you."

Henry Jackson said, "Tell 'em we ain't landing till the money does."

"OK," Johnson returned. "We'll land after he lands."

Captain Haas told his copilot to determine if Captain Wright's jetliner could be contacted. Johnson began the attempt to talk direct.

"Southern 905—this is Southern 49."

"Go ahead, sir—this is 905."

Haas said to Johnson, "Find out who's on board."

"Do you have a company official on board?" Johnson asked.

Captain Wright spotted the navigation lights and beacon of Flight 49 ahead of him. Believing the craft to be the inbound from Atlanta, he said, "I believe that's 963 in front of us. We're seventy miles out."

Johnson said, "OK, who has the company official or company representative on?"

Captain Wright repeated, "There's an aircraft 963. They're inbound. They're in front of us, and we're showing sixty-eight miles out. We tried to talk to 'em. We couldn't get 'em."

Confused by the report from the Chicago inbound, Haas told Johnson, "Find out how many aircraft we've got up here."

Johnson asked the controller, "We understand there are two other Southern aircraft inbound. Could you confirm this?"

"Stand by. I'll check it out."

It was now 4:16 A.M. Captain Wright continued to descend from an altitude of eleven thousand feet. He would level off at four thousand feet and proceed under the directions of the controller.

After landing at Toronto, Captain Godwin's party was picked up by an airport vehicle and rushed to the terminal building. They were taken to the security division office,

where they were greeted by Deputy Chief Douglas Burrows of the Mississauga District police bureau. Burrows
volunteered his services in delivering the ransom money to
the hijacked aircraft. The temperature was hovering in the
mid-thirties. Burrows didn't relish the prospects of strip-
ping down to his shorts to make delivery of the money, but
knew someone had it to do.

George Gross thanked the lawman for his offer, but told
him of his plan to try to talk the hijackers into exchanging
the pirated aircraft and passengers for the money, one of
the DC-9's, and a fresh crew. Gross and Wheeler left the
four crewmen behind and were escorted to the control
tower.

Arrival control continued to guide the approach of Captain Wright's jetliner while communicating with the third
company aircraft.

"Southern 49—this is Arrival."

"49—go ahead," acknowledged Johnson.

"OK, we have a doctor in the unit, and he's at my
position. Do you wish to converse with him?"

"Stand by."

Donna was called forward for a condition report on Alvin
Fortson.

A few minutes later Johnson radioed, "OK—Arrival—
this is Southern 49. Be advised the passenger is on oxygen.
Appears to be better than he was. Over."

"Roger—we check that, 49; and with respect to your
previous query as to whether another—that is, a third—of
your company aircraft is involved, that is negative."

Johnson replied, "OK—905, you still on this frequency?"

"Yeah, go ahead, Hal."

"OK—you the one out of Kenn—uh—out of Chicago?"

"Yeah—we're bringing some station manager, I believe,
in."

"Thank you."

Arrival interjected, "And Southern 49, the doctor's going
to speak with you now."

"OK, go ahead."

"Captain, my name is Flynn—Dr. Kevin Flynn, F-L-Y-N-N, general physician, and I'd like to offer my services to help the passenger in distress. Can you tell me his present condition, please?"

Haas talked with the doctor.

"Well—he appears to be a lot better than he was. He's still on oxygen, and as long as we keep him on oxygen he appears to be doing all right. He had some nitroglycerine tablets with him and also some nasal spray mist. I do not know if the stewardesses have administered either of the items."

"Ah—Captain, can you give me a history of the collapse? What time it occurred and his immediate condition following collapse?"

"OK—it was several hours ago, I believe, and he was coughing and had trouble breathing, so the stews got him on oxygen right away."

The doctor asked if Fortson's skin was cold and clammy and if he was sweating. Haas told the doctor to stand by while he checked with the stewardesses.

Shortly, he reported, "They say his skin was cold; he looked extremely pale."

"Ah—Captain, I understand the passenger is aged approximately eighty years old. Is this correct?"

"Affirmative. He is in his eighties."

Dr. Flynn inquired if the ailing Fortson was accompanied by a relative who might have information on his previous medical history. Informed that the old gentleman had been hospitalized with pneumonia recently and that no one accompanied him, the doctor asked, "What is your altitude, please?"

Haas reported his altitude at twenty thousand feet, although the cabin altitude was equivalent to one thousand feet.

Flynn offered his diagnosis.

"Captain—it would seem to be that this man has likely suffered a coronary thrombosis, and I would feel that he should receive urgent medical attention on arrival at a hospital. Can this be arranged?"

Haas turned to Henry Jackson, who gave him a non-committal look before answering.

"Maybe sometime during daylight hours."

"Captain, you may have a dead passenger on board by that time. Can I speak to the hijacker in charge, perhaps try to arrange for—ah—landing the aircraft a little sooner to take the passenger off?"

Captain Haas advised that the conversation was being monitored and that the hijacker said the man could perhaps come off sometime after landing.

Flynn pressed. "Captain, is there a physician on board or a trained nurse or somebody to give expert opinion on the man's condition?"

He was told there was neither a doctor nor a nurse on board.

Jackson was becoming annoyed at the doctor's persistence. Flynn was trying to help as he continued to question.

"I assume that the hijacker is listening to my conversation; and if so, I think you should realize that a man of eighty to eighty-five years with a history of sudden collapse would—ah—certainly would indicate shock, and his circulation is not likely to stand a type of excitement and lack of expert care that he's not likely to get in the next few hours. Over?"

Realizing the remarks were directed to him, Jackson exploded into the microphone.

"Hey, Doc—look here! You know why I'm up here? 'Cause I couldn't take a certain type of pressure that the people were putting on me for nothing, too. Now look—the man is OK. And the only way he might be taken off is—is in daylight hours. Now, we've done the best we can. We've accommodated him as best we could. Now this is it!"

Dr. Flynn stepped away from the microphone and stood by for another opportunity to talk to the hijacked aircraft. Haas and Johnson were glad to hear the voice of the arrival controller again.

"We check your remarks, Southern 49. This is the controller back on. Southern 905, turn right, heading 140; descend to three thousand and slow to 180 knots."

Captain Wright confirmed, "180—140—down to three."

"Roger," said the controller. "Southern 905 is seven miles from the Juliette beacon."

"OK."

After giving further instructions, the money-laden plane with its FBI contingent aboard was cleared to land. Light rain continued with fog. A heavy layer of clouds hung over the airport.

The physician came back on the radio.

"This is Dr. Flynn here again. I'm speaking now to the hijacker. Would you consider landing this aircraft and taking off again before daylight hours?"

Haas and Johnson watched Henry Jackson for his reaction. The gunman showed his disdain for the doctor's inquiry but remained silent.

Flynn persisted, "Southern 49—did you receive my last message? This is the doctor speaking . . ."

Unintentionally, the doctor was about to ignite a powder keg.

"Captain," he begged, "can I speak to the hijacker again, please?"

Jackson was now on his feet, shaking his head and wishing he and Flynn were face to face.

Captain Haas tried to defuse the explosive situation. "This is Southern 49—he doesn't want to talk."

Flynn would not be denied.

"He must be aware that if this passenger fails to survive, he's got a more serious charge to be considered. There's no doubt in my mind that this passenger has been provoked into a heart attack by the excitement on board; and, therefore, I would not doubt that any further delay in treatment would be his responsibility."

Haas had not wanted to offend the doctor, but the time had come to be blunt about it.

"This is Southern 49—request the doctor off the frequency."

"Yes, I'm now going off."

Again, Jackson exploded into the mike.

"This _____ plane gonna blow up in a minute and all these people are goin' straight up with it. No flapjacks here about one man now!"

The hijacker handed the microphone back to the copilot. Johnson inquired, "Approach—this is Southern 49—is the other aircraft on the ground?"

The time was 4:31 Saturday morning. Arrival had turned the Chicago inbound over to the tower. After checking, the controller replied, "905 is just touching."

Johnson advised, "OK—he's just touching down, and we're ready for approach."

"Roger—descend to four thousand; and what is your present heading?"

We're on a heading of 030 and down to four thousand."

"Roger," said the controller. "Roll out heading 050."

"OK, Approach—be advised that prior to our touching down, the money should be transferred from our other aircraft to the fuel truck. The food, the parachutes, and . . ."

Jackson interrupted with instructions.

The copilot continued, "There should be only one man on the fuel truck; he should be ready to come to our aircraft immediately on our touching down."

"We check that, Southern 49."

"OK, Approach, and we want this man in swimming trunks."

"All right."

"We don't want anything funny now. They've got some grenades in here, and we don't want this thing to blow up."

The controller turned to his assistant, asking if he got the information from the last transmission. He repeated, "They want a man in swimming trunks—one man only, in the fuel truck; he's got to have the parachutes and the food and the money."

Flight 49 continued to descend. It was now at an altitude

of eleven thousand feet and was approximately five to eight minutes away from making its third landing since the hijacking began.

Henry Jackson's head ached. He rubbed his bloodshot eyes, regretting that Karen had not locked the liquor cabinet sooner than she did. The doctor's remarks still hammered on his brain. Calling Lou up to the cockpit, Jackson said, "When we get on the ground, make them people keep their heads down on their laps; and watch those doors. Shoot the first mother that messes up."

"Yeah, Smooth, we'll take care of things," Moore promised.

The Detroit office of the FBI was on the telephone to the Toronto approach center. They had rounded up Lou's half-brother, Sherman. Attempts were underway to establish a connection with the pirated craft in hopes the relative could talk the hijackers into giving up. The attempt had to be discontinued; it had momentarily caused interference in radio communications between the center and the hijacked plane.

Testing to make sure communications had been restored, the controller said, "Southern 49—this is a radio check—how do you read?"

"Loud and clear," came the response.

"All right."

"Southern 49—say your altitude now."

"Ten thousand."

"OK—you're twenty-three miles from touchdown."

"Say again the distance," Johnson requested.

"Twenty-two miles from touchdown."

"Twenty-two miles."

"Roger, and, for your information, Sherman wants to talk to one of the hijackers."

"Is that our station manager?" Johnson inquired.

"It's the brother of one of the hijackers—Sherman—we've got him on the telephone."

Flight 49 crossed the outer marker ten miles from the end of the runway. The aircraft was on a straight-in approach to runway 5 Right.

First officer Johnson maintained constant communication with the controller who reported the tower's clearance to land.

"OK—we have landing clearance, and we can descend to 2500 feet now till we get the glide slope. Right?"

"That's correct, 49."

"OK—Approach, advise our company or someone there that we would like a couple of containers of coffee thrown aboard the aircraft also."

"Will do."

Confirming his altimeter reading, Johnson advised Approach that he was showing 2974.

"Keep an eye on us," he urged.

"Yep—we're watching—and you're five miles from the outer marker."

There was a brief pause.

"You're two and a half miles from the outer marker now. Would you like the approach lights turned up? Then you can advise me when you want them turned down."

"OK."

Arrival instructed the tower operator to increase the brightness of the runway approach lights. The tower increased the intensity to a setting of three. Approach asked the tower operator, watching the blip on his radarscope, "Got him eyeballed?"

"Yep."

The exchange between the two ground controllers continued.

"Confirm he's on the ground?"

"Yes—he's down."

Gross and Wheeler breathed a sigh of relief. It was a momentary breather, however. They feared what could happen next with the fate of Flight 49 in the hands of the three unpredictable terrorists. They hoped they would be successful in arranging the release of the passengers and aircraft. Then if they could convince the gunmen to exchange planes . . .

Henry Jackson instructed the captain to roll to the end of the nearly ten-thousand-foot runway, turn around, and park so that he could be ready to make another takeoff run.

Lou Moore and Mel Cale patrolled the aisle, shouting instructions for the weary hostages to keep their heads down.

Haas told Jackson that it would be necessary to return to the approach end of the runway for parking, in the event the aircraft should have to make a departure under instrument-flight rules.

The hijacker accepted the necessity. Permission was requested of the controller.

"OK," said the operator. "You can taxi down twenty-three, left to position, and hold on 5 Right."

Approach control advised the tower of the maneuver.

"OK, let us know when the fuel trucks can go out there."

"Yep."

Reaching the end of the runway, Captain Haas did a turnaround and brought the jetliner to a halt. The engines would remain on, as would the powerful lights mounted externally on the wings and just forward of the engines on either side of the aircraft. Through the dense fog, observers in the tower focused binoculars on the hijacked aircraft. Hoping that there would be no delay in refueling and that all of the requested items were ready, Haas spoke into his mike.

"This is Southern 49. We need the fuel truck out here right away now with the money and the parachutes and all the provisions: the food, the coffee, some water, and some stimulants for the crew."

Standing by in the tower, Gross remarked to Wheeler, "Billy Bob knows it's against regulations for pilots to take stimulants." He was unaware that the hijackers had insisted the crew obtain the drugs to enable the airmen to stay awake.

Jackson was on his feet in the cockpit, holding the revolver in one hand and a grenade in the other. Captain Haas was permitted to speak into the mike only when told to do so and to say only what the hijacker wanted said. It was a procedure to which Haas was unaccustomed. He was beginning to feel like a wooden dummy with the gunman manipulating the strings as he transmitted further instructions.

"There's to be no one on the fuel truck except the driver . . ."

Jackson spoke in the background. "And the fuel truck's bringing everything."

Haas continued, "And the fuel truck is to bring everything out here; he's only to make one trip. Over."

"OK," acknowledged the controller. "That is the driver only."

"That's right—the driver only—in his swimming trunks. He can only make one trip out here, so he needs to bring the fuel, money, parachutes, and everything the first time."

"We check that."

The tower operator was kept busy running between two consoles of radio equipment, relaying information to ground attendants and the assemblage of lawmen. Reporting to the controller, he said, "John, I'm back in the normal position. Got me running in circles. Go ahead."

"OK—as soon as possible they want the fuel truck out to the aircraft, driven by only one person, in swimming trunks, and with all the requested provisions on the truck. He's to make one, and one only, trip out there."

Time passed. Each minute seemed like an hour to Haas and Johnson. Both men were excellent physical specimens, but the prolonged conditions of duress had tightened their nerves and muscles. They wished for a cup of coffee, or anything, to help them remain alert. There was no chance Jackson would let them drift off to sleep, not with his constant haranguing. But they had to fight to remain mentally alert in order to deal with their captors. The need for fuel and other supplies having been transmitted ahead long before the aircraft landed, Jackson had expected that a fuel truck would come speeding up the moment Flight 49 parked. He was riled as he watched the hands creep by on the instrument panel clock. Five minutes—ten minutes—fifteen. Haas, Johnson, and their captor searched the darkness for the lights of the fuel truck.

Lou Moore stuck his head in the cockpit. "Hey, Smooth, what's going on?" he asked.

"Ain't nothin', man. That's the trouble," Jackson replied.

"You want me to get their attention with this grenade?" Lou agitated.

Haas was instructed to check on matters.

Haas spoke wearily into the mike. "We need to know if the truck is on its way, and we need to know which way it'll be approaching the airplane from. We need the truck out here right away!"

"Yes, sir, I've relayed the request," said the controller; "we'll attempt to find out just where the truck is, and I'll keep you advised as to the direction from which it will be approaching."

The old familiar waiting game was underway. Wear them down. That's what authorities were hoping would happen. Then the hijackers might be receptive to the offer that was coming.

The three gunmen grew more leery by the minute. Lou Moore stood near the front of the passenger cabin and listened to Mel Cale, who said, "They're just stalling for time. They're waitin' for daybreak so they can see what they're shootin' at."

"Yeah, maybe so," Lou agreed. He was in no mood to listen.

"We're gonna have to take this thing down yonder and crash it like I said," Cale suggested. "We ain't gettin' nowhere here."

"Hey, Smooth," Lou yelled to Jackson, "hurry 'em up before they get dumb and we have to start shootin' these passengers."

The remark stabbed like a dagger at the awareness of each hostage. Marge Brennan clutched the hand of young

Patrick. She was sure her heart had stopped momentarily.

Concern for the passengers and crew was uppermost among the dozens of officials and lawmen gathered at various locations in the terminal facility and around the airport. But they did not realize the psychopathic nature of the three hijackers. Faced with a dilemma, the gunmen could be easily provoked to commit violence.

Sensing the tension growing within himself, Captain Haas could imagine what was going on in Jackson's mind.

"Let me ask them again about the fuel truck," Haas suggested.

"Ask 'em," instructed the hijacker.

"Arrival—Southern 49. We need that fuel truck out here or we're going to have to take off again, and we only have seven thousand pounds of fuel," Haas said.

George Gross stepped forward prepared to receive the controller's mike.

"OK—Southern 49, we have a company representative here who wants to talk to you. Stand by."

Gross took the mike.

"Southern 49 . . ."

"Go ahead."

"This is Gross. We would like to request, or to have you request, that they release the passengers."

"OK, George."

Haas waited for Jackson's response. The request was not among the hijacker's top priorities. He was thinking in terms of the ransom money and other things demanded.

Gross became impatient. "Go ahead," he said.

"OK—Billy Bob here. They said just pay the money out here and they're going to do what they want to do. They may release the passengers and crew; they may release the passengers and keep the crew."

"Uh—Billy Bob—we've got some money. I don't know how much because it came in from another city."

"Let's get this thing outa here," Jackson demanded. "They were told they'd better have *all* the money together before we ever came up here."

"Henry," Haas said, "we don't have enough fuel to get back to the United States border."

"To _____ with the United States border," Jackson raged.

Mel was standing in the cockpit entrance. The younger hijacker said, "Let's take this thing to Tennessee and blow up the whole _____ world! The company don't care about us! Detroit don't care about us! The country don't care about us!"

The microphone had been open during a part of the arguing. Gross said, "Southern 49, say again."

"George, it's Billy Bob here. I said just bring the money on out here and give us some fuel. They're going to do what they want to do. They may let the passengers go and keep the crew. They may let the crew and the passengers go—but that's going to be their prerogative. Other than that we take off for Oak Ridge, Tennessee, to crash into the atomic works down there. And we don't have but 7300 pounds of fuel. So we don't have enough to make it to the United States border."

Gross perspired. The hijackers had backed him into a corner. Groping for words, he hoped to conceal the fact that the money flown in from Chicago was far below their demand.

"Uh—Billy Bob—we brought this money in on another aircraft, and at this point I don't know how much there is; but I know it's considerably less than they're asking for. Now we can give them what we've got, but at this time of night—this is the best we can do."

Jackson pressed, "Ask them how much money they got."

Why doesn't George just say they've got more money than they can count, Haas pondered, *and that they're backing the trucks up over here to bring it out to us if we'll just stay long enough?*

The hijackers had never seen ten million dollars and had no conception of its bulk or weight. Whatever had been flown to Toronto would probably take days to count.

Fearing the answer, he asked again for a tally of the

amount on hand.

Gross sought to avoid a precise figure.

"We have not been in contact with the other aircraft yet—it just landed. It's going to take a few minutes before we can get to these people. Can you stand by?"

"Stand by—stand by—stand by—to hell with that bull," Cale said. "I say let's get going."

Speaking to Captain Haas, Jackson said, "Let's go—that's enough of this stalling."

"George, we're going to be taking off here if you can't tell us how much both airplanes got together here," Haas advised.

"There's only one aircraft," Gross said. "We were unable to raise it on the radio; the crew has not come in yet. It's going to take a few minutes before they get in."

"OK—can you give me the radio frequency they're operating on?"

"No; they're shut down on the ramp somewhere en route to the terminal building. We've also got a fresh crew if you would like some relief. You sound pretty tired—we've got another crew to put on here."

The hijacked crew was tired and in need of relief, but there was no way the pirates would make an exchange.

"They say they got the freshest crew they could get right now," Haas reported.

Discouraged, Gross asked again that they stand by while a check on the money was being made.

Johnson tired of remaining passive to the conversation. Pressing the mike button, the copilot spoke. "George— expedite all you can here . . ."

"Expedite." That did it!

To Jackson, who didn't know the meaning of the word, it sounded menacing. Raising his pistol to strike Johnson, the hijacker said, "I told you guys before about speakin' outa turn. I'm gonna change your way of speakin' if I have to cram this gun down your throat . . ."

Seething with rage, Jackson grabbed the mike. Leaning down, he peered through the cockpit window in the direction of the control tower.

"Hey—looka here—if that man ain't out here with the money and everything else in five minutes, we're taking this big, baggly mother off. Somebody better be out here in five minutes with the payroll or, like I said, we'll just do what we have to do right here."

Gross had talked finally with the security division office, where the Chicago crew was holding with the funds.

Awaiting a reply to Jackson's threat, Haas radioed, "Go ahead."

Gross' voice came back on the radio.

"We think we've got $500,000. I'll have to check that, but that's the information we had from Chicago now. We think that's the figure—stand by."

Jackson still had the mike.

"You tell whoever it is to take that $500,000 and they know what they can do with it. Get the fuel truck out here—just get the fuel truck out here!"

Anger had so tightened his vocal chords that Jackson could hardly speak.

"Well, get—well, get it—or we'll blow this mother up. If they ain't got it now, we'll take care of the rest of it. Now I'm gonna pull the pins on these grenades—see what you get up there. We told them what we wanted before we came over to this place."

"Well, we're getting it out there as fast as we can. He's on the way, Southern 49," Gross said.

Captain Haas came back on the radio. In a tired voice he minimized his words.

"49 . . ."

"The fuel tender is on the way. It's just finished servicing another aircraft—it's en route—be there in just a minute."

"He wants to know if he's got everything with him," Haas said.

"I believe he does—if he doesn't we'll have it behind him very shortly," Gross promised.

The arrival controller inquired of the tower, "Have you

got the Royal Police on the frequency? And where is the fuel truck—is he with them?"

The fuel truck was parked at Gate 34, waiting for police clearance to proceed to the hijacked aircraft. Lawmen were unable to agree on whether to send the money.

Slumped in his seat, Haas radioed, "Listen—we're pushing up flowers out here if that's not the fuel truck coming out here, George."

"It's coming out, Billy Bob. He's been tied up fueling another aircraft and he's on the way out."

"They say send that truck out or we're going out right now."

"The truck's on the way. Don't you see it?"

Haas stared through the cockpit windows—to the left—straight ahead—to the right—and slowly back again.

He could see nothing.

Lying, he said, "OK—I believe we see him over here. Is he by himself?"

Gross answered, "He's by himself. It takes a little time to get all this stuff together. He's on the way; and if he's short anything, we'll pick it up and bring it along."

It was now well past 5:00 in the morning as Flight 49 sat on the runway at Toronto. Repeated pleas from the captain for fuel, ransom money, and provisions had gone unheeded. The hijackers had rejected attempts to exchange the aircraft and those on board for another aircraft and crew. And lawmen had played a dangerous game of delays while trying to devise a feasible way of mounting a surprise assault on the pirates. The waiting game had about run its course. A further delay might bring deathly consequences. The gunmen held the upper hand. There was nothing left to do but refuel the aircraft and prepare to deal with the threatened bombing of the nuclear facility at Oak Ridge.

Putting the fuel truck in gear, the driver released the hand brake. Windshield wipers sounded a steady beat, sweeping the rain from the glass-enclosed front of the cab.

Southern 49 was parked more than a mile away. Ground fog and rain made the going slow. The driver steered down the far side of the airfield, where he would approach the aircraft from a taxiway.

Helpless ground authorities could only stand by and wait. Seven minutes had elapsed since the last radio transmission from the hijacked aircraft. They were seven minutes of hell for the captain and his copilot. Jackson argued for an immediate departure. Haas countered each demand with a reminder of the aircraft's low fuel status.

"I'll give you one last chance to find out where that fuel truck is," Jackson said.

Haas would try to get the truth. He hoped those in the tower realized the gravity of the situation as he keyed his mike to speak.

"Where is the fuel truck now? Fellow, where is that gas truck? 49."

George Gross answered.

"It's en route from gate 34 right now."

"Tell him to step on it, George."

"He's going. Billy Bob?"

"Yes . . . where is he?"

"It's on the way, and they picked up the money just a minute ago off the other aircraft; and it's on the way."

"OK—push him on, George."

"Right."

Several minutes passed. Haas, Johnson, and Jackson searched the distant end of the runway for any sign of the fuel tender.

Haas radioed, "We don't see the truck. Where is he now?"

The familiar voice of Gross advised that the truck was about three-quarters of a mile away.

"Look in your eleven o'clock position and you'll be able to see him," Gross assured.

Inching along in the fog, the vehicle driver was unable to

see twenty feet ahead. He was having great difficulty staying on the pavement.

"Billy Bob . . ." radioed Gross.

"Yes, George?"

"The money's going to have to come behind the truck. I'm sorry, but they missed it. The truck's coming; it's already left the ramp, and the money will be right behind it—unless they want the truck to go back and pick it up."

Haas felt that the weight of the world had just descended.

"Bring the fuel on out here, and leave the car there."

"All right."

Confused reports were channeled to the tower by the Royal Police. A first report had the fuel truck en route to the aircraft without the money. Now, Gross relayed a later report.

"I think we've got the money on the truck, Billy Bob; we're still trying to check that out. He's on the way."

Henry Jackson leaned down to Haas' mike.

"Do you want me to blow this mother up right now? Who do you think you're playing with? Make up your mind what you'll gonna do . . . ."

"Well, we're trying to satisfy as fast as we can. It's just gonna take time," Gross said.

The arrival controller queried the captain on the aircraft's departure plans.

"Just get that gas truck out here in a hurry," Haas said.

"Roger, 49."

Captain Haas knew Jackson wasn't pretending. He felt the cylindrical shape of the grenade being held against the base of his skull.

"Take this mother over to Montreal. Maybe we'll get somebody's attention there," Jackson ordered.

As the crew eased the fuel-control levers forward, the jetliner began a slow roll down the runway.

"This is Southern 49. Listen, we're going to have to have flight directions to Montreal. We don't have enough gas to even get off of here. So . . ."

"OK—we check," said the controller. "It's Montreal."

Harold Johnson spoke into the mike. "I believe I blocked you out. We're taxiing out, fixing to start going right now."

"We check that. Hold up. It's on the way at about eleven o'clock—ten–thirty now. You should see the chap."

"OK—you tell him to push on, eleven o'clock, our position."

"It should be eleven o'clock—ten-thirty position."

"He's on the taxiway now, Southern 49."

"That him blinking his light?"

"Yeah—that's him."

"OK—tell him to hurry on now."

The vehicle was not equipped with a radio. So there was no way of communicating instructions to the driver, who was just crossing runway 32.

Haas watched as the blinking lights atop the vehicle cast a yellow glow through the fog.

"What is that truck carrying, exactly?" he radioed.

"Billy Bob, he's carrying jet fuel. The money is coming in a car behind him," Gross reported.

"Roger—they say they don't want to see no car or they'll blow this airplane up."

"It's all right," Gross said. "Tell them that we're going to have to get the money out to them. He can send the truck back and get it, or we can send it out in a car or however they want to get it, but, uh . . ."

"Send the truck," Haas said.

"Do you see the truck?"

"We see the truck."

"Do you want to go ahead and fuel it first and then pick the money up? That's the only option you've really got. There's no communication with the truck—you're going to have to tell him what to do. He doesn't have a radio."

"OK."

"If you want the money sent in another vehicle, we can do that."

"Just the gas."

"OK—you're going to have to tell him that if you want him to go back."

Gross was trying to overcome the failure to place the money aboard the fuel tender. But Haas and Johnson wished he would drop the subject before it struck another discordant nerve with the hijackers.

Having been forced to roll out on the runway a few minutes earlier, the airliner was now about a thousand feet from the threshold of runway 5. Approaching from behind the aircraft, the driver of the truck maneuvered by the right-wing tip and positioned the vehicle for refueling.

Gross spoke into the mike again.

"If you want him to go back and pick up the money, you're going to have to tell him that. We're not going to send any other vehicle out unless you tell us to."

There was no response from the hijacked aircraft.

"You read that, Southern 49?"

Silence.

For the next ten minutes the gunmen wouldn't permit radio transmission from the jetliner. They had too much else to do while guarding the passenger compartment, the crew, and maintaining watch on the fuel attendant.

Perceiving a more relaxed atmosphere, Captain Haas inquired what they wanted to do about picking up the money. Jackson reaffirmed they wanted none of the ransom demand from the airline. He told the captain to determine what was going on in Detroit, what the city was doing to put up the ten million dollars.

Haas did as he was told.

"Hello—tower, this is Southern 49."

Afraid the prolonged silence aboard Flight 49 had meant violence, Gross, Wheeler, and the operator were relieved to hear the captain's voice. They listened intently.

"They want to know what the man in Detroit is doing about getting some money together. They wanted the money from Detroit in the first place. I tried to tell them we didn't have too much money down here at Southern."

Gross answered.

"Billy Bob—I'll have to check it out. I haven't heard from Detroit since we got in here, and that's about two hours old. They were working on it at the time. They had called in the city council, and the mayor was working with the bankers."

After a brief pause, Gross asked, "Southern 49—do you want the money that's here? We're holding it at the gate for the truck to pick up."

"How much?"

"It is a half of a million dollars."

There was no reply. Jackson's attention was focused on the fuel attendant. It was 5:37 A.M.; just over ten hours had passed since the ordeal began.

Seeking to renew the conversation, Gross keyed his mike.

"Southern 49—do you read?"

"49—go ahead."

"What do you want to do about this money?"

Budgeting his words, Haas said, "I want to know if you got the ten million together."

"We don't have it here—we're working on it in several cities. We're not going to have it here immediately. We've got some of it coming—putting it together in Atlanta right now. But we don't have it all here."

Then Gross switched the subject to the ailing passenger aboard the jetliner.

"Uh—Southern—we would like to get the ill passenger off the airplane if we can."

"OK—if they'll let him get off," Haas said.

Jackson was consulted about the request.

"He says that passenger gets off when they get ten million here, and the rest of the passengers, except for the crew; and we need stimulants to keep on going."

The need for something with which to check the flight crew's weariness was obvious. Haas' speech was weak and beginning to ramble.

"Pilots can't use stimulants," Gross reminded. He failed to comprehend that the hijackers were dictating a new set of regulations.

Mel Cale took his turn to respond.

"If you care anything about this ill passenger—as you say—you got to get that money together because no one leaves this plane until we get ten million dollars. Like I say—if somebody about dead you better go open up Fort Knox. We're gonna put down there at Oak Ridge . . . ." His thoughts trailed off.

"Uh—we're opening up Atlanta now," Gross replied, "but it's going to take a little while to get all this money together; and that's where it's going to be, except for the money that is already waiting here if you want to pick it up. Tell us how you want to get it."

Gross pretended to have heard from the mayor of Detroit.

"Southern 49, I got a report for you from the mayor."

"OK—go ahead with the message."

"Message is that the mayor is working on it now in Detroit. He's got some at this point; we don't know how much . . . ."

Jackson and Moore listened attentively.

". . . But it's coming from several banks. He's got the same problem we have: There are no banks open this time of night. They all have time locks in the vault, and we're having trouble getting the money. He and the city council are working on it—can probably have some of it for you."

Lou Moore spoke into the mike.

"Be advised we are going to make one more stop. We are going to ride circle for an hour, and we're supposed to pick it up. We're not going to be stopping all over the place for a half-million here and a half-million there."

"Well, then," Gross offered, "you better make that stop Atlanta. I think we have a better chance of putting it together there than the mayor does. Our people are working on it now and have been. Do you want to pick this money up here at the gate?"

Jackson said, "Is he back on that jazz again? Tell him we want what we oughta get from Detroit."

Captain Haas radioed the hijacker's comment.

"George, they want the money from Detroit, from Mayor Gribbs. How he gets it they don't care—they want it from Detroit!"

"All right, we will convey that message to Detroit. Is that your next stop?"

"Billy Bob, we've still got the problem of getting this much money together. I recommend that you go direct to Atlanta—ah—we will depart Toronto and stop in Detroit and pick up what he's got, and you can add what's available in Atlanta."

The hijackers had not changed their minds about the threat to Oak Ridge. But for the next twenty minutes they argued among themselves about whether to wait until daylight for a departure. They decided on an immediate takeoff. And they still wanted pep pills for the crew.

"Tower—Southern 49 here," Haas radioed. "Does this gas truck have the stimulants on board?"

"Stand by—say it again."

"Does this gas truck have pills or stimulants on board out here?"

"Negative. We didn't have any stimulants with us, Billy Bob. Pilots are not permitted to use stimulants."

Refueling was completed. The attendant closed the fuel panel, entered the cab of the vehicle, and pulled away.

Copilot Harold Johnson took over communications with the controller.

"OK—Southern 49 is ready to take off."

"I heard that," said the tower operator.

"Let me know when the runway is clear," instructed the controller.

"Yes, I heard that, Clare."

"OK—Southern 49, we check your request; and just as soon as the tower confirms the runway is clear, I'll have takeoff clearance for you."

George Gross lifted the flaps of his suit coat and shoved

his hands deep in his pockets. He felt the weight of defeat.

"You did all you could, George," Frank Wheeler consoled.

"I don't feel we did anything but make an unnecessary trip up here," he said dejectedly.

It was 6:15 A.M. when the fuel truck cleared the runway and Flight 49 lifted off the runway.

"We are airborne—get us up to about twenty thousand to begin with."

"Roger."

5
Dive Bomber

For those gathered in the distant observation post of the control tower, the wayward jetliner provided an eerie spectacle as it disappeared into the dense fog. There were doubts that it would be seen again in one piece.

The nervous excitement of the three flight attendants and pilots who had flown to Toronto aboard Godwin's airliner was replaced by a temporary relief that they would be spared, at least a while longer, a confrontation with the hijackers.

George Gross had not abandoned hopes of delivering the ransom demand in exchange for the pirated aircraft and its hostages. The passengers didn't know they had been in Canada for almost two hours, and they didn't know where they were going next. They had no trouble, however, sensing the anger of their captors, whose plans had been frustrated once again.

While the hijacked aircraft was still within range of the Toronto controller's radio, Gross decided to try again to head off the menacing threat to the Oak Ridge nuclear facility.

Fred Parham stood at his side, protecting the heavy suitcase of money, as Gross radioed the aircraft.

"Southern 49 . . ."

"Go ahead," copilot Johnson replied.

Lou Moore sat on the cockpit jump seat, listening.

"Can you stop in Detroit? There's money waiting for you in Detroit," Gross said.

"How much?" Moore wanted to know.

"Not positive—I think it's a half-million dollars—maybe more by this time, and probably will be more when the banks open."

"Look here," Moore said, "we done got down to the wire now. This is it. We're on our way to Oak Ridge. You say you got a half-million down there. By the time we get to Oak Ridge somebody better run on over to Detroit and pick that stuff up there, too. If that money ain't together by the time we get to Oak Ridge, we're putting this airplane down. Like I said—we're not coming down with this bull no more."

"Where do you want to pick up the money?" Gross inquired.

Harold Johnson turned to watch Moore's face. The hijacker was in no mood to play games.

Johnson interceded, "George, we're not going to pick up anything till we—until we pick up ten million dollars."

"Where do you want to pick it up?" Gross continued.

Moore pressed the button on his microphone.

"You just get it together—we'll let you know. I ain't talking no nonsense. Just have it somewhere near Oak Ridge. That's where we'll be."

Moore's repeated references to Oak Ridge had been heard by hostages forward in the cabin.

"Oak Ridge . . . Oak Ridge . . . Oak Ridge . . ." they whispered, one by one, until news of the aircraft's destination reached the rear of the cabin. The constant fear that had confronted the hostages for over ten hours turned to stark terror. Ghastly visions of the World War II explosions at Hiroshima and Nagasaki filled their minds. What could be done to end this madness that now mushroomed into a threatened atomic holocaust?

Gross continued to try to reason with the unreasoning madman. He appealed for a landing at Atlanta.

"That's where we can get the money together first. And it's about thirty minutes from Oak Ridge," he argued.

"Hear this," Moore shot back. "We're not going to Atlanta—hear it?—we're not going to Atlanta. If it's thirty minutes, get someone down there and get to where we are, or, like I said, we're putting this mother down. We're not going to Atlanta, OK?"

"How about Knoxville?" Gross queried.

Harold Johnson interceded again. Moore was seething with rage over the persistent pleadings on the radio.

"George—he's already told you to just get the money together," Johnson reminded.

"Roger—we'll continue to work on it."

Controllers cleared the hijacked aircraft to a flight level of 33,000 feet and placed it on a heading for Oak Ridge.

Captain Haas worried over the gravity of the situation confronting him. He wondered if the time had come to attempt to overpower the hijackers. During his entire flight career it had been drummed into his head that, as captain, he should protect the people aboard, then the aircraft, then himself. To become locked in a struggle with the armed bandits would almost certainly result in his and Harold's death and send the airliner plummeting to earth in a fiery crash that would kill everybody aboard. He would have to think of some other way to overcome the threatened use of his aircraft as a dive bomber.

Henry Jackson was hungry. The galley was completely out of provisions. There was no coffee, no food—nothing except a few olives and cherries, which the hijacker consumed. They did little to satisfy his ravenous appetite.

When the gunman finished, he walked down the aisle to the row of seats where Marcia Timbers sat. Slumping down into an empty seat beside her, he placed his arm around her shoulder.

"I'd like to steal you," he said.

Unnerved by the hijacker's sudden approach, Marcia said, "I'm a flight attendant with Delta Airlines, and I would like to offer my assistance to these two flights attendants. They've been working all night and morning."

She would do anything to get out of the situation in which she found herself. Tensely, she waited for Jackson's answer.

"Sure—go ahead," he permitted.

Marcia hadn't expected the ease with which she extri-

cated herself from the presence of the gunman. But Jackson
wanted to get some more sleep before the aircraft arrived at
Oak Ridge.

Donna was seated forward in the cabin. Marcia introduced herself and explained that she, too, was a flight
attendant.

"For what airline?" Donna asked.

"Delta," Marcia answered, "and I'd like to help you and
the other attendant."

Turning to Karen, who was seated beside her, Donna
said, "What do you think?"

"I don't think it'd be a good idea," Karen replied. "We're
familiar with the aircraft, and she isn't; and should something go wrong, those guys would blame us."

Karen had another reason for rejecting the offer. She and
Donna had received special company training in methods
of dealing with hijackers. She wasn't sure Marcia had had
similar training.

Disappointed, Miss Timbers returned to her seat. She
wanted to take another seat, but was afraid that Jackson
would be provoked if she did.

Sitting down, Marcia was asked by the gunman, "What's
the matter, baby?"

"They said they didn't need my help," she replied.

Courting her favor, Jackson said he'd talk to the two
attendants.

Getting up, he went to where Donna and Karen were
seated.

"That girl says she's a stewardess, too, and wants to help
out. Why don't you want her to?" he asked.

"We just think it best for everybody aboard that we do
the job," Karen answered.

"Well—I want you to let her work if that's what she
wants," Jackson said.

"Henry—we know where everything is, and she
doesn't," Karen alibied. "She might make a mistake, and
then you all would blame us."

Jackson understood. He dropped the subject.

Taking the nearest empty seat, the gunman dozed off again.

By early Saturday morning news had reached relatives of the hostages that their husbands, wives, fathers, and mothers had been hijacked.

Dottie Halberstadt learned of the hijacking from television reports. She knew it was the flight Alex always took for his weekend return from Birmingham.

Jack Eley's wife had sought information from the airline when her husband failed to arrive home late Friday night. During the early-morning hours she received official notification that Jack was a hijack hostage. She knew he was as concerned about her and his family as they were about him. That's the kind of man he was.

Marge Brennan's husband, Bill, had cancelled plans to ride in the horse show. Instead, he remained in his hotel room in order to maintain constant contact with the Federal Aviation Administration.

Mary Melton's daughter, Elizabeth, learned that her mother was among the hijack victims when she telephoned the airline's headquarters in Atlanta.

Southern's station manager, Jess Murray, had broken the news in Orlando to Allyson Senft, Linda Menke, Nancy Morkill, and Calvin Fortson.

Nancy returned to her motel room at nearby Winter Park, where she and her daughters, Lisa, Carol, and Ann, hurriedly packed their suitcases for the return drive to Miami. They hoped there would be another time when Frank could join them for a visit to Disney World.

Of all the families concerned, only Bruce Barnes' wife, Susan, his young son, David, and daughters, Stephanie and Kathy, were unaware of his whereabouts. Bruce's travel plans were often made suddenly and took him in many directions. He had not had time to phone his wife that he was flying to Puerto Rico. He was glad Susan didn't know where he was. She wouldn't have to spend all that time worrying and maybe trying to hide her fear from the children. Now all he wanted to do was to get off of the hijacked plane, fly home to Corono del Mar, sit down, hug his family, and sleep. After he slept he would get up and hug his family again and again.

Yvonne Godwin and Sherry Stempel had remained through the night in the airline operations center. Everybody in the center shared a helpless concern for the crew and hostages as the airliner made its way toward Oak Ridge.

General manager Graydon Hall had spent the night telephoning banking connections in an effort to raise the ransom demand.

As Southern 49 continued its perilous flight southward, Lou Moore sat in the cockpit, raving wildly about what would happen if the money wasn't turned over soon. He had added another demand to the growing list of extortion items. President Nixon was to sign a document stating that the ransom was to be a grant from the United States government.

Haas and Johnson knew that the demand would be impossible to fulfill, but agreed they would try to establish a telephone patch to the White House. That's what the gunman wanted so he could relay the demand in person. The president was at his Key Biscayne, Florida, retreat for the weekend.

Karen asked Moore to get one of his accomplices to relieve him in the cockpit. She wanted to talk to him in the rear of the cabin.

Jackson was awakened by the gunman to stand watch in his place.

Standing in the rear of the passenger compartment, Karen stared up at the hijacker. In a feisty tone of voice she asked, "What's all this stuff about going into Oak Ridge?"

"You've been eavesdropping," he accused.

"And you're breaking your promise that we would be OK—that you were not going to hurt anybody," she said. "Now you say you're gonna nose us down."

"Well," he answered, "don't worry about it."

"I think it's something to be worried about if you're gonna kill me," countered the flight attendant.

"Don't worry about it. You're gonna be OK," he promised.

She acted relieved, but she really wasn't. She had no faith in anything he said.

The hour was approaching 9:00 A.M. Captain Godwin trailed the hijacked airliner, which was in sight twenty miles ahead on the horizon. Aboard the chase plane, Fred Parham sat with the suitcase of money for which he had signed at Chicago. In addition to the crew members and company officials who had boarded in Atlanta, the aircraft carried the force of FBI agents who had been picked up in Toronto.

It had been decided that Godwin's aircraft would proceed to Knoxville in the hope of luring the pirated ship to the Tennessee city.

An early-morning fog and overcast skies hung over the nuclear-test facility. But by midmorning skies would clear.

Alerted to the bombing threat, officials at the nuclear laboratory were busy shutting down three massive reactors. Normally, there would have been thirteen thousand employees on duty. However, the weekend work force consisted of only two hundred.

It was the first time any real threat had ever been made to Oak Ridge. By a shutting down of power to the reactors, only a localized release of radioactive material would result should the threat be carried out.

The Y-12 and the X compounds had been singled out by Cale as the intended targets on the ground. One of the compounds served as the site for manufacturing nuclear weapons components, while the other manufactured radioactive fuel for nuclear generators.

A planned evacuation of the sprawling complex would follow a shutdown of reactors.

Involvement of the Atomic Energy Commission in the hijacking heightened public attention in the piracy. The

ever-increasing circle of events included the city of Detroit, the Federal Aviation Administration, the FBI, and
the White House. Underway were plans to bring into play
the Navy and the Air Force.

When Flight 49 arrived over Oak Ridge, the nuclear site
was still obscured from view by cloud cover. Captain Haas
was ordered to circle over the vicinity while the sun burned
off the haze. Drifting eastward with the wind, the jetliner
maneuvered over the sparsely populated wilds of the Great
Smoky Mountains. The time was fast approaching when the
captain would have to make an appeal for another refueling
stop.

Mel Cale relieved Henry Jackson of cockpit guard duty.

Returning to the cabin, Jackson sat down beside Mary
Melton. The gray-haired grandmother had been unable to
sleep during the night.

Jackson told her, "I've been watching you, and I wonder
why you don't like me."

"I don't dislike you," she said. "I just can't understand
why you're doing this. What do you think you're going to
accomplish?"

"Well," he answered, "we are mad at the whole human
race, and Detroit owes us a great deal of money for the
injustices they've done to us. We're gonna get all this
money and go to Cuba where we'll be appreciated."

"What makes you think you'll be better off in Cuba?" she
questioned.

"Doesn't Castro stand for the oppressed, and hasn't he
welcomed people trying to get away from political persecu-
tion?" he wanted to know.

"You might be kidding yourselves. You don't know for
sure how people are treated there. And you'd be a
foreigner," she reminded.

"We're not worried about how Castro will receive us,"
Jackson said. "He'll be glad to have us bring all those
United States dollars, and we can live like kings for the rest
of our lives."

"Maybe so," she agreed. But she believed the hijackers

were kidding themselves about their prospects in Cuba.

Glancing out the window, she asked, "Where are we?"

"We're over Oak Ridge," he replied. "But don't be nervous. We're gonna take good care of you. Nothing's gonna happen unless people don't do as they're told."

Cale called Jackson back to the cockpit.

"The captain says we're running out of fuel," the younger hijacker reported.

"Well, we're not gonna need any more fuel if they don't come up with ten million dollars pretty soon," Jackson observed.

"Henry—you know they're working on getting the money together," Haas reminded.

"Ohio and Indiana aren't far from here. You can get fuel there," he suggested.

"Listen, Henry, the closest big field that we can reach with the fuel we have is at Lexington. I was just into Blue Grass field last week. I'm familiar with the airport. How about our going there?" Haas inquired.

"I guess that'd be OK," Jackson responded.

Copilot Johnson radioed air traffic controllers with a request for a heading to Lexington.

It was 9:35 Saturday morning when Flight 49 touched down in Kentucky. Looks of anxiety returned to the three captors. The flight to Lexington had been so brief they were confident that lawmen had been unable to prepare for their arrival. But they couldn't be sure. Southern 49 was on the ground for its first daytime landing. The hijackers had to be extra cautious. The down positions of the sunshades obscured their view of the surroundings outside.

Lou Moore stood at the seat occupied by young Pat Brennan. The window on Pat's side faced the terminal building, the direction from which the fuel truck would be approaching. Constantly waving a gun in the youngster's face, Moore instructed Pat to raise the shade. He looked out. Seeing nothing, he told Pat to lower the shade. Repeatedly the gunman menaced the youngster with his pis-

tol while ordering the shade raised and lowered. Just as he
was about to lower the shade a fifth time, Pat said, "Here
they come."

"What do you mean, they?" snapped the alarmed gunman.

"I mean—here it comes—the fuel truck—there's just one
man in it," he corrected himself.

Refueling was accomplished without delay. Southern 49
was back in the air twenty minutes after it had landed. The
deranged gunmen ordered the jetliner to return to Oak
Ridge.

Navy Reserve lieutenant commander Robert Moore sat
in the cockpit of a DC-6 passenger aircraft at the naval air
station ten miles north of Atlanta.

A commercial airline pilot, Moore was on weekend duty
with naval air reserve replacement unit 54. He and his
copilot were reading down the checklist and preparing for
departure on a routine training flight. Eight other reservists
occupied seats in the cabin. They would be aloft to log
training time.

A voice came over the radio to the aircraft.

"Navy 689—this is Operations."

"Go ahead, Operations—this is 689," Moore acknowledged.

"You are to make an immediate departure under priority
1 clearance, diverting to Hartsfield International Airport at
Atlanta. You will be met by a special agent of the FBI under
whose direction you are to proceed on a mission in connection with the hijacking of Southern Airways Flight 49."

Operations concluded its transmission with an authoriza-
tion for Moore and his crew to remain on the mission for as
long as the commander considered it necessary.

Moore didn't know just what his role would be, but he
was no stranger to hijackings. An Eastern Airlines jet he
was copiloting had been taken over by a hijacker several
years earlier and ordered to Cuba.

Within ten minutes the Navy plane touched down at Hartsfield, where ground controllers directed the DC-6 to a Southern Airways gate at the terminal building.

Arriving at the designated position, special agent Karl Bresko of Detroit went aboard and presented his credentials to Commander Moore. Bresko was accompanied by twenty other FBI agents, who were heavily armed with an assortment of weapons: Thompson submachine guns, shotguns loaded with rifle slugs, and high-powered telescopic rifles.

"Our assigned mission is to shadow the hijacked airliner and maintain the capability of instant reaction to future orders," Bresko told Moore.

"We will be of whatever assistance possible," Moore said. "But, as the aircraft commander, I am responsible for the actions of those aboard. I would request your agreement at the outset that no one is to leave this aircraft except with my permission and that there is to be no armed intervention with the hijacked aircraft unless its captain requests aid."

"You have my complete agreement," Bresko said.

Coughing to a start, the DC-6 engines propelled the aircraft away from the terminal building and along the taxiway.

Before giving instructions for takeoff, ground controllers radioed the military plane.

"Navy 689—Navy 689—it is requested that you return to the chocks."

"Roger—roger," Moore acknowledged.

Although there had been no explanation given for the requested return to the loading gate, Commander Moore proceeded in accordance with instructions.

When the craft was parked once again, its passenger door swung open to receive seven bulletproof vests and seven riot helmets. The protective items were among the latest demands of the hijackers.

The door was closed and secured.

Moore taxied again toward his assigned takeoff runway.

Ground control contacted the aircraft with new instructions.

"Navy 689 has priority clearance and is to proceed directly to Lexington, Kentucky."

Commander Moore acknowledged the orders as he rolled out to the end of the runway. The twenty-two-year-old propeller-driven aircraft lumbered down the airstrip and took off to the north.

Less than five minutes later, while the aircraft was climbing to its assigned altitude, air-traffic controllers diverted the flight to Knoxville.

A growing attitude of impatience was reflected by the hijackers as Southern 49 renewed its circling pattern of holding over Oak Ridge. Ground authorities transmitted numerous reports to the jetliner that the ransom money and other items were being assembled for delivery. But the pirates had come to distrust such reports.

Mel Cale and Lou Moore stood in the passageway leading to the cockpit, arguing that the time had come to make good on the threatened bombing of the nuclear complex.

That time was running out worried Haas and Johnson. They could only hope that authorities were doing something on the ground other than talking and stalling.

"Look," Haas said, "they are bringing the money you've demanded down from Detroit on a Lear jet. You heard them say that. Now you said you didn't want to harm the passengers and crew . . . ."

The captain continued his appeal in a soft manner calculated to calm the hijackers.

"Now listen, Lou," he asked, "what time have you got?"

Moore looked at his wristwatch.

"It's ten o'clock," he answered.

Haas said, "I've got ten o'clock, too."

Lou looked at his watch again, then at Haas' watch. He looked at the clock mounted on the instrument panel. It was set on Eastern Standard Time and read eleven o'clock.

"Let's give them until noon," Haas suggested. "Do you

concur?"

Confused by the discrepancy in time between his watch and the cockpit clock, Moore hesitated before answering.

"OK—we're gonna give 'em till noon," the hijacker promised.

Haas breathed a sigh of relief. He had bought an extra hour. Ground authorities were momentarily confused when the captain informed them of the new deadline. It was eleven o'clock in the Air Traffic Control Center. Alertly, the controller realized that the deadline was based on Central Standard Time.

"You have ten o'clock?" he queried.

"That's right," Haas confirmed. "They're giving us until noon, and you'd better start doing something fast."

Unwittingly, the hijackers had extended their deadline until one o'clock.

Moore turned to the passengers and threatened, "If they don't meet our demands by noon, we're gonna blow this thing up."

Cale echoed the threat.

"I was born to die; and if I have to take all of you with me, that's all right with me. We're gonna make this thing look worse than Munich."

He was making reference to the massacre of eleven members of the Israeli Olympic team several months earlier.

At Knoxville's McGhee-Tyson Airport, relatives of Cale and Moore were standing by, waiting for a chance to talk with the gunmen by radio. Law-enforcement authorities had rounded them up at their homes near Oak Ridge during the early-morning hours.

Cale's aged grandmother promised that if she got the chance, she would smack the young hijacker's jaws and pull him off of the aircraft.

Captain Godwin had parked his DC-9 chase plane on the apron at the terminal building. Commander Moore's military shadow aircraft was parked alongside. FBI personnel carried by the two aircraft were augmented by an additional force from Knoxville. Altogether the number of federal agents had grown to over forty.

At the request of the FBI, Godwin conducted an orientation tour of the exterior of his DC-9. It and the hijacked airliner were identical except in one respect. Southern 49 was equipped with ventral passenger steps in the tail compartment. Godwin's DC-9 was equipped with only retractable passenger steps forward in the cabin. Lawmen were primarily interested in the various avenues of entrance that might be used to board the hijacked aircraft should it land at Knoxville.

Another feature of interest to the agents was the built-in power unit located in the tail compartment of the jetliner. The device provides air pressure for the starting of the two engines. Godwin demonstrated how the unit could be shut down externally. But, he pointed out, this action should be accomplished only if the engines were first shut down; and the hijackers had not permitted this since the piracy began.

Finally, the orientation concentrated on the aircraft's two main landing gears. Mounted on each gear were two big tires of twenty-ply rubber. The agents questioned Godwin on the possibility of deflating the tires with small-arms fire. The captain suggested it would take high-powered rifle fire to do the job.

The agents asked if it would be possible for the jetliner to take off with flat tires. Godwin consulted technical and maintenance personnel, then reported their opinion that deflation of the tires would disable the airliner—that it would be impossible for it to gain the required takeoff speed of 140 miles per hour. It was a theoretical answer that had never been tested.

The walk-around briefing ended. Lawmen stood by, awaiting future developments. The acting FBI director, L. Patrick Gray III, maintained contact with the field agents from his Connecticut home, where he was spending the weekend.

Meanwhile, Billy Bob's wife was restless at home.

Ann Haas decided she had to get out of the house for a breath of fresh air. She needed to be alone, to get away from the small gathering of friends and relatives who had joined her and the children at Twin Gables. Most of all, she needed to leave behind for a few minutes the hundreds of cherished household items that symbolized the deep love she and Billy Bob held for each other.

There were his books—mostly about history—that he enjoyed reading. The collection filled a long glass-enclosed bookcase that stood against the wall in the main entry hall. There were books of lasting bindery, and there were others that represented the equivalent of paperbacks from the nineteenth century. Some of the books were written in German and French. The captain had vowed he would learn to read them someday.

Foot-high replicas of American Revolutionary soldiers stood on one shelf of the bookcase. A regimental artillery officer and a general staff officer stood side by side, resplendent in their colorful uniforms. There was one in the uniform of the Second Maryland Infantry of 1777 and another from the Virginia Light Dragoon.

A bust of Gen. Robert E. Lee occupied a place of prominence atop the bookcase. Lee was Haas' favorite Civil War hero. Sitting to the right of the bust was a toy coronation carriage made of papier-maché and iron. Well preserved, it had been one of Billy Bob's childhood toys.

Ann and Bill had collected five antique clocks for their home. They were fondest of the nine-foot-high grandfather clock that stood in the hallway. Dating from the eighteenth century, the clock's weights and pendulum were of solid iron. Handpainted scenes from Scotland, Ireland, England, and Wales adorned the face of the timepiece. A Scotsman wearing kilts stood beside an inscription which beckoned, "Come Unto My Platae." A lassie cuddled beneath the cape to escape the amorous pursuit of a young lad.

From the Victorian-style armoire in the master bedroom, Ann selected a rust-colored pair of slacks and a contrasting floral blouse, a combination that complemented the sultry beauty of her face and her reddish-brown hair.

When she had finished dressing, she walked into the adjacent sunroom for a few moments of solitude. It was a cheerful and airy room filled with colorful wicker furniture. Beside the French doors stood a player piano that Billy Bob had completely rebuilt.

Hanging on the wall above the piano was a collection of glass-enclosed butterflies of Brazil. A gift from Billy Bob to Ann, the collection included red, green, and black butterflies surrounded by dried flowers.

A talented painter, Billy Bob had started an oil of magnolia blossoms five years earlier. It hung on the wall, incomplete. Procrastination was one of his faults. Ann often chided him for putting off things. But he would remind her of the need to have patience.

Patience and calmness were two hallmarks of his character. Those qualities now enabled him to live through the most severe ordeal of his life.

Taking her father's pickup truck, Ann drove the short distance west on Highway 57 to Panky's General Store to shop for several items.

When she entered the store, proprietor Lebert Baker was listening to a radio report of the hijacking. The reporter said the aircraft continued to circle over Oak Ridge, with the hijackers claiming they would make good on their bomb threat if their noon deadline were not met.

Mr. Baker commented to Ann, "Now isn't that something—threatening to kill all of those innocent people?"

Ann asked, "Mr. Baker, would you believe that's Bill flying that aircraft?"

"Oh, no," he answered in a shocked tone of voice. It was bad enough that people he didn't know were threatened. But to know that his friend and neighbor was among those who might die at any moment frightened him even more.

Tears filled Baker's eyes, and he disappeared to the back of the store.

Ann selected the few items she needed and left.

Returning home, she found a group of reporters assembled in the unpaved drive that led to the rear of the home. They would get no statement from her or her relatives and neighbors. They would have to content themselves with color reports about the old home and its surroundings. But the character of Twin Gables told much about the character of its doting owners.

Not an imposing structure by La Grange standards, the home sat back from the road about a hundred feet.

Lined with shoulder-high boxwoods, a brick walkway led the way to the front porch. Old oaks, elms, magnolias, and a tall holly tree bearing red berries dotted the front lawn.

Positioned to the right of the walkway was a one-horse sleigh. On the other side of the neatly manicured lawn sat a refurbished black buggy, its four wheels painted a bright yellow. Billy Bob frequently hitched a horse to the contraption, leading the animal around the farm while Betsy and John sat on the two-seater, enjoying the ride.

Behind the home stood a red barn surrounded by four acres of cleared and fenced pastureland. A big block of salt was kept in the pasture to entice the frequent visit of seven velvet-nosed deer. Billy Bob and the children stood often at the back door of the house for a good nose-to-glass view of the animals romping and playing.

It was lunchtime when Ann got home. She fixed a sandwich for John and sat down with the youngster while he nibbled impatiently. At first he was silent. Then he asked, "Mama—aren't we going to pick up Daddy?"

"We'll go pick up Daddy when he gets in, Johnny," she answered.

"All right," he said and took a few more bites of the sandwich.

Looking up at his mother, John asked, "Has Daddy's plane crashed?"

Emphatically, Ann said, "No, Johnny."

The youngster took several more bites.

Looking up again, he inquired, "Has Daddy got a jacker

on board?"

Hesitantly, she confirmed Johnny's suspicion.

The youngster wanted to know if the hijacker had a gun.

"Yes, Johnny," she admitted, "the hijacker does have a gun—but Daddy can take care of the situation. Don't worry."

"Don't you worry either, Mama," he said. "Daddy will get a big stick and beat the jacker's booty-who."

That sometimes happened to Johnny when he misbehaved. His father would take a switch to the sitting-down part of Johnny's anatomy. If it could mend his ways, it would surely work on a hijacker. And how the youngster would like to be there to see it happen.

Personnel employed by airports and fixed-base operators throughout the southeast were following the hijacking story as it developed from minute to minute. There was much good-natured kidding mixed with serious concern over the news—for no one was able to anticipate where the pirated plane might land next. Anyone could become a part of the drama as it continued to unfold.

The Hangar One line manager at Lovell Field in Chattanooga, Fred Vogt, was in the airport terminal building en route to get some fuel tickets signed when he passed through the Southern Airway's office. Jokingly, the lanky twenty-eight-year-old fuel attendant told airline employees in the office: "If that airplane of yours comes to Chattanooga, just don't call us. We don't know how to fuel Southern jets."

Fred was extremely concerned for the well-being of the hostages aboard Flight 49. He had been praying through the night and morning for their safety. Even if the pirated craft should wind up in Chattanooga, Fred didn't anticipate that he might become involved. Another fixed-base operator at the airport was under contract to provide fuel for the fleet of Southern Airway's planes. Hangar One was owned by the president of Southern, Frank Hulse. To avoid a conflict of interest, the airline made its fuel purchases from Tennessee Airmotive across the field.

At that moment Hulse's wife, Mary, whom he fondly called "Mother Dear," was doing what she could to help raise the ransom demand. Vacationing at their winter home at Key West, Florida, while her husband was on a business trip to Grand Cayman Island, Mrs. Hulse had mounted a one-woman door-to-door solicitation campaign.

Agonized at the results, the rotund little lady had been unable to collect more than seventy dollars toward the fund.

Mel Cale's wife spoke into a microphone at the Knoxville Airport terminal facility.

"Why are you up there doing that?" she pleaded.

At first the hijacker was surprised to hear her voice on the cockpit speaker.

She asked again, "Mel—why are you doing what you are? You should be here with the children and me. Give up before it's too late."

Cale picked up the microphone mounted in a bracket on the cockpit bulkhead.

"I'm following in my brother's footsteps," he replied. "I'll see you. I won't be long—I won't be long."

Aeronautical Radio, Incorporated, a widespread communications network that serves as a private air-to-ground link for the aviation industry, was ready with the requested hookup to the White House.

Deciding he should be the one to talk to the president of the United States, Henry Jackson stood by in the cockpit.

The caller identified himself as John Ehrlichman, the president's chief domestic advisor.

In an irritated tone of voice the caller inquired, "And who am I speaking to?"

Haas and Johnson nearly fainted. *Has the White House connected us with someone who is totally unbriefed?* they wondered.

"You know very well you're talking to a hijacked airliner that's over Oak Ridge," Jackson growled.

"And what is the nature of your call?" came the inquiry.

"We want a letter, signed by the president, declaring that our ten-million-dollar ransom demand is to be a grant from the federal government and that we won't be prosecuted," Jackson explained.

The caller responded in a detached tone, "Well, I don't know about that—that would take considerable time to accomplish."

Incensed at his inability to negotiate with the "establishment," Jackson shouted into the microphone, "You don't have any more time."

Slamming the mike back into its mounting bracket, the hijacker refused to pursue the matter.

Holding a grenade against the base of Haas' skull, Jackson had lost his mind.

"Dive it! Dive it!" he commanded.

Haas pushed forward on the control yoke. The aircraft started downward in a slow spiral. The sudden turn of events quickened the heartbeats of the hostages. What had gone wrong? Was this it? This was it, and it would do no good to beg for mercy. The nightmare would be over in a moment, and they would all be dead.

Downward . . . downward . . . downward . . .

The air screamed by outside. The altimeter turned in a backward motion.

Jackson watched through the cockpit windows as the cloud formations rushed by. Yelling above the noise of screaming air, the beserk pirate said, "The company don't care about us—the people don't care—the president don't care. This is the only thing left to do."

Obviously bent on suicide, he intended to take everybody aboard to their deaths as well.

Cloud cover still obscured the ground from view as the jetliner continued its downward plunge.

Air-traffic controllers watched as the blip on their radarscopes traced the descending path.

"The money demanded is en route to Knoxville," announced the voice on the cockpit radio.

Harold Johnson watched the expression on Jackson's face as the copilot reached for his microphone.

"We have no more time left," he said. "We must have an assurance that the demand will be met. There can be no more delay."

The voice responded that the fast-approaching Lear jet was about one hundred miles north of Knoxville with its valuable cargo.

"When is it to arrive?" Johnson asked.

"It is racing to meet the deadline," assured the voice.

Jackson's grenade was still pressed against the captain's head. For the first time since the aircraft had begun its dive, Haas spoke:

"Listen, Henry—you've almost accomplished your goal. You heard the man say the money would be in Knoxville in a few minutes. Before long you'll all be millionaires—rich! If this continues, you'll be dead in a matter of minutes. Your bones—the bones of the passengers—the bones of thousands—maybe millions of people on the ground, including the relatives of Mel and Lou—will be scattered to the winds. There'll be your flesh and the skin of others clinging to the trees for miles around."

Jackson envisioned the grim scene.

He wasn't suicidal after all.

"Tell that Lear to land ahead of us at Knoxville. And it'd better show up with all of the money. This is the last chance we're giving," he warned.

Haas eased back on the controls, righting the jetliner in a horizontal attitude.

Ash-faced, the hostages wiped at the sweat on their brows and in their eyes. They didn't know what had happened as they collapsed from nervous exhaustion into the backs of their seats.

The hands on the instrument panel clock were closing on one o'clock.

Harold Johnson advised controllers that the hijacked aircraft would follow the Lear jet in landing at Knoxville.

"Roger," acknowledged the controller.

The Lear pilot reported his position as he entered the air space over Knoxville and requested approach clearance.

"Get behind the Lear," Jackson instructed.

The hijacker wanted to see the aircraft.

Haas and Johnson searched the sky to the north.

"Got him eyeballed at three o'clock," Johnson said.

The money carrier was beginning its turn to enter the air pattern.

Captain Haas maneuvered in the direction of the speedier and smaller craft as it turned while descending toward the airport. Captain Haas had placed the DC-9 in a wide orbit to enable the smaller jet to land first.

Jackson kept an eye on the Lear.

"Tell that plane to go to Chattanooga," he ordered.

Haas and Johnson were stunned by the change of plans. Seemingly the hijackers would never stay anywhere long enough to receive the money.

Johnson spoke into his microphone, "They want that Lear to go to Chattanooga with the money."

"Roger—they want the Lear to go to Chattanooga," repeated the controller.

It would be about a fifteen-minute flight.

There was a mad scramble on the ground at Knoxville as FBI agents and flight personnel raced to get aboard the civilian and military chase planes. Within minutes Captain Godwin was airborne. Commander Moore followed in his slower-moving DC-6.

Henry Jackson told Haas to catch up with the Lear, which had quickly changed course for Chattanooga.

"There ain't no way I can catch up with that plane," Haas said.

Jackson challenged the captain.

"You told us that Lear was a real slow plane when it was coming down here. Now you tell us you can't catch it."

Haas had known all along that the smaller jet had been headed south at a speed as fast as sound. Now he worried that he had talked himself into a bad situation.

"It's not that the Lear is so much faster—it's just that he

got a head start on us because of the big circle we made over Knoxville. But we'll try to catch him," the captain promised.

Godwin's jetliner climbed out beneath the hijacked aircraft and sped toward Chattanooga with its flying arsenal of FBI agents.

Haas shoved the throttles forward until the high-speed clacker sounded its warning in the cockpit.

Jackson thought a machine gun had gone off.

"What's that noise?" he asked.

Haas explained that it came from a warning device that signaled the crew they were flying faster than they should for the aircraft's altitude.

Jackson listened to the clacker for a few minutes before he told Haas to slow down and silence the annoyance.

Alex Halberstadt stopped Lou Moore in the cabin.

"Look—this has been fun up to a point," he said.

Showing the gunman his empty cigarette pack, Alex said, "It's now become serious. I'm out of anything to smoke."

"OK," Moore said. In a rare display of solicitous concern, the bandit told Halberstadt they'd have cigarettes put on board at Chattanooga, to which they were headed.

"What do I do in the meantime?" Alex asked.

"Wait just a minute," he advised.

Moments later the gunman returned with several cigarettes he had bummed from other hostages.

"We'll get some cigarettes and food put on in Chattanooga," Moore said.

That sounded good to Halberstadt. He was not a heavy smoker, but he felt more comfortable with something other than an empty pack. And he was hungry. It had been some twenty hours since he and the other hostages had eaten.

6
Ransom Delivery

Fred Vogt was sitting at his desk just inside the big lobby and office of Hangar One. A dozen light aircraft were parked outside the fixed-base facility, located about a hundred yards south of and on the same side of the airport as the main terminal building.

On the left front corner of the desk Fred kept ever-present his favorite book, the Bible. When work activity slowed enough, he occupied his time by studying the Scriptures. He was and is a strong believer. His wife, Brenda, a teacher at a Bible college, shared his convictions.

The line manager had swapped work schedules with a fellow employee who wanted the day off.

Taking advantage of a brief lull in activity, Fred phoned his wife at their home to tell her about the hijacked aircraft being inbound to Chattanooga. So that she wouldn't worry, he reminded Brenda that the other fixed-base operator had the refueling contract for the airline.

The short line on his telephone rang.

"Hold on a minute, honey; let me answer this other line," he said.

An official in the Southern Airways office at the terminal building was calling. Fred was advised that the pirated craft was due to land about 1:30 and that the airline would like to use one of the Hangar One fuel tenders for the necessary refueling operation.

"Sure, I'll bring over the best truck we have," he said.

Punching the blinking-light button on the telephone, Vogt spoke to his wife again. "Honey, we're gonna provide the truck that's gonna be refueling the aircraft. I don't know just how they're gonna do it, but don't be concerned."

Fred was afraid Brenda might become somewhat hysterical, since she always had his safety and welfare at heart. However, she took the news calmly.

"OK—now you be careful," Brenda said.

"I will," he promised.

She didn't urge him to stay away from the hijacked aircraft, which led Vogt to believe that the Lord had his hand on him.

Fred went outside, climbed in the cab of a big yellow-and-red fuel truck, and drove the short distance to the airline's loading ramp at the terminal building. Pulling up on the side of the concourse that jutted out from the structure, he parked the vehicle and went inside.

Asked if he would refuel Flight 49 when it arrived, he answered, "If I can possibly get somebody else to do it, I don't want to be the one."

In addition to being married, the fuel attendant was the father of a six-month-old baby girl, Heather. He had to consider the possibility of something's going wrong and his getting injured or killed.

It was as if he had not objected. Officials got an old pair of trousers and cut off the legs, leaving the pocket linings hanging below the new length. Fred couldn't move for the crowd of FBI agents moving about in the room. He wondered why one of them wasn't prepared to refuel the aircraft as he reluctantly went into a back room to put on what remained of the trousers.

Approaching Chattanooga, the trio of bandits was getting more nervous than ever. They talked among themselves about the three cabin doors, two of which were forward in the passenger compartment; the other was located in the tail section. Nodding toward the doors as they talked, they studied ways to defend against lawmen should they attack. They hoped the last-minute switch to a landing at Chattanooga had caught ground authorities off guard. But they were unaware of the two chase planes that were dogging their trail with more than forty armed FBI agents in pursuit.

Mel Cale sought assurances from Karen that no one could open the doors from the outside.

"I know you can be trusted—you'll level with me," he said. "Can those doors be opened from the outside?"

"Yes," Karen answered, "but they would have to have a tall ladder to do so, and you would see them approaching the aircraft."

He was relieved and would be very alert once the aircraft was on the ground.

Vogt phoned one of his employees at Hangar One.

"I want you to come over here and bring that tall ladder lying next to the building," he instructed.

Fred specified the ladder with the protective rubber on the upper two-thirds. He didn't want to scratch or otherwise damage the skin of the hijacked aircraft.

When the employee delivered the ladder, Fred asked, "Would you go out there and refuel the aircraft instead of me?"

Laughing, the employee rejected the request. "No—I'm not running around out there in my underwear."

Fred was not angered at the man's refusal, but he was upset over his bemused attitude—his ability to find humor in the situation. He resisted firing him on the spot.

Vogt placed the ladder atop the fuel tender and went back inside. It was too chilly to be standing around outside in short pants and a T-shirt.

There must have been a dozen people trying to talk on the telephone at the same time when Fred picked up the straight line to the control tower. He had to shout into the mouthpiece to make himself heard.

"Hey—I'm the one who's gonna be goin' out to the aircraft when it arrives. I want you to listen to me."

The harsh sound of voices became silent.

"Now, look," Fred said, "if there's a doctor in the terminal building, I want him out there the minute I get shot. And if there's any shootin' outa this thing—get all the ambulances out there that you can. And get one especially for me. Don't forget me."

A doctor had been summoned to stand by in event of an emergency. No one had thought to have an ambulance on hand.

Harold Johnson radioed the pilot of the speedy Lear jet that was advancing on Chattanooga.

"We don't know how much money you have on board. These people want to know."

"We have all the bags—they are filled," came the answer.

"Are you checking the amount?"

"We have the amount requested on board," assured the pilot.

The small executive aircraft touched down on the runway a few minutes later and taxiied to the terminal building with the millions of currency it had flown first to Knoxville and then to Chattanooga. The pilot had not been told how much the United States mail sacks contained. He had just been told to arrive safely.

Lovell Field's terminal building was rapidly becoming a scene of bedlam. Hundreds of persons crowded all available windows to stake out a vantage point in hopes of catching a glimpse of the hijacked airliner when it arrived. Scores of FBI agents had been summoned from nearby points. They raced from one point to another, their jackets flapping open to reveal guns strapped to their sides.

The federal agents were joined by dozens of local law enforcement personnel from the Tennessee Bureau of Investigation, the State Patrol, the Hamilton County and Chattanooga Police Departments.

Outside the building crowds of curious spectators, armed with cameras, binoculars, and portable radios tuned to police radio frequencies converged on the area. They had learned of Flight 49's expected arrival from news broadcast. Police cordoned off roads leading to the facility, but not before hundreds had infiltrated the site. A railroad track paralleling the airport road was lined with spectators. There were men, women, and children making up the ghoulish crowds that had assembled.

As news spread, workers at a nearby shopping center adjacent to the eastern approach of runway 2 left their jobs to watch for the plane's arrival. Peanut and popcorn vendors appeared among them. Only a high-wire fence stood between the spectators and the end of the runway.

Airline officials coordinated their activities with the FBI. Over two dozen boxes of fried-chicken lunches had been rounded up, along with trays of sandwiches, soft drinks, containers of tea and coffee, bulletproof vests, and riot helmets. Even a six-pack of beer had been sent for. It was not among the list of items demanded by the hijackers. But stimulants were requested. A doctor had suggested that the beer would produce neutralizing effects on the stimulants should they be consumed by the bandits. Otherwise, it was predictable that when the effects of the stimulants wore off, the hijackers would become disoriented and totally irrational.

Vogt watched as the provisions were loaded atop the catwalk of the fuel tender. He wondered how he would ever get all of the supplies down alone. Each of the bulletproof vests weighed approximately forty pounds. They would have to be carried down the truck's vertical ladder and up a steep ladder to the aircraft.

Sacks of money nearly filled the cab of the vehicle.

It was after one o'clock on Saturday afternoon when approach control radioed the hijacked aircraft as it held over Lookout Mountain, to the west of the city.

"Southern 49—I have been advised that the airport manager is trying to arrange for everything to be placed aboard the fuel truck. They'll have your request complied with as soon as possible."

"Tell 'em to hurry," said Harold Johnson.

"Southern 49—stop your descent at four thousand feet," advised the controller.

"OK—we're gonna have to go back up. Tell them to get

the money and fuel truck ready so we can land."

"Understand you're going back up. Fly a heading of zero-four-five. And what altitude do you want to hold at, Southern?"

In a tired voice, Johnson said, "At six thousand. We're just gonna hold till you get that fuel truck loaded."

"OK," acknowledged the controller.

Godwin's aircraft loaded with FBI agents and company officials reported in at a ten-thousand-foot altitude.

Commander Moore's Navy craft was bringing up the rear with an additional force of twenty-seven agents.

Ground authorities had initiated delaying procedures to give the two arms-laden shadow planes an opportunity to land ahead of Flight 49.

The hijackers were aware that the other Southern jet-liner was in the air space. They were not concerned, know-ing it had aboard the half-million dollars that had been refused earlier in Toronto. They were not aware of the FBI agents on board; nor were they aware of the Navy chase plane that had joined the pursuit operation.

Copilot Johnson transmitted additional instructions to airport authorities.

"Southern 49—advise the airport manager that the fuel truck is to be parked on a taxiway, not on the runway. When we stop the aircraft, he will proceed on to the runway and fuel us with the engines running."

"OK."

"He will have the money on board?" Johnson inquired.

"As far as we know—they have the instructions."

"OK—check it out. Make sure the airport manager un-derstands."

"OK—well, all of this is being monitored, and the crew ahead of you is hearing this. They will comply with the instructions."

Ominously, Johnson warned, "You must have the money when we land, or we'll go back to Oak Ridge."

"Understand."

Captain Haas was trying to organize his thoughts to make

another appeal to the hijackers for the release of the hostages. If nothing else were accomplished at Chattanooga, he wanted to get the passengers freed. Every passing minute endangered their well-being. Haas knew the pirates wouldn't be in a receptive mood, though, unless all of their demands were met. He worried that the trio still planned to keep the hostages. Why else would they have insisted that so many box lunches be placed aboard? Nonetheless, he would make a strong appeal. The plan he had worked out was sound—if he could only convince them of that.

Much would depend on how things went while they were on the ground. The least little thing could frighten the gunmen into a sudden departure and spoil his plan. Haas and Johnson were exhausted. But if they could just get the hostages off of the aircraft, they might be in a better position to end the hijacking by force. The captain didn't want to risk his life and that of his crew, but their safety was endangered more and more as the two pilots neared an end of their physical and mental endurance.

Normally, the captain and copilot alternated on each leg of a flight. But this had not been a normal flight. Johnson had done such a good job of maintaining contact with ground authorities that Haas had relied upon him to function in that capacity ever since the takeover. Consequently, the captain had been at the controls without relief for some twenty hours. And he had been without sleep for more than thirty hours.

Young Pat Brennan was nearing a breaking point. Although only fourteen, he was a big lad. Cale and Moore had used the window at the seat occupied by Pat as their constant lookout port during each landing. The youngster didn't know just how much longer he could take the menacing of their guns and grenades. Each time they came near, his Irish temper boiled.

Speaking to his mother, seated across the aisle, Pat told her of a growing compulsion to engage the hijackers in physical combat. He realized he would likely emerge a loser, but Pat's buildup of tension was rapidly becoming uncontrollable.

Marge listened and offered no comment. She was the
kind of mother who raised her children in a home atmosphere free of exposure to drinking and profanity. Carefully,
she calculated the shock value of what she was about to do.

Leaning toward the youngster's seat, Marge asked, "Son,
do you know any dirty jokes?"

He wondered why she would ask such a question, and he
was uncertain how he should answer.

"Well, do you?" she insisted.

Didn't every teenager? She knew that, Pat thought. Did
she think he was any different? Chagrined, he admitted he
knew a few dirty jokes. Hoping to lessen the impact of his
admission, he said he didn't know many, however.

"Then tell me a dirty joke," Marge appealed.

Editing his thoughts for the least dirty joke he knew, Pat
reluctantly began relating the story. Purposefully, he
selected a very short story to get its telling over with as
quickly as possible.

Afterward, Marge related what she considered a dirty
joke.

For the next fifteen minutes, mother and son sat exchanging jokes until Marge could sense that Pat had overcome the anxieties that had been about to land him in a
great deal of trouble.

The crowd of spectators steadily mounted around the
airport's boundary fence.

Chattanooga's police chief, Jerry Pitts, ordered all uniformed officers to keep out of sight when the hijacked
plane landed. Civilian-clad federal agents and state officers
would have to control the sightseers the best they could.

Captain Bob Pipkin, flying copilot to Godwin, radioed
the approach controller with information that a portion of
the items demanded by the hijackers was aboard the chase
plane.

"We need Flight 49's permission to land to off-board a

part of the money and other items," Pipkin said.

The controller acknowledged while giving instructions for the aircraft to continue its approach.

Contacting the hijacked aircraft, the controller said, "Southern 49, the aircraft off Knoxville with some of the items requested is inbound to Chattanooga about twenty miles out and will land when you request it."

"Tell 'em to hurry up and land before we do," Johnson radioed back; "have him clear the runway and get the items loaded so we can get them."

Pipkin communicated directly with the pirated craft.

"963 to 904—we are ready to come on down and meet you and lay the items out."

Godwin's aircraft was cleared for its final approach.

Commander Moore maneuvered in a lazy circle some distance away and out of sight of the hijacked jetliner. Controllers were aware of the Navy plane's presence in the vicinity. They were also aware of its mission and planned to clear it for a landing right behind the Southern chase plane.

The weather was clear and crisp. A moderate wind swept across Lovell Field at ten miles an hour from the north.

Harold Johnson relayed additional instructions from the hijackers. "These items that are aboard the other aircraft are to be placed on a baggage cart—repeat—on a baggage cart—by a lady driver. Bring them to our aircraft, and we will board them through the copilot's sliding window. A lady driver—no other vehicle—and she will wait until the fuel truck leaves to bring her items out."

Police-radio frequencies crackled, with the voice of the dispatcher sending dozens of units from point to point in and around the airport. Police transmissions were being devoted entirely to airport-crowd control. Heavily traveled Brainerd Road, a main thoroughfare leading to the airport from the city, had become very congested. The problem was complicated by the large number of shoppers leaving from and arriving at the big Eastgate Shopping Center about two miles from the airport. Spectators would command an excellent view of the hijacked aircraft as it made its low approach to runway 2.

Godwin's jetliner touched down and taxied to the terminal building, where it parked alongside of the Lear jet at gates 1 and 2. Quickly boarding the aircraft, FBI agents took charge of the suitcase of money in the possession of Fred Parham. The currency was transferred to a mail sack, which the agents split open. An impressive-looking document also was stuffed into the sack.

Captain Pipkin remained seated in the cockpit of the parked chase plane. A mechanic aboard the aircraft expressed concern that the hijacked aircraft's engines had not been oiled since leaving Memphis the day before. Pipkin radioed Flight 49 with a reminder that something should be done to receive oil while on the ground.

"You are cautioned about not having oiled those engines. We'll do anything you want to do—shut down one at a time—but you should make some plans to put some oil in those engines."

Johnson asked, "Can it be put in with them running?"

"Negative," Pipkin advised. "The pressure will blow the oil out. You can shut down one at a time, and we'll do it as quickly as you want."

There was no answer from Johnson as to what would be done. The hijackers hadn't permitted a shutdown of the engines anywhere else, and they weren't contemplating one at Chattanooga. The problem would have to be discussed with them.

A crowd of about thirty local pilots and employees surged out on the ramp in front of Tennessee Airmotive. Pipkin reminded the tower operator that the hijackers didn't want to see anybody moving on the ramp or any other part of the airport.

"We're moving them out now," said the operator.

A second Lear jet bearing an additional cargo of money landed on runway 32, a strip that intersected the other runway. The pilot was instructed to report to the tower after parking.

Commander Moore was on the ground, maneuvering the

Navy DC-6 into a parking position on the opposite side of the terminal concourse.

"That's as far as we can hide you," said the ground controller.

Fred Vogt had discovered the mechanic aboard Godwin's chase plane. He asked him if he would be willing to refuel the hijacked aircraft in his place.

The mechanic agreed.

Fred took him to the parked fuel tender and began instructing the man in the proper operation of its pumping controls. He showed him what to do to correct any number of malfunctions that could occur.

While Vogt was instructing the mechanic, the FBI continued to load supplies aboard the truck. It was beginning to look like Santa's sleigh, with all of the items demanded stacked atop the vehicle.

Out of the corner of his eye, Fred caught sight of a Catholic priest trotting out from the concourse with an FBI agent.

Throwing up his arms, Fred motioned the priest back.

"I don't need him—I don't want him out here giving me the last rites—I'm in touch with the Lord already, and I don't want any interference from that priest."

Vogt couldn't get out of his mind the threats made by the hijackers that if anything went wrong, they would make things look "worse than Munich." Having first made the threat over Oak Ridge, they had renewed it en route to Chattanooga.

The line manager was confident that he could go out and get the job done as it should be. He had been a Christian ever since he was a nineteen-year-old Navy recruit, and he had faith that when he died he would go to heaven. It bothered him that he didn't know whether the mechanic was prepared to die.

Looking up at the mechanic, seated in the cab of the truck, Fred then asked the Lord for guidance. *If You want me out there, I know there's no greater place than to be in God's will*, he prayed. He meditated on his belief that in many instances God received more glory in a person's death than in his life.

"Get down outa the truck," he told the mechanic. "There are simply too many things that could go wrong with this contraption. You might not be able to fix it."

The mechanic assured him he could handle the situation.

"Naw—if you get out there and start fumbling around, they'll tag you as an FBI agent; and you'd get shot. Besides, you don't have your trousers cut off," Vogt said.

The fuel attendant had been so busy while the FBI loaded supplies aboard the vehicle that he hadn't noticed that his tall ladder had been buried under the provisions. And that would be the first thing he would need when he got to the aircraft.

Aboard Flight 49 a slight change of plans was taking place. The hijackers decided that the fuel truck should deliver everything in one trip. There would be no need for a lady driver and a baggage cart.

"Put everything on the truck—hurry—run—they're getting short. Expedite . . ." radioed Johnson.

He had slipped again. The word "expedite" brought the cold steel muzzle of Henry Jackson's revolver up against his throat.

"We've told you for the last time to say only what we tell you to say," Jackson shouted.

Plainly, the gunman was a trigger squeeze away from committing murder.

Approach control assured the hijacked jetliner that everything would be ready in another minute.

"Hurry—give us an approach," Johnson pleaded.

"Turn left to a heading of three-six-zero."

"OK," Johnson acknowledged, "get that truck out on the midfield taxiway and have him ready to come to the aircraft when we land—otherwise, we keep going."

"Yeah—I understand," answered the controller.

Police units 64 and 65 were dispatched to the big vacant field behind Gibson's Discount Store on Brainerd Road.

Crowds of people lined the fence. News cameramen were climbing the barrier to get up near the runway.

Vogt was driving the fuel tender to the intersection of the two runways. He thought he would never get there at the rate he was going, but there was nothing he could do about the problem. There were so many sacks of money beside him in the cab that he was unable to shift into second gear, and the heavy load was restricting him to a speed of four miles an hour. He thought how glad everybody should be that he was an honest man. Had somebody without scruples and the ability to get the truck in high gear been driving, he might have gone off with all of the money.

Eventually the truck made it to the intersection. Vogt brought the vehicle to a halt. Sitting in the cab, waiting, Fred thought, *Now, Lord—I've got a definite conviction you don't want me out here.*

Without hesitating he turned the tanker around and headed back in the direction of the terminal building.

Captain Haas was making his final turn seven miles south of the Fort Oglethorpe, Georgia, air intersection. The aircraft was cleared to descend to three thousand feet.

Harold Johnson radioed: "This is Southern 49—do you have that fueler loaded with the money, provisions, and everything else?"

From his darkened and windowless room in the terminal building, the approach controller was unable to observe that the fuel truck was returning.

"All instructions have been complied with, and the truck is on the way to the runway," he said.

"OK—get him on the midfield taxiway, and when we stop have him proceed up slowly . . . ."

Jackson corrected the copilot.

"Have him come up fast," Johnson said.

"Roger."

A lone FBI agent waved frantically as Vogt neared the terminal building. He signaled him over to where he stood on the ramp.

Fred motored in that direction.

When he pulled up, there was another baggage cart of money sacks sitting there.

Cramming the money into the already-bulging cab of the vehicle, the agent ordered, "OK—get back out there."

Fred didn't protest. Thinking he had misunderstood the Lord's will a few minutes earlier, he concluded that he had just been sent back for the forgotten money.

Slowly the long yellow-and-red fuel tender creeped back toward the runway intersection.

Nagging doubts returned to the fuel attendant after he reached the holding position. Seeking the only kind of assurance that meant anything to him, Fred wondered, *Lord, do you really want me out here?*

He was sure the answer was in the affirmative—that God didn't want him to leave again, but to stay there.

Vogt thought, *Now this is really funny, sittin' out here.* The air was almost still. It was quiet. There was no radio in the cab of his truck, so he had no way of communicating with anybody. He was all alone and face to face with whatever his destiny might be.

Getting out of the cab, he climbed up on top of the vehicle. Standing there in his cut-off pants and white T-shirt with a noise-suppressor set worn loosely around his neck, he watched the sky to the southeast for the arrival of Flight 49.

A number of FBI sharpshooters positioned themselves in the concealments afforded by drainage ditches and culverts.

Fred glimpsed the jetliner as it came into view over the big shopping center two miles away. The necks of thousands of spectators craned upward for a look as the twin-engined craft descended for its landing.

It was 1:35 P.M.

Vogt got down from the top of the vehicle. He sat in the cab, waiting for the airliner to roll out, turn around, and head back to the end of the runway, where it would park.

"Lower all those window shades," Lou Moore instructed

the hostages, "and keep your seat belts fastened, with your heads down on your laps. The first one that raises his head is gonna get it blown off."

Obediently, the hostages lowered the sunshades. Then they leaned their heads forward on their laps insofar as possible. For some it was an uncomfortable position. For others it was an impossible position.

Karen knelt in the galley, unfastening from their retaining cleats the straps that secured the emergency evacuation chute to the right cabin door.

"Get up from there," Moore barked.

"I'm just getting this slide unfastened so you can open the door and receive the supplies," she explained.

"You crazy or somethin'? We ain't opening that door or any other," he told her.

She was told to take her seat and keep her head down like everybody else.

Moore and Cale began stalking the aisle, stopping frequently to order a sunshade raised so they could look outside.

Dick Senft didn't have his head down far enough to satisfy Moore. He was built too generously around the midsection to reach lower. A pistol swipe against his head convinced the rotund executive he could do better.

Strange feelings came over Senft. At first he thought the hijacker was joking. Then he thought it couldn't be happening. Anger, anxiety, and fear followed in rapid succession.

Approach control announced that the airport was closed to all inbound traffic until further notice. A passenger flight from Atlanta was diverted elsewhere. A southbound flight from Cincinnati was diverted, while another was placed on hold over Knoxville. Numerous private aircraft on the ground at Lovell Field were stranded.

The number of spectators that ringed the airport had grown to an estimated two thousand, with many adults carrying children on their shoulders.

As the jetliner taxied back toward the end of the runway to turn around and park in a takeoff position, Henry

Jackson observed the huge throngs gathered along the fence. He had not seen this type of spectacle anywhere before. It made him tense and nervous.

"They're gonna have to get rid of those people if we stay here," he warned.

Trying to allay his fears, Captain Haas said, "Look, Henry, you all are celebrities. These people have been hearing about you on the news broadcasts. Your names have probably been on radio and television throughout the country."

Jackson liked the ring of the word "celebrity." It made him feel important.

Calmed by Haas' unintended flattery, he said, "Yeah—maybe so."

Turning around to Moore, who was standing guard with Cale in the cabin, Jackson announced, "Hey, man—we're celebrities."

"Yeah—but I don't like that big audience out there," Moore said.

Haas pointed out it would take a batallion of police or soldiers to clear the crowd.

"You don't want that, do you?" he asked.

A bright green light flashed from the distant control tower. It was the signal Fred Vogt had been watching for to start down the runway behind the hijacked aircraft. He hadn't wanted to follow too closely in the wake of the jet thrust.

Straining under its heavy load, the fuel truck chugged along slowly. Vogt was concerned that the captain would think he was being deliberately slow. But there was no way to shift out of low gear unless he opened the passenger door and shoved some of the money out.

Driving down the runway, Fred was compelled to have one last talk with his maker.

Now, Lord—this is real funny. Here I am—I might die here in a few minutes. I'd like a verse of Scripture. Bring somethin' to mind that might kinda help me.

Fred was amazed that he was not scared. He was re-

minded of D. L. Moody's response when asked if he had
the grace to die. Moody had said he didn't have such grace,
but that he would have when the time came. Fred felt that
the time had come for him and that he had been endowed
with the necessary grace. That was the reason he was not
scared.

He had hoped that the Lord would call to his mind
something like Philippians 4:13: "I can do all things through
Christ which strengtheneth me."

But he was stunned by the verse that came to mind
instead.

It was Psalm 116:15: "Precious in the sight of the Lord is
the death of his saints."

Well, that settled that, he thought. Although content, he
was fully convinced he was about to die. The only thing the
Lord hadn't told him was when. He didn't worry about it,
though.

Vogt pulled up and parked in front of the aircraft's right
wing. Lou Moore, who had replaced Jackson in the cockpit,
stuck his pistol out of the window and motioned the fuel
attendant to come to the copilot's window.

Setting the brakes, Vogt jumped down from the cab.
Running around to the rear of the truck, he climbed up on
the tanker to get his tall ladder. Seeing it was buried under
what appeared to be a ton of provisions, Fred wondered
what to do. Without the ten-foot ladder he wouldn't be able
to reach the cockpit window to receive instructions.

Looking back at Moore, he started to unload the provisions in an orderly fashion. But the hijacker motioned
impatiently for him to hurry and get over to the aircraft.

For another brief moment Fred studied the problem of
the buried ladder. Then the thought occurred to him that
since he was not scared, the hijackers might suspect him to
be an FBI agent.

He thought, *Now, Lord, since I'm not afraid, help me to
at least appear to be frightened.*

Without considering that the hostages on board hadn't
eaten anything for almost twenty hours, Vogt began throw-

ing trays of food and soft drinks off of the truck to the ground.

At last he was able to remove the ladder. But not before he had dumped six cases of soft drinks and four trays of sandwiches onto the runway at the side of the truck.

Captain Haas and his first officer were horrified at the sight. They feared the fuel attendant was so nervous that Moore would shoot him. They thought his stumbling about on top of the truck—the knocking off of food—was a product of Fred's nerves. If he was not that scared and was really an FBI agent, they thought he deserved an Oscar for acting.

Taking the ladder over to the aircraft, Vogt leaned it up against the right side, beneath the copilot's sliding window. Backing off, he removed his cut-off trousers to reveal he wasn't armed.

Moore continued to wave his pistol in a menacing manner, which prompted Fred to climb the ladder in a hurry.

The hijacker leaned over and told him to calm down.

"Now—if you do everything like we tell you nobody's gonna get hurt. Just take your time. You got all the time in the world. Slow down. You speed up, and somebody's gonna get hurt."

Then Moore added a final word of warning.

"Whatever you do, don't throw any more food on the ground. Do you understand?"

Fred nodded.

"Are you sure you understand—no more food on the ground?"

Vogt understood. He just didn't understand how hungry the hijackers were, and they didn't want the food they were going to eat thrown on the ground.

"Now, listen," Moore said. "I'm gonna tell you what to bring up here, and you do it like I tell you. First, bring those bulletproof vests."

The lanky six-footer returned to the truck. Time and time again he struggled down off of the tanker, crossed the short runway distance to the ladder, and climbed up to pass the heavy objects through the small opening.

As each vest was taken aboard, the hijackers put them on. Haas and Johnson felt they had been demoted. No longer did the gunmen wear the captain and copilot jackets and caps.

Fred worried about the dress shoes he was wearing. The mixture of clothing was incongruous. Dress shoes, under-wear, and noise suppressors . . . an unlikely combination. He was afraid the shoes might mark him as an FBI agent. He hoped the thought wouldn't occur to the hijackers.

Reaching the top of the ladder on his third climb, Fred asked Moore if he could put his cut-off trousers back on.

"Yeah, go ahead. It's probably pretty cold out there," Moore agreed.

It wasn't the temperature that bothered Fred as much as the embarrassment resulting from his appearance. Putting his pants on, Vogt repeated trips between the truck and the aircraft until he had delivered the seven vests and helmets.

His next trip was an easy one. The gunmen wanted the six-pack of beer they had spotted atop the truck.

Handing the beer through the window, Fred realized how easy it would be to blow the heads off of the hijackers if only he had a gun. Such an act would not be counter to his morals, either. He would be putting an end to the immorality of a hijacking and kidnapping. But not being empowered by the law to take another person's life, he probably wouldn't have used a gun if he had had one.

Going back to the truck, Fred removed a box containing more than two dozen buckets of fried chicken.

Standing on a rung of the aircraft ladder, the box held above his head, the attendant felt it become lighter as each bucket was removed by the hijackers and passed through to Donna and Karen for stowage. They stacked them on an empty seat near the front of the cabin.

Sleeping under a blanket when the aircraft landed, a male hostage awakened to the smell of food. It had been placed on a seat beside him. Mary Melton's head was turned in his direction. She watched as the man's hand slipped deftly out from under the blanket, down into one of the buckets, and out with a piece of chicken. Both the man and the chicken disappeared again under the blanket.

Beer that had been taken aboard was rapidly consumed by the hijack trio. It made Haas and Johnson yearn for something to drink. They were beginning to feel dehydrated, not having taken any liquid into their bodies for more than twelve hours.

Volatile Henry Jackson relieved Lou Moore in the cockpit. Vogt, a gun enthusiast, admiringly eyed the chrome-plated .38 revolver Jackson used in reinforcing the instructions he gave. The cold steel muzzle of the gun was held at the bridge of Fred's nose while Jackson talked. Perhaps the beer had made the gunman drunk, but Fred was quickly impressed with the fact that Jackson was more histrionic than Moore had been.

"Get me the stimulants," the hijacker ordered.

An envelope containing the pills was in Vogt's right hip pocket. At first he didn't understand Jackson, who was drowned out by the noise of the running engines. Jerkily, he removed the noise suppressors from his ears. Holding on to the edge of the cockpit window with his left hand, Fred asked Jackson to repeat his instructions.

"Get the stimulants," he shouted.

Fred's right hand swung toward his hip pocket. He heard the click of the claw-shaped hammer open on Jackson's gun. The hijacker apparently thought Vogt was reaching for a pistol. He would blow his head off.

"This is it—this is it," Jackson said as he extended his arm toward the cockpit window while backing off.

Vogt thought, *Now, Lord—what should I do about this? I could easily faint and fall off of the ladder.* But the Lord told him to stay where he was. So he did.

The copilot leaned forward into the instrument panel. Vogt thought, *Why, you dirty dog, sit back there and block his aim.*

Captain Haas reached out with his right hand, gently placing it on Jackson's gun-holding hand.

"Henry—don't shoot the little ole boy," he said softly; "he's petrified with fear. He's trying to do everything you all tell him to do. Let me talk to him."

Jackson dropped his arm.

"Talk to him. But if he's got a gun, I'll kill him," the hijacker threatened.

Haas leaned across to the window. Winking at Fred, he spoke above the noise of the engines.

"Now just be calm—be cool. Do exactly what you're told to do, and you won't be hurt. But if you keep jumping around out there like you've got the St. Vitas dances, you're gonna blow the whole works. Do you understand?"

Fred said he did.

"You just take your time. Now give me the pills," Haas said.

With a slow, arclike sweep of his right arm, Fred again reached for his right rear pocket. Reversing the motion, he brought the envelope up behind him, paused, and placed it in Haas' hand. The captain handed the envelope to Jackson. Then he slumped down in his seat. Narrowly, the killing had been averted.

Jackson stuffed the revolver down in his belt.

"Go get the money now," the hijacker ordered.

Vogt got down and went to the truck. Opening the cab door, he pulled out several big cloth sacks of money. Dragging them behind, he started across the short distance toward the aircraft. The sack containing the impressive-looking document began spilling its contents. Caught by the wind, the document blew over against the nose wheel, where it became lodged. Vogt was unaware of the trail of money being left behind on the runway until he turned to see why the load was getting lighter. Throwing the sacks down, he began gathering up the currency.

Stuffing the money back in the sack, he struggled up the ladder to make the first ransom delivery through the cockpit window.

As each sack was received by the extortionists, it was passed back to Donna and Karen in the front of the cabin.

"Start counting," Jackson instructed.

There was so much money in ten- and twenty-dollar denominations that it would take days for the two girls to count it all. Kneeling at the front row of seats, the flight attendants were soon dwarfed by the stacks. Within a few minutes the accumulation was so great that Moore and Cale had to drag some of the sacks to the rear of the cabin.

Moore wanted the document demanded from the president.

Jackson was more concerned about the ever-growing crowds lining the airport perimeter fence about a hundred yards away. He wanted them moved back.

Copilot Johnson radioed the tower:

"We've got a bunch of people outside the fence that need to be moved back."

Police dispatched four additional units of plainclothesmen to the troublesome area at the east end of the field.

Units were also called for at a cemetery on Shallowford Road, at the far end of the field, where spectators were tromping through the graveyard to view the scene.

"Get those people away from the fence," Johnson repeated.

"Cars are leaving now," said the tower operator.

"Make sure they're on the other side of the fence—not on the taxiway or runway," Johnson cautioned.

"OK—we got that, 49."

Moore stuck his head in the cockpit entrance.

"Find out where the document is," he said.

"Check with our company—find out where the document is. Where is the document?" Johnson radioed.

Several minutes later authorities responded, "The document is with the money."

"OK—the document is with the money."

"They advise you will have to open the money to find it," said the operator.

The crowd of spectators surged with excitement.

"Those people over to the left of the aircraft—get 'em outa here," Johnson insisted.

A small group had made it onto the field from the cemetery.

"And there's a whole bunch of people in the other direction . . . on the right . . . on the other side of the fence. Get them moved."

"Southern 49—Roger."

"Be sure none of those cars comes down by us."

There was no way to get to the small group on the field without sending out a police vehicle. The tower operator asked Johnson for advice.

"Southern 49—we have a car ready to come out and remove the people. Is it all right if he comes out down the taxiway or runway?"

Johnson checked with Jackson before answering.

"We don't want to see any cars on the ramp or the runway or the taxiway out here. You can send them around the road. But don't send them out here where we are."

"Roger—understand."

The tower reminded the crew that the engines needed to be oiled.

Vogt was standing atop the aircraft ladder when he heard Moore complain that he couldn't find the document.

Thinking the document academic, Captain Haas said, "Lou—you are all millionaires. You don't need a piece of paper to prove it. You've got the money to show for it."

Moore hadn't thought about it that way.

Turning to the hostages, the hijacker proclaimed:

"What about that, folks? We are millionaires!"

Vogt told Jackson there was a piece of paper beneath the nose of the aircraft, and he thought it might be the document for which they were looking.

"Do you want me to get it?" asked the attendant.

"No, leave it there," Jackson advised. He didn't want Fred out of his sight. But on his next trip down he walked over and retrieved the paper anyway. It was delivered to the hijackers.

Waving the document before the hostages, Moore said the president had made them all millionaires. But after inspecting the document, Moore was not too impressed. The purported presidential seal looked more like a fancy notary seal. And the signature lacked a look of authenticity. The document had been contrived hastily by the FBI.

Vogt finished delivering aboard all of the items demanded. Standing on the ladder and waiting for additional instructions, the attendant was told by Jackson to fuel the aircraft.

When Vogt reached the ground, Moore reached out the cockpit widow and toppled the ladder. The attendant didn't like that. It was an expensive ladder, and he tried to keep the company's equipment in good shape. Now the ladder lay right in the path of the aircraft's main right wheels. He would have to rescue it before the plane moved.

Climbing up in the cab of the truck, Vogt maneuvered the vehicle the short distance to the right wing tip. Jumping out of the cab, he looked up toward the cockpit window, where Silvertooth stood waving his arms. The hijacker wanted the attendant back up to the window in a hurry. Vogt was pleased. It gave him a chance to rescue his ladder.

When Vogt reached the window, Moore shouted to him that the fuel truck was rolling out of control toward the edge of the runway. Fred had forgotten to set the air brakes on the big vehicle.

"Go stop it," Moore yelled.

"Get to it fast," said Harold Johnson.

If the big wheels of the truck rolled off the concrete, they likely would become mired in the soft earth at the edge of the runway.

Fred jumped off of the ladder.

Running as fast as he could, he reached the tanker just in time. A couple of inches more, and the vehicle would have left the strip. Setting the brakes, Vogt got down out of the cab again. Unreeling a long hose, he pulled the end over and connected it to the fuel-intake opening beneath the wing.

Returning to the truck, he switched on the pumping mechanism, then went back to the wing tip, where he picked up a hose attachment known as the dead man's switch. The safety device had to be hand held in a closed position for the fuel to flow.

Glancing in the direction of the fuselage, his eyes searched for the ladder. Again the hijackers had slammed it to the ground. He thought, *Those dirty dogs are going to bang up my ladder something awful.*

Fred would have to hold the dead man's switch for the next twelve minutes. This gave him time in which to consult the Lord about his next move. So he kneeled down under the wing and began praying.

Amused at the sight, the hijackers laughed. They thought the attendant had become so scared he was praying for his life.

Karen shamed the bandits for their ridicule.

The trio wouldn't have thought it so funny had they known what Fred was about to do. He first asked divine blessings for all of the hostages and crew members, believing they needed all the prayerful consideration they could get.

Then he said, "Now, Lord—a lotta times we pray for what we wanta pray and not what we're supposed to pray. What do you want me to pray?"

Vogt felt a conviction that the Lord wanted him to pray that his will be done regarding the hijackers. Fred prayed that God's will would befall the deranged trio as he invoked the Levitical laws regarding the fate intended for kidnappers—death. Vogt doubted that the criminal system of justice in the United States would result in a death sentence. He was confident the Supreme Judge would see that justice was done.

Henry Jackson stepped back into the cockpit. He wanted to know where the parachutes were.

Harold Johnson showed him a list he had made, enumerating the items to be boarded in Chattanooga.

"You didn't tell me you wanted the parachutes put on

here. If you had, I would have written them down,"
Johnson said.

"OK—I guess that was my fault," Jackson replied.

Captain Haas said, "Henry, while you and Lou are both
up here, there's something I want to talk to you about."

"Yeah, what's that?" Jackson asked.

"Southern 49—this is Chattanooga Tower," said the voice
on the overhead radio speaker.

Haas reached over and turned down the volume.

"I'd like to talk to you about those people back there," the
captain continued.

"What about them?" Moore inquired.

"You've got your money—you've got the document—
you've got everything you asked for. Why not let the
people off here?" Haas appealed.

"Well, I don't know about that," Jackson said.

"I know what you're afraid of," Haas suggested; "you're
afraid the FBI will charge through the doors and begin
shooting if they're opened."

"Yeah, that's exactly what they'd do," Moore feared.

"Well, listen—let me tell you how we can get the people
off without that happening," Haas argued.

"We're listening," Jackson said.

"We don't have to open the forward side doors. We can
line the passengers up in close single file, facing the rear of
the cabin—drop those steps in the tail compartment—and
have the people run down in a hurry. It could be done in a
matter of not more than thirty seconds. Now you know the
FBI is not going to be shooting while the passengers are
getting off. And as soon as the last foot hits the runway,
we'll suck the steps back up and take off. Then we'll take
you anywhere you want to go. What do you say?"

Henry looked toward the rear of the aircraft. He agreed
the plan might work.

"The passengers are just a liability from here on out,"
Haas argued. "You don't need hostages any longer. They've
served your purpose. It's senseless and cruel to inflict more
hardship upon them."

"What about the old man—can he walk?" Moore asked.

"Let's find out," Haas suggested.

Calling to Donna in the front of the cabin, Haas asked the flight attendant to determine if Alvin Fortson was strong enough to walk off the plane.

Donna walked back to where the sick gentleman sat.

"Mr. Fortson—it appears that the hijackers are considering releasing the passengers here. Do you feel well enough to walk?"

"Oh, yes—I could make it," he answered.

Donna reported back to the captain.

"Well—what do you say—will you let them go?" he pleaded.

"I guess it'd be OK," he answered.

During the captain's appeal to the hijackers, the tower had made seven attempts to establish radio contact with the aircraft. Authorities were perplexed and worried that there had been no reply. Focusing binoculars on the aircraft, the tower operator could see nothing unusual. The fuel truck was still parked near the right wing.

Speaking into his microphone, the operator said:

"Southern 49—we have a request—a request to know if the passengers can be deplaned now. Everything has been completed."

"Affirmative—yes," Johnson replied weakly.

"Understand the passengers can be deplaned."

"Yes."

"Are you going to proceed with the deplaning?"

"Yes."

"Should we send someone out—or do they—what are your instructions?"

"They will walk."

"Understand they will walk away. We understand that one passenger has had a heart attack. Will he be able to walk?"

"After we leave—he'll be off to the side of the runway. You can send a stretcher."

"Understand."

Another call went out on the police radio to move all

spectators away from the fence. Officials wanted to eliminate any chance that the crowd would interfere with the deplaning. The dispatcher also wanted instructions from his supervisor concerning the need for a bus for the passengers.

"Should we have a bus stand by in case?" he radioed.

The supervising officer radioed back with instructions that a bus be sent to the airport from downtown Chattanooga with a police escort.

Another superior officer radioed orders for a patrol car to commandeer the nearest available bus to the airport.

From fire station 18 a voice radioed the availability of a minibus. The station was located on the airport grounds within the boundary fence.

Vogt had completed the refueling operation. Disconnecting the hose nozzle from the underside of the wing, he ran over to remove his ladder from in front of the wheels.

Moore motioned for him to climb up to the cockpit window. It was to be his twenty-seventh trip up the ladder.

"Did you put oil in the engines?" Moore inquired.

For the first time Fred snapped back at the gunman.

"No, I did not. You didn't tell me to oil the engines, and you told me to not do anything I wasn't told to do," Vogt countered.

"OK. You're right; I didn't tell you to do it," Moore admitted.

A case of oil had been placed on the truck, and the attendant could have accomplished the operation; but it was too late. The hijackers didn't want to take the time that would have been required to pour one can at a time down the oil-filler neck on each engine.

Continued operation of the engines without lubrication would not be safe.

The fuel attendant got down off the ladder. The hijackers wouldn't get another opportunity to abuse his ladder. This time Fred took it with him and placed it at the edge of the runway.

As soon as the attendant removed the truck from its position in front of the right wing, the aircraft engines roared as the jetliner began a takeoff roll down the runway.

Mystified, an FBI observer among the spectators spoke into his walkie-talkie.

"Looks like the plane's taking off," he said.

"49 is leaving?" asked the dispatcher.

"That's right."

"Disregard all units—disregard," the dispatcher instructed.

The voice from the tower queried, "Southern 49—advise intentions."

"Going to Cuba—they want to talk to Castro," came copilot Johnson's reply.

"Understand you're going to Cuba . . . you want to talk to Castro."

"We want flight level 35,000," Johnson reported.

"Flight level 35,000? Stand by," said the controller.

"Navy 689 is cleared for takeoff," acknowledged the tower.

The chase was on again.

Captain Godwin's crew and force of FBI agents scrambled aboard Southern 963. Within a minute and a half, both the Navy and civilian aircraft were off again in pursuit of the hijacked aircraft, which was climbing out on a southerly heading.

"Southern 49, climb and maintain flight level 21,000. We'll get further clearance en route."

"21,000—give us a vector," said Johnson.

"Fly a heading of 180," instructed the controller.

Police at Lovell Field had prepared to send a bus out to pick up the passengers. They thought they could see the heads of some people near the end of the runway.

Ground unit 604 reported in. The plainclothesman said, "The passengers didn't get off. There's no one here but the fuel attendant and his truck."

"Southern 49—we will take your proposed route any time you're ready," said the controller.

"Direct—Havana."

"Direct—Roger."

Fred Vogt walked over and picked up a canned soft drink that was laying on the runway. Popping the top, he swished the liquid around inside his dry mouth before allowing it to be swallowed.

The brief pause for refreshment over, Fred climbed up in the cab of the fuel truck and began the drive back to the terminal building. Free of the ransom money, he could move at top speed.

Within a few minutes he was nearing the main concourse.

Dozens of FBI agents waited for his return. They were eager to interrogate the attendant. Stunned, they watched as Fred suddenly stopped the vehicle out on the runway.

Reversing direction, Vogt headed back out on the field. He had forgotten his indispensable ladder. He sure was glad to have remembered. He knew that once the FBI agents got to him, he would probably be more confused than ever.

Arriving back at the end of the runway, Vogt carefully placed the ladder aboard the truck and then sped toward the terminal facility once again.

Walking inside, the fuel attendant was deluged with questions.

"Now—you all just wait a minute," he told the agents. "I'm gonna go call my wife before I talk to anybody."

During the brief telephone conversation Brenda told her husband she had been praying constantly; and at one point she had had a conviction that he had been shot and killed. Fred told her of the near-shooting that almost cost his life.

Ending the conversation, Vogt returned to the room full of lawmen.

"Did Jackson wear an Afro-style haircut?" they asked.

Fred said he didn't know. He just knew one of the hijackers looked like a Mao-Mao.

After the interrogation Vogt was faced with the problem of newsmen, who agitated outside of the building for an interview. Company officials had instructed him to maintain silence.

Knowing his way around the airport, Vogt slipped away from the prying questions of the newsmen and took an evasive route back to Hangar One. He was relieved to be out of the limelight and was anxious to thank the Lord for his safe return.

Captain and Mrs. William R. Haas with his Gold Medal Award for aviation heroism
(Photo by Wilborn and Associates, Kansas City, Mo.).

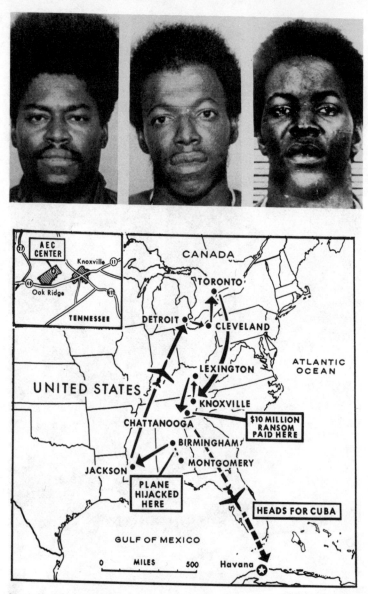

(Top) The United States government charged these men with air piracy in the skyjacking of Flight 49. They are (left to right): Henry D. Jackson, Jr., Louis Moore, and Melvin C. Cale (United Press International Photo). *(Bottom)* A map of the first flight to Cuba. Southern Airways actually paid $2,000,000 of the demanded $10,000,000 ransom money (United Press International Photo).

(*Top*) Southern officials and law-enforcement personnel plot their strategy. Captain Jim Godwin, pilot of the chase plane, is at left (Photo courtesy of Captain Haas). (*Bottom*) John W. Burns, agent in charge of the Cleveland FBI, talks with newsmen (United Press International Photo).

(Top) Flight 49 at Toronto International Airport. One of the skyjackers is looking out the middle cockpit window (United Press International Photo). *(Bottom)* Fred Vogt returns to the Chattanooga terminal after delivering the ransom money to the plane (United Press International Photo).

(Top) Flight 49 as it leaves Chattanooga. *(Bottom)* Lynn Thompson, administrative aide to Orlando Mayor Carl Langford, holds one of the plane's tires that was shot out at Orlando (Photo by Wide World Photos).

(Top) After meeting Premier Castro, the crew and passengers are given a banquet (left to right): Holman, Juan, Haas, Ellis, and Morkill (Photo courtesy of Captain Haas). *(Bottom)* Preparing to leave Cuba (left to right, foreground): Ellis, Johnson, and Holman; (background) Haas (Photo courtesy of Frank W. Morkill).

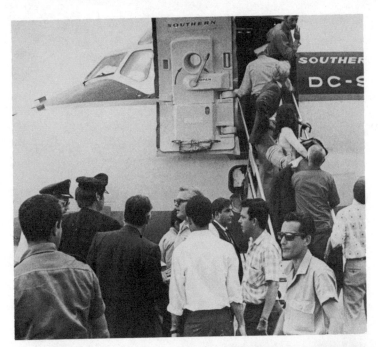

(Top) Leaving Havana—Johnson (hat cocked) talks with Captain Bob Pipkin and Frank Morkill (left, center) (Photo courtesy of Captain Haas). *(Bottom)* A mother and her child return to the States (United Press International Photo).

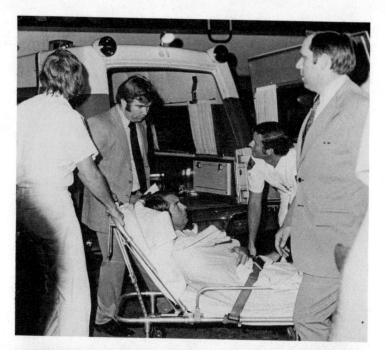

(Top) Johnson arriving in Miami (Photo by Wide World Photos). *(Bottom)* The passengers after their release (Photo by Wide World Photos).

(Top) Back in Memphis, Tennessee, on November 12, 1972 (Memphis Press Scimitar Photo by Saul Brown). *(Bottom)* Left to right are Captain Haas, Captain L. E. Hines, who was skyjacked in October of 1972, Congressman Harley O. Staggers, and Captain John J. O'Donnell, president of the ALPA (Congressional Photo).

(Top) The signed photo from Senator Robert C. Byrd tells the story. Byrd (right) is with Haas (left) and Judge James F. Gartland of the Airline Pilots Association (US Senate Photo). *(Bottom)* Captain and Mrs. Haas and Mr. and Mrs. M. J. A. Glover of Lloyds of London (Photo courtesy of Captain Haas).

7

Sanctuary Sought

Haas and Johnson felt like pelicans in an aviary.

"Open wide," Henry Jackson said.

As each of the pilots opened his mouth, the hijacker popped one of the stimulant pills into it. They were being made guinea pigs just in case the pills were poison instead of what had been demanded.

Jackson watched Haas' throat for a few seconds.

"I haven't seen you swallow," he said.

Touching the tip of his gun barrel to Haas' throat, the bandit gave encouragement.

"Maybe this will help," he suggested.

It helped. Haas gulped it down.

Johnson swallowed his pill.

Then Jackson stepped just inside the cabin to repeat the procedure with Donna and Karen, who willingly consumed the capsules.

After waiting about five minutes, Jackson decided from the reactions of the crew members that there would be no ill effects. The extortionist downed one and shared some of the remaining capsules with his two accomplices.

Departure from Chattanooga had been ordered so suddenly and without warning that Haas had not had an opportunity to obtain an explanation.

"You promised you'd free the hostages at Chattanooga. Why did you go back on your word?" he inquired.

"Didn't you see that car start out from the terminal building?" he asked.

Haas had not seen the vehicle.

"We said there was to be no movement of any cars, and they were sending one out there," Jackson said.

Silently, the captain uttered an unflattering oath for whoever had been so unthinking on the ground. He had been so close to getting the weary hostages released. He wouldn't allow himself to brood over the matter, thinking it best to deal with the reality of the situation and to hope the next stop would be the last.

Karen went to the cockpit and tapped Jackson on the shoulder.

"That pill really pepped me up. Lay another one on me," she urged.

"Sure," he said.

Removing one of the capsules from its envelope, he dropped it in her mouth.

Neither Karen, the other crew members, nor the hijackers knew the chemical makeup of the pills. She had gotten a psychological "high" from the first one, although nothing more than harmless sugar had been placed in the gelatin capsules by a Chattanooga doctor.

The physician had delivered the stimulant pills as well as the sugar capsules to Captain Godwin. But he warned of the consequences of putting stimulants aboard, explaining that when the effects wore off, all who had consumed them would become disoriented and highly irrational. Godwin elected to put the sugar aboard.

Henry Jackson wondered what Detroit city officials thought of him and Moore now. They had been forced to "enrich" the hijackers against their will. The gunman was pleased. But he wondered if all of the money had come from Detroit.

"How much money did the company have to put up?" he asked Haas.

"I have no way of knowing," the captain answered.

"Well—get on the radio and find out," Jackson instructed.

The radio had become a means to every end dreamed up by the hijackers. Even Harold had become caught up with the magical responses produced by his communications with ground authorities.

Transmitting the request for information, Johnson said, "These people want to know how much money the company had to come up with to sweeten the pot."

"Bubba" Shanahan intercepted the request aboard the chase plane. Shanahan was flying copilot to Bob Pipkin. The airliner's pilot in command, Jim Godwin, was riding the cockpit observer's seat.

Relaying the inquiry on the company frequency to Southern Airways headquarters in Atlanta, Shanahan waited for the answer.

For the first time it was revealed that the hijackers had been shorted on their demand.

Graydon Hall advised the radio operator in the operations center to tell them that the company had put up the entire two million dollars of ransom.

Shanahan hoped the hijacked airliner wasn't tuned to the company frequency when the headquarters reply was broadcast. Censoring the report, he said, "The company put up a half-million dollars."

Harold Johnson acknowledged receipt of the communication from Shanahan.

Hearing the report on the overhead cockpit speaker, Henry Jackson got off of the observer's seat and went to the back of the cabin. He was gone less than a minute. Dragging a mail sack full of money behind him, he returned in a strangely new, benevolent mood.

Reaching into the sack, he began counting out money.

Alternately, he gave handfuls of the green currency to Haas and Johnson.

"You can do whatever you want with this money—we don't have any axes to grind with the company. You can give it back, but we'd prefer that you and Harold keep it for yourselves," Jackson said.

Deciding to play along with the farce, Haas said, "Well, I'll tell you something, Henry. The company probably had to mortgage its airplanes and won't be able to pay its employees; but you are dealing with the real Frank and Jesse James."

Jackson laughed. He knew about the celebrated Western outlaws.

Jokingly, Haas said, "Harold and I have been flying around for years just waiting to pull off a deal like this. You see, I've got this old house I'm restoring out in La Grange, Tennessee. I can sure use the money."

Taking a piece of paper from his shirt pocket, Johnson quipped, "Yeah—and I've got about five farms out in Arkansas I'd like to buy . . . ."

Jackson thrust some $70,000 on Haas before the captain could beg off. The stacks of tens and twenties lay scattered about the instrument panel and control console. He was out of places in which to stash the money.

"It doesn't pay to be the captain on a DC-9," he complained; "there just aren't enough stowage pockets on this side of the cockpit."

Harold didn't have that problem.

"I can take some more over here," he suggested.

Jackson's generosity continued until the copilot's stowage compartments bulged with about $300,000.

The hijacker was disappointed that the two airmen couldn't accept more of the money. He wanted them to have a half-million dollars.

"You're really beautiful people," Jackson assured.

As the jetliner proceeded on its direct course to Havana, Jackson went into the cabin, where he enlisted the assistance of Lou Moore. Cale went to the cockpit to stand guard.

Announcing to the hostages his plan to share the wealth, Jackson said, "I realize that this has been an inconvenience for most of you and especially you men who have lost a day's work. I know you've got payments to make on your homes and other expenses, so we're gonna reimburse you for your time and trouble."

Counting out three hundred dollars for each hostage, Jackson and Moore began the big giveaway.

Jackson encountered resistance with his first offer. Mary Melton declined the money.

"Take it and buy your girl friend a present," she demurred.

"I have a wife and two lovely children," he replied.

"Well, then, take the money and buy something for your wife and children," she argued, pushing his hand away.

"You take it and buy something for your children," he insisted as he dropped the currency in her lap.

He couldn't understand anyone who would refuse such generosity. Nobody else refused. They weren't given a chance. The hijackers stuffed the money into the shirt pockets of the men and dropped it in the laps of the ladies.

Alex Halberstadt asked Lou Moore if he knew how to play gin rummy.

"Sure, man," the gunman said.

"Then find us a deck of cards, and I'll give you a chance to win back the money," Alex suggested.

"OK," said Moore, as he dashed up to the front of the cabin where Donna, Karen, and Marcia Timbers were counting the extorted funds.

Returning moments later, Moore appeared to have tears in his eyes.

"They ain't got no cards on board," he whined.

Halberstadt regretted that. He was confident the three hijackers would have an impossible task on their hands trying to divide a supposed ten million dollars equally. With his skill at gin rummy, Alex was confident he could have relieved them of at least a million dollars before arriving in Havana.

A few minutes later the complacent and celebrating attitudes of Jackson and Moore waned. A frenzied search was underway for something forward in the cabin.

"All right—who's got it?" Jackson yelled.

No one knew what he was upset about until somebody asked, "Who's got what?"

Jackson and Moore were in a state of near panic.

"Who's got Lou's pistol?" Jackson demanded, sure it was in the possession of one of the hostages.

Donna calmed their fears. Getting up from her kneeling position at the left front row of seats, the flight attendant stepped across the aisle to the galley.

"Nobody's got your pistol. It's right here where you left it while you were looking for a deck of cards," she said.

The hostages stifled their laughter.

Mary Melton had about concluded that Moore was stupid. Now she no longer had any doubts.

Cale, who had turned around to view the scene from the cockpit, was both amused and irritated at his brother's carelessness in misplacing the weapon. He was annoyed that Jackson and Moore had become so preoccupied with partying that they had let down their guard.

The Jacksonville air traffic control center took a hand-off from Flight 49 from Atlanta as the aircraft entered the air space over Florida.

Controller Dave Siegel was working the flight when Harold Johnson radioed the hijackers' request for a telephone link to the president of the United States.

Moore still had doubts about the authenticity of the document received in Chattanooga. Why hadn't he thought of it before? All he had to do was to get the Chief Executive on the telephone and ask him if he signed the document or if someone forged his signature on the paper. Moore was not too sure what kind of reception the trio would receive in Cuba; and if they decided to return to the United States, he wanted an assurance that the money had been made as a grant and that they would be immune from prosecution.

Siegel turned over the request for a direct line to the president to his supervisor. But he knew there was little chance of completing the call. Flight 49 would reach Havana before something so complicated could be accomplished.

Moore had good reason to be apprehensive about placing his fate in the hands of the Cubans. There had not been any firsthand evidence that hijackers enjoyed a safe haven on the Communist island.

Premier Fidel Castro had maintained a tight veil of secrecy around the subject. Hijackings to Cuba were a constant source of irritation to the United States, and the middle-aged revolutionary liked it that way. He liked the ever-increasing pressures brought to bear against the State Department to improve relations between the two countries in order to seal off the island to would-be pirates.

The Bay of Pigs fiasco, the Cuban Missile crisis, the resulting embargo of the island, plots to assassinate the Cuban leader—all served to harden the premier's attitude toward the United States. Hijackings and hijackers gave him a small edge for possible negotiations of some kind at a future date. So it benefited Castro that air pirates were made to at least seem welcome.

Information filtering out of Cuba indicated that hijackers were not receiving cordial treatment as thought, that Cuba was not a land of sugar-plum fairies after all. The trip would more likely be one to the back-breaking labors of a sugarcane field—a hard, sometimes violence-touched life. The most a prisoner could ever hope to earn for his labors was a monthly allowance of forty pesos or about forty dollars.

A few hijackers managed to move on to other Latin American countries or Europe or blended into the fabric of Cuban society. Others suffered imprisonment at the Casa de Transitos ("Hijackers' House") in Havana's Siboney district. The two-story house is a decrepit old mansion kept under guard around the clock. Light blue with peeling paint, the structure holds about twenty of the hijackers who are in Cuba.

Life at Casa de Transitos is one of animated suspension. The hijackers get their forty pesos a month and are occasionally given passes for outside visits. Maggots compete with the prisoners for the daily menu, which compares favorably with slop. The house is home for those who were obviously insane when they arrived. The young and strong were shipped to the sugarcane fields.

About a dozen of the sixty or so hijackers who fled to Cuba chose to return to the United States rather than cope with the life they found on the onetime Caribbean resort island. But they've undergone little questioning because they are in prisons or mental institutions.

Suicide attempts are said to be relatively common. At least one person is reported to have been successful.

Hank Baron, a seventeen-year-old disciple of Cuban revolutionary Ernesto (Che) Guevara, reportedly leaped to his death from the roof of the Hotel Nacional in Havana on February 8, 1971. State Department sources said they had been unable to confirm that the suicide of the Indianapolis youth had happened, although they said there were indications that it took place.

The lives of hijackers in Cuba is not the sort of information the State Department traffics in at the Swiss Embassy, which serves as the United States' intermediary with Cuba.

Captain Godwin's chase aircraft continued to trail behind the hijacked airliner. Before landing at Miami, Godwin planned to follow as far as Marathon Key, where he would fly an orbital pattern until Flight 49 was reported on the ground in Havana. Everybody on board was of the opinion that the piracy was nearing an end, that it would now just be a matter of delivering Jackson, Moore, and Cale to their destination and then returning the hostages to the United States.

Around the nation, millions of people who had been following the event were coming to the same conclusion.

In Washington, the FAA was preparing to close its monitoring of the incident. Across town at the FBI headquarters special agent Bob Gebhardt, who coordinated the bureau's actions with field agents, also believed the episode was ending. He had maintained regular telephone contact with his boss, L. Patrick Gray, at the latter's Connecticut home.

Comm. Robert Moore's Navy DC-6 was nearing the vicinity of Tampa when it was decided to halt the southward pursuit. His aircraft would remain airborne until confirmation was received that Flight 49 was on the ground in Havana. Having a fuel endurance state of six hours, the military-shadow aircraft would have no difficulty in staying aloft for the remaining length of time required. The commander planned to land at Tampa's McDill Air Force Base.

Aboard the pirated jetliner, it had become apparent that the attempt to reach President Nixon would not be successful. However, there was official concern among government authorities that the menacing tactics used by the hijackers at Oak Ridge might be repeated over the presidential retreat at Key Biscayne, Florida. But there was no way Captain Haas would permit the life of the president to be jeopardized by an aircraft under his command. Although he was not in complete control of the situation, he would have crash-landed elsewhere first.

As a precautionary measure, a detachment of the Forty-eighth Fighter Interceptor Squadron was alerted at Homestead Air Force Base, Florida. Should a threat develop, the interceptors were prepared to blast the airliner from the sky if necessary.

Captain Haas wanted to stretch his legs and stiffened body to be as alert as possible for the landing in Cuba. He requested and was given permission to go to the rest room. During his walk down the aisle he stopped to speak briefly with the passengers.

"We're going to make it," he promised. "Just have faith."

The captain asked Alvin Fortson how he was doing.

Fortson replied that he was all right. Haas thought he looked better than when he had last seen him.

"You hang in there. Everything's going to be all right," Haas said.

Henry Jackson was tired. He wondered why the stimulants hadn't helped overcome his weariness. The hijacker felt like he had been drunk for two days. The calmness and elation he, Moore, and Cale had experienced after leaving Chattanooga had worn off. Now, like Moore, he was becoming apprehensive about the next phase of their plan. He was expecting to talk by radio with Castro to seek an assurance of freedom in Cuba. Not being able to speak Spanish worried him. Too, he was concerned that the Cubans might put someone on the radio to imitate Castro. He wouldn't know the difference.

Paranoia gripped his brain on another matter as well. His thoughts went back to the hated policewoman in Detroit. Rage boiled within him as her vision returned to mind. If he could, he would empty the bullets of his .38 into her head. It wasn't so much that he wasn't guilty as accused in the sexual-assault cases. What gnawed at him was his intolerance for the fact that a woman had been responsible for his and Moore's arrest. The two men considered themselves too clever to have been outsmarted by a female. Jackson resented also that his wife had rejected him and moved out, taking with her his proof of manhood—his two children.

Marcia Timbers didn't know at first what the cold steel object was that raised her chin. She had had her head down helping Donna and Karen with the money count. The last person she expected trouble from was Jackson, who stood towering above her as she crouched on her knees at the front of the cabin.

"Get up," said the bandit. As he spoke he lifted her to her feet, with the gun muzzle still against her chin.

Fear struck at her heart. She had thought he was joking, playing games to relieve the tension and pass the time. She had done nothing to provoke him.

"Walk to the back of the cabin," Jackson said through clenched teeth.

Marcia could tell by the angry look in his eyes that he was not joking or playing games. Surely he didn't suspect her of stealing money. That couldn't be it. He would have suspected Donna and Karen, too. Besides, the hijackers had freely given some of the money away.

Terror tightened every nerve in her young body as she started down the aisle. Donna and Karen were mystified. They were sure she was about to be killed. But why? What had she done? They knew every move she had made. The two flight attendants watched helplessly as Jackson marched her to the rear of the cabin.

When Marcia usually walked the aisle as a flight attendant, it always seemed so long. Now the tubular confines of the cabin telescoped inward around her. Tears of fright tumbled from her eyes. Clasping her hands together in an effort to cloak her fear, she knew she had to maintain her emotional control. Sickness invaded her stomach as Jackson shoved her into a vacant seat at the rear of the compartment.

Dropping wearily into the adjacent seat, he jabbed the .38 tip against the underside of her chin. He watched as her startled brown eyes widened and flooded with tears. Her lips faltered as she attempted to speak. But the gunman spoke instead.

"You're a policewoman. Aren't you?" he demanded.

"No—no—no," she cried. "You know I'm not."

"Yes, you are—you've been trying to trap me, haven't you?" he accused.

"No—no," she repeated.

"Do you know what I do to women who cross me?" he asked.

Marcia felt faint.

"What's the worst thing that can happen to a woman?" he pressed.

He was threatening her with rape.

"I can prove I'm not a policewoman if you'll just let me," she pleaded, the tears rolling down her cheeks.

Jackson had lost what little sanity he had left.

"You can't prove nothing," he shot back.

"I can—I can—please just let me get my purse. I can prove who I am. I'm a flight attendant, not a policewoman. Please . . ." she begged in a weak voice.

The gunman considered for a moment. Maybe he could be wrong. She was pretty. He had liked her and had tried to help her earlier when she wanted to assist Donna and Karen.

"Get your purse—and you'd better be telling the truth, or you'll pay for it right here," he told her.

Marcia hurried to the seat where she had placed her purse. The big, burly gunman's livid eyes followed her

walk up the aisle. He hoped she wouldn't be able to prove
him wrong.

Marcia's hands trembled as she removed a wallet from
her blue flight bag. Inside was an official airline identification card bearing her picture as a flight attendant. She
returned to Jackson, who studied the picture. Then he
studied her face.

Slowly he folded the wallet closed and handed it back.
For a moment he sat silently, regretting what he had done.
He had little sorrow in him for anybody. But he was sorry
for her. Placing his arm around her shoulder, he attempted
to kiss her. She withdrew from the advance.

Jackson got up and walked away.

Marcia sat motionless, staring blankly out the cabin
window, the dried tears traced upon her olive complexion.

Relieved at news that the hijacked aircraft was nearing
Cuba, Ann Haas regained her appetite. She hadn't eaten
since the ordeal began. Friends and neighbors had sent a
variety of prepared foods to the home.

The large dining room had taken on the appearance of a
wake. Ann had not wanted to go near the room until now.

Atop the Queen Anne table was baked ham garnished
with pineapple, turkey and dressing, molded gelatin
salads, mashed sweet potatoes crowned with tiny marsh-
mallows, and freshly baked breads in loaves and rolls.

A warm glow of light shined down from the two-tiered
brass chandelier.

The massive empire buffet held a variety of desserts.
There was a German chocolate cake and one of coconut,
along with several types of homemade cookies in different
shapes, sizes, and colors. They had been sent for young
John and Betsy.

The delicate sounds of the St. Michael chimes tolled the
hour of four o'clock as the Swiss clock on the mantel signaled the passing of another hour. Ann and Billy Bob had
bought the beautiful gold clock during a visit to Switzerland. Like all of the other antique clocks in the home, it was

kept in perfect running condition. On each hour and half-hour the different chimes sounded softly and melodiously to fill their rooms with gaiety.

Ann circled the table, placing moderate servings of each dish on a plate. She hesitated in front of the china press that stood against a far wall. Its four shelves held six collector's-item plates Billy Bob loved and admired. They pictured historic shrines the couple had visited. Steeped in history, there was "The Hermitage," Andrew Jackson's home, Jefferson Davis' "Beauvoir" at Biloxi, "The Cabello" at New Orleans across from Jackson Square, "Rosewood" at Natchez, Thomas Jefferson's "Monticello," and "The Palace" at Williamsburg. The shelves also were adorned with a set of oyster plates made of delicate chinaware and a bonbon dish which had been a gift of Billy Bob's great-great-grandmother. At one time the heirloom had been accidentally left in the drawer of a piece of furniture the woman had sold. Haas' Aunt Sue spent six months tracing down the dish to repurchase the keepsake.

Going into a small, cozy alcove just off of the kitchen, Ann sat down at the long, polished wooden table. Heat from the big fireplace radiated to her back, helping her to relax from the strain she had been under. She wished Billy Bob could be there to relax, too. Ann knew he was as exhausted as she was.

Above the table on the wall hung one of her many woven scrolls. The words were in German:

"Wo Glaube Da Liebe;
Wo Liebe Da Friede;
Wo Friede Da Segen;
Wo Segen Da Gott;
Wo Gott Keine Not."

Translated, it was a divine home blessing which served to remind the Haas family that: Where there is faith there is love; where there is love there is peace; where there is peace there is blessing; where there is blessing there is God; and where there is God there is no want.

Ann's eating was interrupted by another of the many calls Southern Airways officials had been making to keep her informed. She was advised that the airliner was about to land in Havana.

Captain Haas circled the island coastline at an altitude of 33,000 feet. An attempt was being made to establish radio contact between the hijackers and Premier Castro.

Haltingly, the Cuban radio operator responded while searching for the correct words in English. Harold Johnson advised the operator that in addition to seeking permission to land at Havana, the three hijackers aboard wanted to speak personally by radio with Castro to ask for assurances that they would not be harmed or imprisoned.

"His Excellency Dr. Castro is not available to talk direct to the men," explained the tenor Cuban voice, "but they may permit to land to talk to authorities at the airport— then they may permit to leave if not wish to stay."

Lou Moore didn't like the suggestion. He wanted to hold out until he could talk to Castro.

Captain Haas suspected that they wouldn't get that chance, that the Cuban leader wasn't inclined to negotiate with hijackers. The captain didn't want to encounter another critical fuel need. Hopefully, he could persuade them to land, making Havana the last stop for the trio.

"Listen, Henry—the people on the ground say you can leave if you don't want to stay. Let's go down and see what they've got to say. Maybe they'll throw a big celebration for you," Haas appealed.

That sounded good to Henry. Why wouldn't they be welcome? They were arriving as multimillionaires.

"Go ahead," Jackson agreed. Lou Moore shrugged and walked away to take a seat as the airliner began its descent to José Marti airport.

Minutes later Flight 49 touched down on runway 5. The time was 4:50 p.m. It was the sixth landing in less than twenty-four hours and the second on foreign soil.

Captain Godwin's aircraft orbited over Marathon Key while the tired crew members and company officials waited for word of Flight 49's landing.

Commander Moore's military shadow operation had terminated at Tampa's McDill Air Force Base, where the DC-6 was placed under tight security because of the many automatic weapons left aboard by FBI agents.

The Navy pilot requested refueling of the aircraft while he, his crew, and the federal lawmen went to dinner. Some of the agents had been on the go for over thirty hours, having been called back to duty after working a full shift the previous day.

Upon their arrival at the officers' club, they received orders from FBI headquarters in Washington that released the contingent from the mission.

After dinner Commander Moore planned to fly the group back to Atlanta, from which point the agents would continue on to their respective duty stations in Knoxville and Detroit.

Taxiing along the José Marti runway, Captain Haas was instructed by the tower operator to proceed along the full length of the 11,483-foot macadam strip and park in front of the terminal building.

8

Impasse

Sharpshooting riflemen—select members of the Cuban internal security force—stationed themselves in positions of concealment on the business side of the José Marti terminal building at Havana airport.

Captain Haas maneuvered the airliner toward a lone ramp attendant, wearing white coveralls and a billed cap, who signaled the hijacked aircraft to its parking place immediately in front of the building. The exterior of the two-story pastel brick facility took on the orange glow of the late-afternoon sun. A long row of maintenance hangars stretched out diagonally to the right of the terminal building, while similar facilities of Cubana, the airline of Cuba, were prominent to the left side.

Henry Jackson and Lou Moore peered out of the cockpit windows at the reception party, who stood near the terminal. They were unnerved by what they saw. The welcoming committee was not what they had anticipated. It was made up of armed Cuban soldiers clad in the familiar olive-green battle uniforms that symbolized Castro's revolutionary army. Tough-looking soldiers, they numbered fifty or more. Milling about in front of the building, they carried carbines slung from their shoulders. Among the soldiers were several officers with holstered sidearms hanging from a webbed ammunition belt at the right hip.

Premier Castro stood out of sight in the control tower high above the terminal. From that position he commanded a view of the hijacked aircraft.

Coming to a stop, the jetliner shared ramp space with a row of other large aircraft. Immediately adjacent was a DC-9 bearing the name and markings of Air Canada.

Another and much larger aircraft, with swept back wings and a tall tail section, was a part of the Soviet Aeroflot fleet. The huge jetliner, with Russian lettering on the sides of its fuselage, had brought a passenger load of East Europeans to vacation on the Communist island.

"Keep the engines running," Jackson told Haas.

An antiquated fuel truck crept up and parked in front of the hijacked airliner.

There emerged from a group of soldiers a high-ranking officer, who walked toward the left side of the aircraft. Wearing a crew cut, the blond-haired officer stopped where he was visible to the captain. He shouted something to the captain. Although the cockpit window was open, Haas couldn't hear what the officer was saying because of the engine noise. Cupping his hand to his ear, the captain shook his head from side to side to let the officer know he couldn't be heard. The officer then motioned for the hijackers to come down to the ground.

Jackson leaned across Haas' back and stuck his head through the open window. He shouted, "We want to talk to Fee–del."

The officer, José Abrantes, Cuba's Deputy Minister of the Interior and Castro's security chief, shouted back. But Jackson couldn't hear him.

Several soldiers rolled a maintenance workstand up to the window.

Abrantes climbed up on the stand and stuck his head in the cockpit window. Jackson held a loaded revolver on him.

"We want to talk to Fee–del," Jackson repeated in a loud voice.

"Eez not possible, señor," Abrantes answered.

"Why not?" Jackson demanded.

"Dr. Castro eez not available," he explained.

"Where is he?" Jackson wanted to know.

"He eez in the country among the people," was the reply.

Waving the pistol in the officer's face, Jackson persisted, "We have millions of dollars to share with him in exchange for safety and freedom. We must talk to him and him only."

"Señor—we do not know when he will return," lied the officer, "but you can leave your weapons and I will talk to you on the ground."

Sticking his pistol in the Cuban's face at close range, Jackson said, "We came here to talk to Fee–del and only Fee–del."

Slowly, Abrantes brought his right hand up and pushed the weapon aside. Captain Haas thought him to be one of the bravest men he had ever seen.

"Come, señor. We talk," he urged.

Jackson was reluctant. He placed the gun in the Cuban's face again.

Abrantes repeated his action of pushing the weapon aside.

"Come. We talk."

Then he turned and got down off of the workstand.

"Whatta you think, Lou?" Jackson asked, seeking encouragement.

"It's beginning to look like we never should've come down here in the first place," Moore answered.

"Well—we're here. We may as well talk," Jackson said.

"Then you go talk to him. I'm staying here," Moore stated.

"OK—while I'm out there you keep me covered," Jackson replied.

Jackson had to suck in his big belly to wiggle through the opening.

Looking up at Jackson, Abrantes reminded him to leave the gun as he turned and walked away. Jackson stuck the weapon inside his shirt, jumped down, and followed the security chief to a point about fifty feet away.

The two men stood facing each other in animated conversation.

Jackson insisted that Castro be asked to come to the airport so he could talk with the Cuban leader. Abrantes insisted the premier was not available. Again, the hijacker wanted to know when Castro would be available.

"Maybe mañana," said Abrantes.

Slowly about two dozen soldiers had moved in, encircling the pair. They pretended they were there just to listen.

Jackson's body sweated from the tropical sun and humidity. He repeated his offer to share with Castro the millions of dollars aboard if the Cuban leader would allow the hijackers safety and freedom in Cuba.

"The matter is one that will have to be considered by the proper political authorities," Abrantes explained.

Where had Jackson heard that before? It came back to him that he had heard it from the voice talking from the White House while the hijacked aircraft circled over Oak Ridge earlier during the day.

"You people sound like a bunch of Washington bureaucrats," Jackson insulted him.

"I'm sorry, señor." Abrantes shrugged. "There are certain procedures that must be followed, whether you're in Washington or Havana."

"I thought this was supposed to be a free country," Jackson argued.

"There is freedom here for the Cuban people," the officer insisted, "but the admission of foreigners addresses itself to proper political authorities."

Laughing, Abrantes added, "Otherwise you must understand our tiny island couldn't hold all of the people who might want to come here."

That seemed reasonable to Jackson, but there were only three foreigners wanting asylum in Cuba at the moment; and he argued that Castro could give his approval immediately. After all, wasn't he a dictator? The hijacker's previous visions of sipping beer and smoking Cuban cigars with Castro were beginning to fade from Jackson's expectations. This was not the attitude he had hoped for. Why were they being treated differently than other hijackers? Or were they? He was beginning to wonder. How could he get himself out of the situation? He had been so busy talking with Abrantes that he had not become alarmed at the assemblage of soldiers around them. He was aware of them, but until now he had considered them friendly. Glancing toward the aircraft, he sweated more and more, while wondering if Lou realized the difficulty he faced.

"Look. We were told that we could come down and leave if we didn't want to stay," Jackson said. He almost said, "if we didn't like it here." The hijacker had already decided he didn't like the Cuban with whom he argued.

"Who gave you that assurance?" asked the officer.

"The voice on the radio to the aircraft," Jackson replied.

"Señor, no one was authorized to give you such an assurance," said Abrantes. "That is a political matter and can be decided only by the proper authorities."

There he goes with that line again, Jackson thought. *It's always the proper authorities deciding for other people wherever you go.*

Aboard the aircraft, Mel Cale patrolled the cabin, keeping an eye on the hostages. He tried to see what Jackson was doing on the ground, but the hijacker was not in view.

Alarmed at the growing number of soldiers who surrounded Jackson and Abrantes, Lou Moore crawled through the cockpit window. Standing on the maintenance platform, he waved his pistol back and forth while shouting to Jackson, "C'mon, Henry—let's get outa here."

Haas and Johnson sensed that an impasse had developed or was about to develop; they might be confronted with yet another crisis created by the deranged trio.

Either Henry couldn't get free of the crowd of soldiers or he hadn't heard Moore's shouts. He was still surrounded.

Lou stuck his head in the cockpit window. Cale had moved into the cockpit to stand guard over the flight crew.

"Hand me my grenade," Moore told his brother. "They've got Henry completely surrounded over there."

Haas wondered, *what is that nut about to do?*

Moore stood on the platform outside of the window, waving a gun in his left hand, the grenade in the other.

"Henry, get outa there. C'mon," he yelled.

Jackson was unable to move. He was hemmed in.

Moore jumped to the ground and started in the direction

of the soldiers, waving the weapons as he went. Cale told Haas to get out of his seat so the hijacker could get a clearer view.

Haas got up and stood at the front of the cabin, with his hands reaching out to the seat backs on either side of the aisle.

Arthur Tonsmière asked what was going on.

Haas explained that two of the hijackers were outside talking to the Cuban soldiers and that some kind of difficulty had developed.

"If there's only one hijacker on board, shouldn't we rush him and overcome him?" Tonsmière asked.

"Perhaps," Haas answered.

The captain had been thinking the same thing, but he knew he would have trouble getting rid of Cale's grenade. Haas didn't doubt his physical ability to overpower the young hijacker. However, he would have ten seconds or less in which to dispose of the hand grenade before it exploded.

If he could just get to the crash axe before Cale realized what was happening, he would split the pirate's head wide open. But he would still have the problem of the grenade. If he tossed it through the cockpit window, the explosive device would land right in the midst of the group of soldiers; and Haas would be in more trouble than he cared to imagine.

Just as he started to make a lunge for the crash axe mounted just inside the cockpit, the decision to attack Cale was taken away from him. Jackson and Moore came scrambling back through the cockpit window.

"Cuba ain't no place for us," Jackson fumed. "This place ain't got nothin' but a bunch of Spanish-talking George Wallaces."

"Yeah—they got some mean-looking cats out there," Moore agreed.

"This is supposed to be a free Cuba?" Jackson asked. "It's as bad as Wallace's Alabama or Maddox's Georgia."

"What are you going to do now?" Haas asked wearily.

Johnson looked up from his seat, waiting for the reply.

"We're gettin' outa here," Jackson replied.

"Where are we going?" the captain inquired.

"I don't know, but we're leaving here," he insisted.

Lou Moore told the hostages in the cabin that those people on the ground wanted to arrest him and Jackson. "Can you believe that?" he asked.

Mary Melton recalled having told Jackson earlier that the hijackers might not be welcome in Cuba. Now they would believe her.

Marcia Timbers trembled at the thought of Jackson's being back aboard the aircraft. She had hoped she would never see him again.

Arthur Tonsmière wished the two hijackers had stayed on the ground just a few minutes longer.

Frank Morkill worried that the impasse meant that the worst was yet to come, that the hijackers would turn their full fury on the flight crew and hostages.

Everybody aboard wondered what the hijackers would do next, where they would want to go, where it would all lead, and when and how it would end.

Not even Jackson, Moore, and Cale knew the answers to those questions. They were rich men without a country, fearful of being jailed should they return to the United States. Maybe they should go to Africa, Cale suggested to Jackson. Surely they would be welcomed there.

"Henry, we're going to need fuel before we can go anywhere," Haas advised. "We're at the mercy of the Cubans on that score."

"They ain't gonna give us no fuel," Jackson said dejectedly.

"They have to, or we'll wind up somewhere out there at the bottom of the sea," Haas warned.

Without waiting for instructions, Harold Johnson radioed a request for refueling. It was an automatic response to the captain's spoken wishes.

Jim Godwin and his crew checked into the airport hotel

in the Miami international terminal building.

He was too tired to eat, but he and his flight crew needed the nourishment. Having been on the move for over thirty hours, he needed rest mostly. After dinner he would go to his room, take a hot bath, and sleep.

Gross, Wheeler, and other management personnel fought weariness as well, as did the FBI agents who had been aboard the Southern chase plane.

At Tampa, Commander Moore and his group prepared to board the Navy DC-6 for the return flight northward.

The contingent of Cuban security forces remained on the scene at José Marti airport. José Abrantes reported to the control tower, where he and Castro discussed the security chief's encounter with Jackson.

Thirty minutes had passed since Harold Johnson requested fuel. Nothing had happened. A fuel truck sat in front of the aircraft's nose section, blocking the jetliner.

Repeatedly, Johnson tried to persuade authorities to respond to the request. United States officials had appealed through the Swiss Embassy in Havana that the Cubans detain the airliner if possible. Apparently the Cubans planned to do just that.

Numerous radio contacts were exchanged with the control-tower operator regarding fuel needs. Johnson was told that ground personnel didn't know how to refuel a DC-9. He knew they were lying. Otherwise the Air Canada DC-9 wouldn't be in Havana. It was known that the Canadian jetliner made regular flights to Cuba. The tower operator also expressed doubt that the proper kind of fuel was available. Johnson knew that was a lie, too.

Henry Jackson was unyielding in his demand that the hijackers be flown elsewhere.

Word was received in the cockpit that one of the hostages in the cabin could speak fluent Spanish. He offered assistance in communicating with the control tower.

The Spanish-speaking hostage was Frank Morkill.

"We don't need anybody up here," Jackson reacted.

"Listen, Henry," Haas replied, "if there's anybody back there who can help us, get them up here quick!"

Jackson relented.

"Bring him up," he told Moore.

Silvertooth walked toward the rear of the cabin. "Where is the passenger who speaks Spanish?" he asked.

Morkill raised his hand.

"Come with me," the hijacker said.

Morkill and Moore went forward to the cockpit, and Frank introduced himself to the captain. He said, "I'm here to assist the captain in any way possible. I'll do whatever the captain desires."

Haas explained the problem—that prior to the landing, the hijackers had understood they would be able to negotiate directly with Premier Castro. They had not been able to do so and wanted to leave.

"Unless we get fuel, and unless the vehicle is removed from our path, we can't move," Haas said. "We don't seem to be able to communicate the desperate situation that exists. Will you help?"

Morkill said he would try to be of assistance.

He was handed the microphone mounted in a bracket on the bulkhead behind the copilot's seat.

The graying management consultant spoke into the instrument as he depressed a button on its side.

"José Marti Tower . . . my name is Frank Morkill. I'm among the hostages being held aboard the Southern Airways aircraft. I speak Spanish. In an effort to help the captain I have volunteered to serve as a voice link between the aircraft and the tower. I speak only for the captain."

Morkill described the desperate situation aboard.

"This has been going on for over twenty hours," he said. "The hijackers are extremely agitated because they thought they had an agreement before landing that they would be permitted to talk with Premier Castro."

"We understand, señor," assured the tower spokesman, "but the prior agreement you mention was not made; there was no such agreement made or implied. We're not empowered to speak for government authorities. We can only pass on the hijackers' request to the proper political functionaries."

Jackson and Moore leaned forward against Morkill's back from their standing position in the narrow passageway between the cockpit and cabin. They listened to the two-way conversation.

"Tell that guy to hook us up with the authorities," Jackson instructed.

"Is that the captain's wish?" Morkill asked Haas.

"Do whatever you can, Frank," Haas replied.

"Would it be possible to establish a voice link between the proper authorities and the aircraft?" Morkill asked the tower operator.

"Señor, we regret that such a link is not possible at this time," came the reply.

"Then tell 'em to get us some fuel so we can leave," Jackson interjected.

Haas asked Morkill to have the tower contact Swiss authorities in Havana, who would arrange for payment of service to the aircraft.

Morkill repeated the request.

The tower operator advised that the Swiss authorities had been notified and were en route to the airport. But the tower said refueling would have to be authorized by the proper political authorities.

"Unless the hijackers can talk to Premier Castro, they want to leave Cuba," Morkill radioed.

"You may assure them that they will be treated fairly, that no harm will come to them if they will disembark without weapons," replied the operator.

Morkill translated each of the tower exchanges for the hijackers.

Jackson rejected the suggestion that the pirates leave the aircraft.

"They've already tried to arrest us once," Moore reminded. "They must think we're fools. We ain't gettin' off again unless Fee–del is standing right down there."

Angered more each minute, Jackson said if the hijackers had to do it to get action, they'd begin shooting the hostages one by one and throwing dead bodies out the window.

Morkill feared that the gunman would do just that and that he might be the first victim.

Communicating the threat to the tower, the translator said, "I cannot emphasize strongly enough the extremely volatile atmosphere—the highly charged and dangerous situation we face on board. Our captors are threatening to shoot us one by one and throw our bodies from the aircraft if you do not comply with their request."

Again the operator gave assurances that attempts were being made to contact the proper political authorities. José Abrantes and his security forces were putting into motion a plan to try and apprehend the pirates. He would like to get his hands on Jackson and Moore for their earlier threats on the ground.

About a half-dozen armed security troops were hoping to sneak up on the rear of the aircraft in a fire truck. They thought it might be possible to gain entry into the aircraft through the rear cabin steps.

Morkill realized that the Cubans were stalling. He was well acquainted with the Latin way of doing things. From years of experience he had learned to detect their deliberate foot-dragging procedures. He had often been irritated by their seeming lethargy, and he was growing impatient now as the Cubans gambled with the lives of those aboard.

"Looks like we're gonna have to start shooting," Moore warned.

Morkill appealed again for action.

"The situation aboard is rapidly deteriorating," he told the tower. "The hijackers are still threatening to shoot the hostages in order to get fuel."

"Señor, we hope to be in touch with the political authorities soon," said the operator.

Henry Jackson said, "Tell 'em we want the fuel and we

want it now. We can take off and circle while they get Castro on the radio."

Morkill repeated the request.

"We are not sure we have the right type of fuel at this location," said the operator.

"Advise them we need JP4," Haas said.

Morkill transmitted the fuel specifications.

The Cuban in the tower came up with another alibi.

"We do not have specific knowledge of DC-9 fueling operations and cannot assume responsibility," the tower informed.

Continuing to speak Spanish, Morkill said he realized that those in charge of the airport were trying to help by stalling, but that the hijackers' demands simply had to be met—else serious trouble was likely to take place at any moment.

"Please be patient and try to keep a calm atmosphere aboard," replied the tower.

Morkill would have to do something more than he had been able to do so far to get action.

Turning to Jackson, he said, "When I get back on the radio, stick that pistol up against my nose."

Morkill depressed the button, keying the microphone. Leaning forward so the tower official could see him through the cockpit window, the translator spoke while Jackson held the pistol where requested.

"Señor—the three desperate banditos are going to blow my brains out . . ."

Captain Haas raised his hands as if to shield his eyes from the sight of an impending murder.

"For God's sake, please comply with their demands. I'm just the first about to be killed."

Horrified, the tower operator radioed instructions to the fuel truck that was blocking the path of the hijacked aircraft. The vehicle began moving toward the right wing tip for refueling.

"It worked, Frank—it looks like they're going to refuel us," Haas said.

"Yeah—they were giving us the ole Latin stall for some reason," he said.

"Listen, Frank," said Haas, "get on the radio to the tower and request permission for the first officer to disembark through the cockpit window to supervise the refueling."

Morkill relayed the request.

"Si, señor—it will be OK," replied the tower operator.

"You make sure they're gonna let me back on board, captain," Harold Johnson said.

Without waiting for the captain to tell him what to do, Morkill spoke into the microphone.

"We'd like an assurance that the copilot will be permitted to return to the aircraft after refueling," he stated. "We would be endangered if forced to take off with only one flight crew member on board."

"Si, señor—the copilot may return to the aircraft afterward," assured the tower.

"We must be fueled with the right type of fuel, since it is to be used for takeoff," cautioned Morkill.

"Si, señor—it is jet fuel," answered the tower.

Harold Johnson squeezed his six-foot body through the cockpit window. Using the emergency descent rope, he dropped to the ground. Breaking his fall, he sustained painful rope burns to his hands as he tried to grip the small webbed band.

Walking over to the fuel attendant, he was unable to make himself understood. The truck operator couldn't speak English. Johnson smelled of the fuel. It had the distinct odor of kerosene and was clear in color.

Satisfied that it was the correct type of fuel and that the attendant knew what he was doing, Johnson struggled back up the rope and took his seat in the cockpit. Several layers of flesh in the palms of his hands were badly peeled along the life lines.

The time was coming up on seven o'clock.

Fuel gauges on the cockpit instrument panel had moved up by approximately fourteen thousand pounds as the old tanker truck pumped fuel into the wing tanks.

Jackson and Moore had lost their patience. They wanted to be on the move again. The aircraft had been on the gound for almost an hour—too long, in their estimation.

"Let's get going," Jackson said.

"They haven't finished the refueling," Haas answered.

"We can get more fuel somewhere else," Jackson insisted.

Haas was about to object again when Cale ran up to the cockpit.

"There's a truck moving toward us back there. Looks like it has soldiers in it," he reported.

Holding a grenade to the captain's head, Jackson threatened to set off the device if there were any further delay.

Johnson signaled to the fuel attendant. The hose was disconnected from the wing intake line.

Within minutes the Havana airport's size diminished in appearance as the aircraft climbed through the dusky sky and headed north over the Caribbean.

Flight 49 was off again on the tenth leg of its long odyssey.

9
Flight to Europe

Frank Morkill had been ordered back to his seat in the cabin, where he sat brooding, playing over in his mind his actions in the cockpit and his conversation with the tower operator. The more he thought about it, the deeper he dug for himself a kind of double hell. Blaming himself for over-playing his hand, he thought maybe the Cubans could have ended the hijacking while on the ground in Havana. He had been his usual impatient self with Latin slowness. *But perhaps this time,* he thought, *I have not given them credit for their stalling tactics.* Morkill was sure he had blown it. He was fed up with himself. There must have been others aboard who spoke Spanish. Wishing he had just kept out of everything, he sank into a deep feeling of depression.

Henry Jackson and Lou Moore stood at the entrance to the cockpit, talking over their next move. Captain Haas had offered to circle above the northern coast of Cuba while additional attempts could be made to establish radio contact with Premier Castro. But the two pirates had rejected the offer, concluding it wouldn't do any good. They wanted no part of Cuba.

Preoccupied with plotting what to do next and where to go with their millions of dollars, they had agreed that Captain Haas could land at the naval air station at Key West to top off the wing tanks with fuel. To reach the destination they had in mind would require all the fuel the aircraft could take on and then some.

Captain Godwin was soaking in a hot bath when the telephone rang in his hotel room. He was tempted to ignore the jangling nuisance. Whoever was calling had better have something on his mind important enough to interrupt the captain's relaxation.

"Hello," he answered gruffly.

Southern Airway's Miami station manager, O. B. Matthews, was on the line.

"Captain—we have just received word that Southern 49 is airborne again on a northerly course out of Cuba," he reported.

"He's probably inbound to Miami after letting the hijackers off in Havana," Godwin speculated.

"No, sir—the hijackers are still directing the flight. They didn't stay in Cuba," Matthews said.

"For pity's sake, what's going on then?" the captain asked.

"We don't know for sure, but we thought you would want to get back downstairs to your aircraft," the station manager replied.

"Yeah—thanks," Godwin said.

Hurriedly, the captain dressed and headed back to the airline's Miami operations center in the terminal building.

When he arrived, further word had been received that the hijacked airliner would be landing at Key West within a matter of minutes.

George Gross was on the telephone to the duty officer at the Boca Chica naval air station. The company official was pleading with the Navy officer to somehow block the aircraft to prevent its leaving the base once on the ground. But he was told that such action would require the approval of the base's commanding officer.

"Then get his approval," Gross stormed.

The commanding officer was not available, Gross was informed.

Godwin, his crew, and company officials were joined by the two dozen armed FBI agents who had accompanied them to Miami.

The group would stand by to await developments.

In Washington, the special hijacking command posts at

both the FAA and the FBI headquarters were reactivated.

Acting FBI director L. Patrick Gray telephoned Southern Airways' executive vice-president and general manager, Graydon Hall, in Atlanta, to confer on the situation.

Gray suggested that the hijacking would have to be terminated by force.

Hall was distraught after the conversation. Leaving his executive-office suite, he walked down the corridor and rounded the corner to the operations center. Telling a few key personnel about the FBI plan, his eyes were glazed and reddened with tears. His hands shook noticeably. Somebody appeared with a drink of whiskey, suggesting he have a drink to compose himself. Hall returned to the solitude of his office.

The prospect of ending the hijacking by force was repugnant to all of the airline people. Debate had raged over the issue throughout the day among those aboard the chase plane. Armed intervention violated the sacrosanct domain of the pilot in command. But the growing risk of death or injury to those aboard the pirated aircraft had increased with each passing minute. While Haas and Johnson had been able to maintain their mental alertness, company officials believed the flight crew's physical endurance to be comparable to their own—nearing the limit. What they had to consider was the grave possibility of losing the crew, the passengers, and the aircraft.

Another critical consideration centered around the low oil supply in the engines of the hijacked aircraft. The twin turbines had been running continuously without additional oil. Each engine normally consumed oil at the rate of one pint per hour. Within a few more hours of operation, the sixteen-quart capacity of each engine would be exhausted; and the lubricant was vital to the continued movement of the bearings in the main turbine shafts of each engine. The hijacked aircraft was rapidly approaching a point when its engines could fail, producing disastrous results.

At Key West, where Southern 49 was being refueled, Captain Haas radioed a request that the engines be oiled.

But the only lubricant available was for propeller-driven engines, not jets.

Somehow he had to persuade the hijackers to release the hostages. Turning to Jackson, he renewed his appeal for freeing the passengers.

"Henry, listen to me about those people back there. You don't need them anymore. Let them go while we're here. We'll take you wherever you want to go," he said.

"Well . . . I don't know," Jackson answered.

Haas continued his plea.

"It's quiet here and safe. It's dark, and the only movement on the airfield since we've been here is that fuel truck out there. Let me tell you what we can do," Haas suggested.

"Yeah—I'm listening," Jackson said indifferently while looking out of the right-side cockpit window toward the fuel tender.

"Well," Haas said, "we can just drop the back steps and let the people off. After taking off, we'll radio the control tower to send a bus out to pick up the people. Authorities won't know anything about what's happened until we've gone."

The plan sounded safe enough to Jackson, who said, "Well—we'll think about it. It might be a good idea."

During the refueling, Mel Cale sat on the armrest of Morkill's seat.

"Look," Morkill said, "if you guys have got a plan, let us in on it. We are all in the same boat together. We want to help you accomplish this mission of yours. It is the only hope for all of us. If you haven't got a plan, let us help you formulate one."

Cale didn't reply. He just stared at the tired and frightened hostage who still brooded over his actions while he had been in Havana.

None of the passengers knew where they were. Alex Halberstadt thought the aircraft had landed in Haiti. Mary Melton believed she was somewhere in Central America. Others concluded that it didn't matter where they were.

They were still held captive, and that was what mattered.

Suddenly, the aircraft was moving again.

An hour had elapsed during the refueling operation at Boca Chica naval air station. The long stay on the ground had made the three gunmen shaky and nervous. And the pirates had decided to continue holding the hostages despite the captain's plea for their release.

It was 8:15 P.M. as Captain Haas maneuvered clear of the fuel truck. Engines roaring, the jetliner sped down the runway to become airborne.

Mel Cale had been forward talking with Jackson and Moore during the takeoff. Returning to Frank Morkill's seat, he motioned the hostage to the rear of the cabin.

"We have a plan," Cale revealed. "We're going to Switzerland."

FAA controllers in the Miami air traffic control center huddled around the radarscope as Southern 49 winged away from Key West on its new heading to the East. They were puzzled over the new direction.

"Southern 49—advise your intentions," the controller radioed.

"Our destination is Switzerland," replied copilot Johnson.

Captain Godwin was on the telephone to the Miami center when the new destination was announced.

"My God," he exclaimed, "they'll never make it. That aircraft has a range of only fifteen hundred miles."

He asked the controller to inquire about the proposed route to Switzerland.

Relaying the question, the controller spoke into the microphone. "Southern 49—what is your proposed flight course to Switzerland?"

"They are demanding to be flown directly out over the Atlantic," Johnson reported.

The copilot thought the hijackers had lost their minds to even think such a flight possible. A distance of more than four thousand miles of ocean separated landfalls over the Atlantic. They would be at the bottom of the sea if they continued out over the water.

Miami Center inquired about the state of the aircraft's oil supply. "Did you take on oil at Key West?" asked the controller.

"Negative," Johnson reported.

"Are you aware that those engines are in danger of failing at any moment?" the controller pressed.

"Affirmative," Johnson acknowledged; "instrument gauges are already reflecting high exhaust and high oil temperatures."

Henry Jackson listened as the controller continued.

"It is absolutely vital that you put in somewhere for oil," urged the controller.

"Roger—the crew is aware of that," Johnson said.

Proceeding on its flight out over the Atlantic, Captain Haas wondered about the condition of young Keith Didien. Keith and the captain's young daughter, Betsy, were about the same age. All the hijackers had to do to get Haas to do anything they wanted was to threaten to kill the little boy. The captain would have tried to fly the jetliner to Switzerland on one engine before he would allow that to happen. He had been careful to not ask how the little boy was doing, for he didn't want to reveal his weakness for children. But the pirates could have gotten anything from Haas. He would have even written them a check for ten million dollars and tried to work it out before he would allow anything to happen to that boy.

Commander Moore and his Navy DC-6 had reached a position thirty-eight miles south of Tallahassee on the northbound return flight to Atlanta with the cadre of FBI riflemen.

A voice on the radio called out the aircraft's designation numbers.

Moore acknowledged, "This is Navy 689. Go ahead and speak slowly. Keep your transmitter keyed, please. Over."

"This is directed to your aircraft from FBI headquarters in Washington, requesting to speak to Mr. Karl Bresko."

"Yes, sir—he is standing here beside me. Go ahead. I'll relay. We do not have facilities to have you speak directly to him. Over."

"Ten-four. Can the hijacked Southern Airways plane overhear my conversation on this frequency?"

The Navy plane was receiving and transmitting on ultrahigh frequencies, while the hijacked airliner used lower frequency channels.

"It is possible," Moore reported, "but not probable. Over."

"Ten-four. Mr. Bresko, Mr. Hall and I have had conversation; and if you have not, you are to receive instructions at Orlando as to action to be taken in connection with the hijacked aircraft."

"689," Moore acknowledged, "stand by."

The Navy commander told Bresko he interpreted the message as a request to divert to Orlando.

Resuming the conversation, Moore was asked to report his geographical position, fuel state, and the time he would require to reach Orlando.

"Do you have a specific reason for the diversion?" Moore asked.

The FBI spokesman in Washington advised, "The opertion you were involved in is back on again."

Neither Moore nor Bresko completely understood what was happening, but the Navy commander altered his course for the central Florida city.

"This is Navy 689," Moore continued. "Mr. Bresko can now transmit to you. Over."

"Would you repeat that, Navy?"

Bresko recognized the voice on the radio.

"We can read you, Bob Gebhardt; go ahead. This is Bresko, FBI, Detroit."

"Ten-four. Did Mr. Bresko receive the specific instructions given by Mr. Gray?"

"I am not aware of that," Bresko answered.

"INSTRUCTIONS ARE THAT THE HIJACKED CRAFT BE DISABLED WHEN NEXT ·ON THE

GROUND."

The communication link that enabled Bresko to speak directly to Washington introduced radio interference. Moore took over the radio exchange with FBI headquarters.

"Navy 689—roger—roger," Moore said, acknowledging receipt of the instructions.

"Ten-four. I understand the hijacked aircraft is en route to Miami at this time. Is that correct?"

Moore reported information obtained by monitoring the Miami control center.

"At the exact time the aircraft is fifty miles south of Bimini."

Gebhardt advised that the same instructions given Bresko were being transmitted to agents in Miami. Concluding, he said, "It is possible the hijacked plane could land at some remote area. Be alert to that situation and to access routes, and implement the instructions of Mr. Gray."

"Roger—roger," Moore acknowledged.

Both Miami and Orlando were being placed on alert to cover the possibility that the hijacked jetliner might land at either location. Now the task was to persuade the pirates to land at one of the two locations.

Prodded by Godwin, who remained on the telephone to the Miami center, air-traffic controllers in contact with Southern 49 hammered away at the urgent need for engine oil aboard the hijacked airliner.

Pressurization problems also had developed, making the flight even more uncomfortable for those aboard. Frank Morkill had developed a splitting headache.

"Henry," Haas said, "this is now the worst aircraft in the Southern fleet, and Harold and I have got to be the worst crew the airline has on its roster. Why don't we land somewhere and exchange planes? If you're going to Europe you need a four-engine aircraft."

Haas and Johnson would be more than pleased if Jackson went for the idea of switching to a four-engine aircraft.

Neither was qualified beyond twin-engine jets.

"How do we know that guy on the radio is leveling with us?"Jackson asked.

Removing the thick DC-9 operating manual from his flight bag, Haas opened the book to the section on engine performance. Handing it to Jackson, he told him he could verify what the man was saying—that the engines were nearing a state of oil depletion. He reminded the hijacker of the very elementary laws of friction and of what happens when dry metal comes in contact with dry metal.

"Why, those engines could freeze on us any second now," Haas warned.

Jackson was becoming a believer.

"And Henry, more than that is the peril that faces us if we continue on this course out over the ocean," Haas said.

The captain emphasized the limited range of the aircraft, that after flying for fifteen hundred miles out at sea, the jetliner would be out of fuel.

"When that happens," Haas said, "we'll go into the ocean, and I hate to think what will become of us. Even if any of us get out of this thing alive, they'll never find us in the darkness. We'll become a midnight snack for a bunch of man-eating sharks."

That was one prospect Jackson had not considered, and he didn't like the idea of being eaten alive by a school of hungry sharks.

"Turn north then—we can reach Bermuda," Jackson insisted.

Henry had studied his geography. Bermuda was within the aircraft's range.

Haas placed the jetliner on a northerly course.

Air-traffic controllers noticed the changed flight path on their radar screens.

Captain Godwin and George Gross decided it was time to renew their pursuit of the aircraft. Climbing aboard the Southern chase plane, they were followed up the steps by the two dozen FBI agents.

Given priority takeoff clearance, the group was back in

the sky headed north. They would parallel Florida's east coast while keeping track of the hijacked aircraft. It was not known to Godwin and traffic controllers exactly what had happened to change the minds of the hijackers. But they were glad the futile oceanic course eastward had been altered.

"Look, Henry," Haas suggested, "if you are determined to go to Europe, let me tell you what we should do."

"I'm listening," Jackson said.

"Well, we don't have any overseas navigation charts, and we should have them. Too, we need a navigator. I'd probably get us lost at sea somewhere, since Harold and I are not qualified as navigators. We could land at, say, Jacksonville or Charleston and get the oil, fuel, food, and perhaps even an Air Force plane to lead us up through Newfoundland and Iceland and across that way. It would be risky, but I think we might make it in that direction."

Unaware of Haas' suggested plan, air-traffic controllers picked up the same theme in their continued radio contacts with the hijacked aircraft. Except they were urging that the hijacked airliner land at Orlando.

"Orlando . . . Orlando . . . Orlando . . ." was repeated over and over in appeals from the ground.

The critical need for oil, the pressurization problem, the lack of navigation charts—all of these things were beginning to bother Jackson as much as Haas. The pirate wasn't keen on landing at military air bases such as Haas had suggested. Orlando appealed to him more. He wasn't aware that Orlando shared its jetport with the Air Force.

"We'll land at Orlando," Jackson instructed.

"Why not continue on to Jacksonville or Charleston?" Haas appealed.

Growing weary of decision-making, the hijacker placed his grenade against Haas' head. Obviously irritated, Jackson repeated his order. "I said go to Orlando. And tell them to be ready for us with all of those things you say we need."

Haas felt uneasy. He didn't know exactly why. It was just

instinct. But because there had been so much urging from ground authorities to land at Orlando, he sensed that something bad was sitting up there waiting for their arrival.

He turned the aircraft northwestward and headed for the Florida coastline.

Harold Johnson asked controllers to give the crew a vector heading for Orlando and radioed ahead for the requested overseas charts, a navigator, oil, and fuel.

"The plans are to continue the flight to Switzerland," he advised.

Southern 49 estimated 9:15 P.M. as its arrival time at McCoy Jetport at Orlando.

10
Encounter

It was nine o'clock, according to the instrument panel clock in the DC-6 cockpit. The Navy aircraft had slowed its speed upon entering the traffic pattern over Orlando Jetport at McCoy Air Force Base.

From an altitude of eleven thousand feet, Commander Moore spotted the incoming hijacked aircraft below and three miles out on its final leg of the approach to runway 36, right. Landing lights on the wings of the jetliner cast a silvery path ahead and downward through the black sky.

Hoping to slip into the airport undetected, Moore reached for an overhead panel, flipping into the off positions the switches for his aircraft's rotating beacons, anticollision lights, and the red and green navigation lights. Then he doused all of the interior lights, leaving only a faint glow coming from the cockpit gauges. The military shadow of Flight 49 would lurk above in the pattern while the pirated craft proceeded toward touchdown.

Several miles to the south, Captain Godwin's DC-9 was closing in on Orlando. Hearing the air-traffic controller radio a straight-in approach to Flight 49, Godwin throttled back to permit the hijacked airliner to land first. Unaware of the Navy plane's blacked-out configuration, Godwin had also blacked out all of the exterior and interior lights aboard his aircraft.

Ground traffic at the airport was at a standstill. The FBI had taken over command of the airport, with Orlando and Orange County police at their disposal. The busy Beeline Expressway, adjacent to the airport, had been sealed off to comply with the hijackers' demands that all traffic be stopped. A number of commercial jetliners ready for departure sat silently and motionless where they had been when the tower froze all movement on the ramps and taxiways. With the exception of the three aircraft involved in the hijacking, all inbound flights were being diverted.

Among the outbound passengers stranded in the terminal building were members of a European tour group, who were winding up their visit to the United States with a trip to Disney World.

Bob Perri was mad. He had come to the jetport to meet his mother's flight and was unable to get any information as to when it might be permitted to land.

Mrs. Bill Strick of Toledo had driven to Orlando with three children, who ranged in age from five to thirteen. She was to meet her husband's flight and go on vacation. Unable to find out anything, she, too, was angered and scared; and two of the children were crying.

Fredda Coulter of nearby Winter Park wouldn't be able to board her flight to Palm Beach in time for a date. Now she was unable to get a taxi to return home.

A number of curiosity seekers milled about in the terminal building.

Brady Weeks, a mechanic for Delta Airlines, telephoned Southern Airways in Atlanta to advise that he would not be permitted to ram a steel rod into the engine turbine blades of the hijacked aircraft as planned. His supervisor had vetoed the mechanic's involvement.

FBI agents aboard the two pursuit planes looked out through the cabin windows, trying to focus on the runways below to get a view of their quarry. Nervously, the sharpshooters gripped their firearms. Although outnumbered, the hijackers would hold a decided advantage in having the protective shields of the aircraft and its hostages.

At the military side of the airdrome, a bank of high-intensity floodlights illuminating the Air Force ramp were shut down, plunging the huge concrete apron into an eerie darkness. Commander Moore had radioed a request for the blackout to enable him to maneuver toward Flight 49's position once the Navy craft was on the ground. A ghostly appearance of near-abandonment spread across the sprawling airport facility as the normally brilliant myriad of lights gave way to darkness. Out on the field, a mixture of purplish, amber, red, and green lights outlined the two long, parallel runways and connecting taxiways.

The airport manager, Richard Gossett, positioned his official vehicle at a vantage point near the terminal building where he could command a view of both runways. Three FBI agents from Orlando sat in the car with him, monitoring radio communications between the tower and Flight 49. They listened and watched as the airliner's lights traced its descent on the distant horizon.

The stage was set for a showdown with the maniacal pirates.

Losing altitude gradually, Commander Moore watched as the hijacked aircraft touched down.

"Southern 49 is on the ground," verified the voice on the tower radio.

The Navy plane turned on its left downwind leg to runway 36, right. Observers aboard the craft watched as Captain Haas rolled out to the 3200-foot marker, stopped, reversed direction, and returned the aircraft to a getaway position eight hundred feet from the approach end of the runway.

Seeing he could not land undetected on runway 36, right, Moore extended flight of the DC-6 to the parallel 36, left, runway.

Just as the aircraft landed, Moore pressed the button on his microphone and said, "This is Navy 689 requesting permission to stop and taxi back to the end of the runway."

"Negative," replied the tower operator. "Proceed all the way to the end of the runway immediately."

Moore was disturbed at the order and the tower operator's seeming failure to know what was going on. But the Navy airman was unaware of the rapidly approaching DC-9 chase plane coming in on his tail. Unwilling to break security by divulging his mission through further radio communication with the tower, Moore cursed the necessity of rolling to the end of the twelve-thousand-foot runway, but complied dutifully.

Captain Godwin brought his flying arsenal in for a landing on 36, left. Rubber screeched as the four main-wheel tires made contact with the runway. Simultaneously, he pressed his feet forward on the brake pedals while reversing the powerful thrust of the engines. Pitching forward on its nose wheel, the speedy jet slowed its forward momentum and reluctantly rocked to a stop. Godwin turned the aircraft around and taxied back even with Flight 49's position on the parallel runway. Two dozen lawmen aboard jerked open the wing exit windows, quickly filing out and descending off of the wings to the pavement.

The cadre of FBI agents, armed with an assortment of firearms and walkie-talkies, fanned out. Slowly and cautiously, they crouched and crawled their way toward the rear of the hijacked aircraft. A thousand feet of grassland separated them from their intended target, the full length of which was illuminated by its wing and engine floodlights.

After disgorging the riflemen and in total darkness, Captain Godwin began the long taxi trip toward the main terminal building.

Commander Moore's DC-6, with its load of FBI agents, had reached the far end of the runway and turned onto the northernmost taxiway. Despite the darkness, the pilot could make out the outline of a motor vehicle blocking his path. Stopping the aircraft, he waited for the driver to move aside. Nothing happened. The vehicle remained stationary. Moore considered sticking his head out the open cockpit window and shouting to the driver, but he knew he couldn't make himself heard above the noise of the four piston engines. He revved up the engines and began inching forward. As the whirling propellers neared the vehicle, the Air Force colonel behind the wheel maneuvered out of the path of the aircraft.

Reporting his position, Moore radioed ground controllers for permission to taxi.

"Negative," came the response.

Hurriedly, Moore advised agent Bresko, standing in the cockpit, of the problem.

"We are two miles from the hijacked aircraft," he said. "Ground control refuses permission to taxi. We are of no assistance to Captain Haas while we are sitting here. What do you suggest?"

Concluding that there had been a breakdown in communications regarding the Navy plane's mission and the identity of those on board, Bresko said:

"We have only one course of action. Taxi with or without permission."

Moore made another request for permission to taxi. Again, the controller said, "Negative. Maintain your position."

The aircraft commander advised the controller of his intention to taxi anyway.

Proceeding for a short distance, the DC-6 encountered another obstacle. It was the darkened bulk of a National Airlines 727. Communications between the civilian and military aircraft were not possible due to the need to maintain radio silence. Moore was beginning to doubt that he would ever get to the hijacked aircraft in time to aid Captain Haas, should he request aid. Now he faced what could be an insurmountable problem.

Calling his load master forward, Moore instructed the crew member to lower himself to the ground by sliding down the emergency escape rope.

"Try to guide us around that 727," he said.

Sticking their heads out of the open cockpit windows on the left and right, Moore and his copilot began moving the DC-6 forward while following hand signals from below.

The limited space on the taxiway provided passage for a single large aircraft with ease. But for the two large aircraft to pass, especially in the darkness, was a hazardous task.

Darkness made the going slow for the assault forces, who were already on the ground. Stealthily, they continued to move toward the hijacked aircraft while trying to stay clear of drainage ditches and the lights shining from the exterior of the DC-9.

With great difficulty, Commander Moore made it around the 727 and was taxiing at top speed in an effort to reach Flight 49. Speaking to agent Bresko, he reaffirmed his mandate that no one, including the FBI agents, was to leave the aircraft except by the Navy commander's orders. Bresko agreed that the hijacked captain would be aided only if he requested aid. Moore and Bresko established priorities for the disembarking of the agents on board. Those carrying high-powered rifles would leave the aircraft first. Next in order would be those armed with automatic weapons such as submachine guns. Last to leave would be the agents having shotguns loaded with rifle slugs.

A crew member briefed the lawmen on the method of lowering to the ground. "Because of the prop blast, you won't be able to use the main-cabin door ladder. You will go out in single file through the overwing exit windows and slide down the flaps on the trailing edge of the wing."

Reassuringly, he said, "That's a drop of only a few feet."

The briefing was concluded; he asked if there were any questions. There were none.

Tension mounted among the agents as the aircraft neared its destination. They feared the possibility of injuring or killing those aboard the hijacked airliner should the hostages become caught in an exchange of gunfire between their captors and FBI riflemen.

Commander Moore was growing uneasy because of the numerous ground vehicles moving around in the darkness. He was concerned that uninformed ground authorities might order immobilization of his aircraft. It was a dreaded possibility!

Uneasiness swept over Captain Haas as well. Flight 49 had been on the ground for ten minutes. His patience had worn thin while he was waiting for the appearance of a fuel truck.

"Harold, get on the radio to the tower and tell that controller to get those charts and that fuel truck out here right away. Tell him to quit stalling. We don't have forever," he said.

Window shades aboard the pirated craft were in a down position. The hostages sat in their seats, uncomfortably leaning forward with their heads resting on their laps.

Lou Moore and Mel Cale, pistols drawn and hand grenades ready, patrolled the aisle. They were not concerned about a threat from the hostages. Stabbing at the nerves of the two gunmen was the constant fear posed by the doors and windows of the aircraft. It was the eighth time the jetliner had been on the ground since the hijacking began and only the third time the aircraft had been on the ground during the night. The darkness outside was an enemy to Moore and Cale, making difficult their guarding of all approaches to the aircraft.

Donna and Karen continued kneeling at the front row of seats forward in the cabin. They had not completed the task of counting the ransom. Periodically, the two flight attendants glanced across the aisle to the galley and took pleasure at the sight of Henry Jackson gathering up garbage to be thrown out the cockpit window. He couldn't tolerate the rancid odor any longer. Some of the refuse had aged for more than twenty-four hours, and he doubted he would ever rid the stench from his nostrils. Henry was convinced he could do without fried chicken for the rest of his life. The soured spoilage made him hold his breath to keep from vomiting.

Michael Goff, a supervisor for Aircraft Service International at McCoy Jetport, pulled up and parked the fuel tender forward of the right wing. Climbing down from the cab, he left the dome light on inside so the hijackers could see that no one was with him. Walking around to a compartment on the side of the truck, Goff removed a case of oil. So that the crew could see and identify what he was carrying, he walked back and forth in front of the aircraft before going toward the right rear engine.

Commander Moore had maneuvered his shadow plane off of the taxiway and was rolling up the runway toward the rear of Flight 49's position. He was within three hundred feet of the jetliner. His eyes searched for any visual signal that might be interpreted as a request by the captain for aid. He could see none as the DC-6 continued inching forward.

The fuel attendant had just finished pouring one can of oil down the engine filler neck when a sudden rash of gunfire erupted. No one had told him that riflemen were anywhere near the aircraft. Jumping down to the ground, Goff ran away from the aircraft, going to the rear and off the runway. He wanted to warn whoever was firing that they could put a bullet into the fuel truck and touch off a tremendous explosion. But he stood helpless, knowing he could never make himself heard above the roar of the engines.

Harold Johnson turned to Captain Haas and reported, "Looks like he's finished oiling the right engine; he's down."

Haas read the oil gauge on the instrument panel.

"Harold, it looks more like he took oil out instead of putting it in," observed the captain.

Seconds later FBI agents sighted in on the main-wheel tires, unleashing a barrage of .30 caliber bullets. The high-powered propellants found their mark but ricocheted off in all directions, failing to penetrate the twenty-ply thickness of rubber.

Hostages in the rear of the cabin wondered about the strange noises they had heard. It sounded like someone was trying to axe their way into the aircraft from beneath their seats.

Calling a halt to the rifle fire, several agents moved up with shotguns. Standing at point-blank range, they pumped dozens of rifled slugs into the tires. At last the rubber was punctured. The aircraft settled discernibly to the left.

Haas detected the downward motion.

"Harold—they're shooting our tires out!"

Henry Jackson looked out the galley window. Not seeing the fuel attendant, he stuck his head in the cockpit, saying, "Cut off the left engine and crank up the right one."

Haas could think of no painless way of breaking the news.

"There's not much sense in cranking up the engine," he said; "we may as well shut them both down. They're shooting our tires out."

Lou Moore was standing in the front of the cabin as the aircraft dropped suddenly on the right side. A look of incredulous disbelief came over his face. Moore went absolutely wild. Snorting like an angered bull, the jaundiced whites of his eyes enlarged, his lips clenched stiffly, and his cheeks puffed with restrained breath. Reaching into the cockpit, he jerked the copilot from his seat. Johnson was sent hurling through the passageway into the cabin in a horizontal position, his head down level with the hijacker's waist.

Thrusting his arm through the open cockpit window on the right, Moore triggered pistol shots in the direction of the fuel truck. Boiling with rage, Jackson joined in the shooting as he stood in the cockpit, firing to the left side.

The hostages raised up to see what was going on. When they saw Jackson fire his gun, they knew the captain had been shot. Who was next?

Jackson turned and entered the cabin. He sent two rounds flying into the galley floor. Screams and shouts from the hostages mixed with the violent discharges.

Copilot Johnson had picked himself up and plopped into the second-row seat on the right. Jackson waved his pistol at the dazed airman.

"Why did you do it? Why? We're gonna kill you, Harold. We're gonna kill a lot of you people," Jackson shouted.

Johnson had become a symbol of contact with authorities, and the crazed gunmen apparently believed he had called for the disabling action.

"Stand up, Harold. You're gonna be the first to die. Stand

up; we're gonna shoot you," Jackson insisted.

Johnson's mouth went dry. The whole aircraft was plunged into chaos.

Mary Melton shouted, "You promised you wouldn't hurt any of us."

Donna and Karen turned pale. Would they be shot after Johnson?

Wild-eyed, the slobbering gunman reiterated, "Stand up on the seat!"

Choking on his words, Harold stammered, "Man—I didn't do anything. It wasn't my fault. I didn't give any signal. Please—don't kill me."

Karen cried, "He didn't do anything—he didn't know. The FBI didn't consult anybody."

"STAND UP ON THE SEAT—STAND UP ON THE SEAT, I SAID. I'M GONNA KILL YOU!" Jackson snarled.

Johnson dove between two seats as a blue streak of fire, accompanied by a deafening roar, belched from the gun muzzle. He was hit by the bullet. Pain shot through his entire body.

"You've broken my arm," he cried in anguish.

Horrified, the passengers wanted to aid the first officer. But the berserk gunman's ferocity mounted.

"STAND UP—YOU'RE GONNA DIE. I SAID—STAND UP!" Jackson screamed.

Harold lay prostrate across Luther Waller's lap. The copilot had taken the bullet in his right arm. He feared he would be shot again and again until his consciousness gave way to death. Where would the next bullet strike? He hoped it would be the last.

Cale ran up to Jackson before he could continue the slaughter he had begun.

"OK, man—no more shooting. We've gotta get out of here."

The younger hijacker sidestepped Jackson and went to the cockpit.

Forward in the cabin there were the scuffling, dragging sounds as the copilot was helped to his feet and thrown back in the cockpit's right seat. Then there was the lurching start of the aircraft's roll, the high revving of the engines, the vibrations of metal, the shuddering of seats. The DC-9 didn't want to move. Then there was the slow turning of the wheels with metal grinding on the runway. As the speed gradually accelerated, Frank Morkill thought, *My God, one of those spooks is sitting in the captain's chair, trying to fly this thing. We have had it; we have really bought it this time.*

A human form was hurled along the runway toward the rotating propellers of the Navy chase plane, which had stopped just behind the jetliner. A bruised and lacerated FBI agent, caught in the jet blast, righted himself as Commander Moore reacted to shut down the two starboard engines of the DC-6.

Captain Haas sat erect in his seat as the aircraft lumbered down the runway. Johnson slumped in his seat, his right sleeve a crimson red. Blood gushed from his arm.

"Harold, don't you faint on me. You've got to help me," Haas said.

Johnson's head rolled from side to side. His vision blurred. Pain radiated throughout his body. Nausea found his stomach.

"I'm not gonna make it, Billy Bob," Johnson groaned.

"You'd better make it, Harold. I need you," Haas said.

A dozen FBI agents ran along in a meaningless pursuit of the rolling aircraft. They were soon outdistanced by the missile's accelerating speed.

Tightly gripping the control column with his left hand, Captain Haas placed the other hand firmly against the fuel-control levers. Steel rims protested against the unyielding runway surface. Large chunks of rubber marked the course of the aircraft's forward momentum. Thirty-five tons of metal, fuel, and human beings propelled toward the end of the runway. Food trays rattled in the galley. The hostages prayed aloud for a miracle, convinced the takeoff attempt would end in their deaths.

Arthur Tonsmière thought, *We're not gonna make it.*

We'll go into a slide. How could we rush these people?
When we go into a slide, they'll be thrown off balance. We'll
all be in it together—crash—burn—we are gone.

Violent rumbling shook the aircraft. Captain Haas was
unable to read the airspeed indicator. He had no way of
knowing how fast the jetliner was moving. It passed the
six-thousand-foot marker, leaving half the runway behind.

The engines strained to build speed. Eighty miles an
hour . . . ninety . . . one hundred . . .

Haas braced for an expected crash into the airport's outer
boundary fence. Flames would likely envelop the ill-fated
aircraft. Then an explosion. *That's how this maddening*
attempt will end, he thought. *Although it will not be me or*
Harold, I hope somebody survives.

A cushion of compressed air ballooned between the aircraft and the runway. Abruptly, the vibrations stopped.
Haas realized that the disabled jetliner was trying to leave
the ground.

"C'mon, baby, c'mon," he urged.

Gently, he eased back on the control column. Upward
the craft struggled. Its flight was smoothing out in a feat of
unbelievable defiance. Haas pulled the control column all
the way back. The jetliner would not be denied its effort to
climb skyward again. The right wing dipped slightly as the
captain reached over to the opposite side of the instrument
panel to retract the landing gear.

Johnson's face was ashen. His voice was weak. But he
looked over to the captain and asked, "When you get time,
would you fasten my seat belt and shoulder harness?"

Compassionately, Haas said, "Well, I've got time right
now, buddy."

He reached over, securing the first officer in his seat.

Although airborne once more, the hostages were
paralyzed with a sickening, moribund fear. They didn't
know how high the aircraft was or how long it would stay in
the air. All hope had been abandoned that they would
survive the endless nightmare. They were resigned to a
disastrous end that could come at any moment.

Observers on the ground wondered if the aircraft could remain airborne. Its left engine left behind a streak of fire one hundred feet long. The flash was caused by an ingestion of rubber from the tires, a chunk of which had been picked up by the turbine during the takeoff roll.

After taking care of his copilot, Captain Haas noted he was climbing at a rate of four thousand feet per minute. Summoning all of his strength, he pushed the control column forward until the craft nosed over to its proper altitude. The captain's eyes drifted back to the first officer, who was using his uninjured left hand in an attempt to perform his normal flight duties.

Haas gave him an approving smile.

11
Return

Stunned by the aircraft's unbelievable takeoff, the Orlando tower operator radioed a strong plea to the hijackers that they permit the jetliner to return and land.

Captain Haas responded.

"Why did they shoot my tires out? Whoever got funny down there sure messed me up. They shot my first officer, and he's no good to me anymore . . . ."

Jackson ordered the captain off the radio.

The tower operator continued his appeal.

"Due to the length of the runway, you should return with those tires in that condition in order to make a safe landing. Did you copy?"

Shouting obscenities into the mike, Jackson said, "You know somebody's shot now, don't you?"

"Will you please return that aircraft here so you can land safely? Your demands will be met."

"Do what?" Jackson asked.

"I say again—will you return that aircraft to this runway? Because of its length you can make a safe landing here. You do not have enough fuel to reach another runway that will accommodate you. I repeat—return here and your demands will be met. We'll change your tires."

"What the _____ did you mess with us for in the beginning?" the hijacker demanded.

"This is Orlando tower. Did you copy? Are you returning?"

Hurling verbal profanities at the tower operator, Jackson concluded with an emphatic "No!"

"You do not have enough fuel to reach another base that will accommodate that aircraft," the tower reminded.

There was no reply from the aircraft.

"This is Orlando. Do you copy? You need to return due to the length of the runway."

Silence.

"Southern 49—this is McCoy."

Jackson and Moore had been too busy trying to decide what to do next. Moore took over the exchange with the tower.

"This is 49," said the hijacker.

"Will you please return and exchange that aircraft for another one?"

"I am sorry, sir," Moore apologetically intoned. "I cannot trust you. We're gonna take this plane down—we're gonna take everybody with us, nose first. We're gonna destroy this plane and everybody on it."

Another more mild-sounding voice began transmitting from the Orlando tower.

"We know your fuel status, and this is the only airport that can handle your situation."

Moore was in no mood to be reasoned with as he answered.

"We're not going to another airport, young man. We're taking this thing down, nose first. Now, we warned you, didn't we? Why would you mess us up like that? Don't you know we still got people on board? And you know why they ain't got off."

"We are still promising anything you want."

Moore interrupted the tower spokesman.

"Now, take this—take this—I won't take no million dollars. I'll land and I'll stuff this grenade anywhere you want it."

"Anything you want," came the reply from the ground.

Moore ended the conversation with a final obscenity for the authorities.

It was Jackson who finally decided where to take the distressed airliner.

"GO BACK TO CUBA!" he commanded.

After what had happened on the ground a few minutes before, the desperate and frustrated trio concluded that Cuba wasn't so bad after all.

Slowly, the Navy chase plane taxied down the runway, trying to avoid ingesting into its engines the numerous spent shotgun casings that littered the strip. Large pieces of tire rubber also created a hazard along the runway.

Commander Moore halted the DC-6 about a hundred yards from where the shooting took place. Haggard and shocked, the cadre of FBI agents climbed aboard.

Although convinced of its futility, Moore decided to continue the mission of shadowing the hijacked aircraft.

Splinters of bone raked the nerves and tissues of Harold Johnson's arm. The first officer was trying to remain conscious and help the captain, but the pain was excruciating.

"I'm not going to make it, captain," he moaned.

"You have got to make it, buddy," Haas said. "I can't have you going into shock on me and fainting. I need your help."

The captain assumed that gunfire had penetrated the skin of the aircraft, damaging the pressurization system. He was unable to make the system work and worried that other vital support systems might have been damaged as well. Without pressurization Haas would have to restrict his flight altitude to a maximum of ten thousand feet to avoid increasing the discomforting effects of higher altitudes.

Safe once more from authorities on the ground, Jackson, Moore, and Cale began calming down. Hoping to further relieve the strained atmosphere, Haas told the gunmen, "Listen—we didn't have a thing to do with the shooting. We didn't betray you. We were all betrayed, and we are all victims."

Nervously, the captain fingered the cigarette pack in his shirt pocket.

"Go ahead—you can smoke," Moore said.

Haas removed a cigarette and placed it between his lips.

Moore started to light it for him.

"I have matches," Haas declined.

Motioning toward Johnson, Haas said, "Look—we've got to do something for him. Go back to the cabin and get a compress for Harold's arm."

"And, Captain, could I have some ice water? I'm burning all over," Johnson pleaded.

"Bring him some ice water, too," Haas said.

A few minutes later one of the gunmen reappeared with a dirty shirt, which he threw over the injured copilot's head. Haas leaned over and loosely knotted the shirt around Harold's right arm. Then he handed him a cup of ice water.

Agent Bresko listened to the aircraft radio in the cockpit of the DC-6. New orders were transmitted from FBI head-quarters in Washington. The instructions were to im-mobilize the hijacked aircraft should the possibility present itself again.

Commander Moore considered the orders to be some-what academic. Southern 49 was already immobilized for all practical purposes. One more landing would likely re-sult in extensive damage to the landing gear and undercar-riage, thus rendering the aircraft incapable of taking off again. That was the least amount of damage that might be expected. There was the possibility that when the jetliner touched down again, it would be ripped into a thousand pieces.

Radar position reports from Miami Center were keeping the DC-6 crew informed of the hijacked aircraft's flight path. The slower shadow plane had been unable to main-tain visual contact with the speedy jetliner.

Commander Moore observed the erratic flight patterns being flown by Captain Haas. Southern 49 was doing a series of irregular, circular, and figure-eight maneuvers over the Key West vicinity. Trying to guess at what was going on, Moore concluded that Haas couldn't have been in more trouble. Severely tired; under constant threat by people who were fanatical, beserk, and unpredictable; low on oil, perhaps low on fuel; and without tires and the assistance of his copilot, he was in a desperate situation.

Moore feared the hijacked aircraft was in imminent danger of ditching at sea. The disabled jetliner was not equipped with life jackets or rafts.

Contacting the Miami center by radio, the Navy airman requested that authorities take air-sea rescue precautions.

The center declined to act on the request, saying it had not received a request for aid from the captain of Southern 49.

Moore's aircraft could eventually catch up with the jetliner if it remained over Key West long enough. But it could only serve as an observer craft in event of a ditching at sea, not having the capability of a water landing.

Using a standing Navy procedure, Moore radioed the Coast Guard rescue station at Opa-Locka, Florida. Declaring himself the unseen sea-air rescue commander, he ordered an amphibian aircraft to take to the air and track Southern 49. Further, he ordered the Coast Guard pilot of the amphibian to aid the jetliner's occupants in any way possible should there be a ditching.

Reports of the Orlando shooting, broadcast over Miami radio stations, were monitored in Havana. Cuban authorities suspected from the southward flight of the stricken airliner that it was again headed for Havana.

A black Mercedes that had sped eastward along the inland highway to Rancho Boyeros arrived at José Marti airport. The tall, bearded, and fatigue-clad occupant, accompanied by two of his top lieutenants, had come to take personal command of emergency operations. Premier Castro summoned all available ambulances and firefighting units for miles around to report to the airport.

The Cuban leader decided every detail, even designating the use of runway 23 for an attempted landing should it occur. The runway was better suited for the deployment of emergency vehicles.

High-powered portable spotlights were ordered into positions on both sides of the airstrip.

Checking the amount of foam on hand for covering the runway, the premier was informed that there was not enough. What was available would be reserved for firefighting purposes.

Emergency medical facilities were brought to the terminal building.

Havana's main hospital was placed on full alert to receive and treat possible crash victims.

Now everybody would wait. That's all that could be done with one exception.

In a generous display of optimism, the Cuban premier put the banquet-room and kitchen staffs in the terminal building to work, preparing for a sumptuous celebration. He hoped there would be cause for one.

Preparations for a crash landing also were underway aboard the disabled jetliner.

Calling Donna and Karen to the cockpit, Captain Haas instructed the flight attendants to stow all loose articles in the cabin as best they could and to thoroughly brief the hostages on emergency procedures.

They had been given a mountainous assignment. There was a two-day accumulation of garbage alone. Donna and Karen would have to somehow find a retaining place for it all.

Coffee had spilled from its container in the galley during the Orlando climb-out, causing a treacherous footing in front of one of the main cabin doors that would be used for evacuating the hostages.

Bulletproof vests and riot helmets lay abandoned on the floor in front of the other cabin door.

Fifteen buckets of uneaten chicken were stacked on a row of seats.

Trays of sandwiches were stashed under another row of seats.

Bundles of money were piled everywhere.

Donna and Karen worked feverishly to stow the assortment of debris in the coat closet and rest rooms. They wanted everything to be just right, but there was no place to secure everything that might be sent flying through the cabin in case of a hard-impact landing.

They would brief the passengers when the jetliner turned on a heading for Havana.

Indecision marked the behavior of the hijackers. Henry Jackson and Lou Moore were at odds with each other.about the return to Cuba. Jackson ordered the captain to proceed to Havana. Within minutes Moore countermanded the order, insisting on remaining over the Key West area awhile longer.

Nearing total exhaustion, Graydon Hall walked over to the operations center radio desk. His tall, wiry stature was bent and stooped from the heavy weight of decision-making during the hijacking. Placing his left hand on the operator's shoulder, he stared down through his rimless glasses.

After a moment of hesitation, Hall asked, "Do you suppose Billy Bob and Harold would land that plane in Miami? Do you think they would do that for me?"

At first the operator thought his hearing was deceiving him. Standing up, he respectfully addressed the senior company executive. "Mr. Hall, you should get some rest. Those two men are not free to make a decision about landing in Miami or anywhere else. Harold has been shot. We don't know whether he is even alive. And Billy is being threatened with death."

Hall didn't appear to have heard the operator. Haltingly, he stammered, "I believe they'd land if we ask them to."

Appeasingly, the operator said, "We'll try, Mr. Hall. We'll try."

Attempts began to contact the distressed airliner.

"Southern 49—Southern 49—do you read Southern Atlanta?"

The frequency was heavy with transmissions between numerous aircraft and Miami air-traffic controllers.

"792 level at two-six-zero."

"452, Miami Center. Roger. Ident."

"452. Ident."

"476, Miami Center. Squawk two-one-zero-zero."

"Southern 49—Southern 49—do you read Southern Atlanta?" the operator tried again.

There was no reply.

Eastern flight 587, somewhere over Florida, answered controllers, "We read you loud and clear. Who do you want us to give the numbers to?"

The operator continued efforts to cut through the incessant chatter on the frequency. Normally, Southern had little difficulty in contacting its high-flying jetliners. But Flight 49's restricted altitude was responsible for the reduced effective range between the hijacked aircraft and its home-base communications center.

Another attempt was broadcast.

"Southern 49—Southern 49—this is Southern Atlanta. Billy Bob, is there any possibility you could consider landing at Miami?"

Captain Haas heard the request, but the hijackers wouldn't permit him to reply.

There was more chatter on the frequency.

"792, Miami Center. Roger."

Lou Moore had come up with a request of his own. He told Haas to get on the radio to the company and tell them what the hijacker wanted.

"Would it be possible you could get a telephone patch with President Nixon? If you could, the hijackers have requested to talk to the president."

It was the first time in more than an hour that the captain's voice had been heard on the radio.

Grouped around the radio console, Southern operations personnel shook their heads in amazement at the request.

Haas waited for a reply to his question.

Extraneous transmissions continued on the channel.

"792, I am unable to say anything about another frequency."

A link to the president would not be easy. Likely it would be impossible.

Buying time while trying to improve communications, the operator queried, "Southern 49—could you climb toward Miami?"

Henry Jackson was back in the cockpit.

"I thought I told you to head for Havana," he said.

The captain explained that Moore had demanded that the aircraft continue over Key West while an attempt was made to contact the president.

Again, Southern Atlanta requested that the airliner climb to the north.

Haas was permitted a one-word response: "Can't."

"Understand, Billy Bob," said the operator.

Then there was silence.

Southern Atlanta personnel had gone into action on the request for a connection with the president.

Several minutes passed before the operator reported, "Southern 49—Southern 49—we are working on a patch to the president."

Several more minutes passed.

Flight 49 continued to hold in a big circle over Key West. The radio frequency was quieter as pilots of other aircraft in the night skies over Florida listened for the outcome of the latest demand by the hijackers.

Broadcasting another assurance, the Southern radio operator advised, "Southern 49—this is Southern Atlanta. We're trying to get the White House for you now."

There was no response.

"Southern 49—Southern 49—if you read me, key the mike button, please," the operator pleaded.

There was only silence.

Looking up at the clock on the wall above his desk, the operator noted it had been ten minutes since the captain had relayed the request for a patch to the president.

Ground-to-air communications were being set up by Aeronautical Radio, which had gotten as far as the White

House switchboard. There the request was turned over to weekend duty aides, who were trying to decide what to do.

Fifteen minutes elapsed from the time the request was originally transmitted from Flight 49.

Radio silence by the hijacked airliner was broken as Captain Haas spoke in a tired but soft voice. "We want a patch to the president of the United States. They want to talk to him. And they want it done immediately."

Haas could be heard taking a deep breath before he released the microphone button.

Atlanta's base chief pilot, David Norvell, was now manning the Southern Airways radio. "Understand, Billy Bob."

In an effort to insure dependable communications with the hijacked aircraft, Norvell asked Haas, "Do you understand if you could fly north, it would help?"

Henry Jackson, standing in the cockpit, shook his head disapprovingly.

Captain Haas radioed, "We're staying exactly where we are now."

A few seconds later Haas cautioned, "We can stay in this area for five minutes only."

"Roger, Billy Bob—five minutes only," said Norvell.

"Eastern 452 level at three-five-zero," reported a commercial jetliner.

Air traffic control replied, "452 at three-five-zero."

Once again Southern Atlanta assured Flight 49 that they were trying to get through to the president.

Captain Haas acknowledged the report. "He is the only one who can help us now."

It was 11:30 P.M.

Orbiting over Key West would have to be discontinued shortly. Captain Haas had burned off all but enough fuel needed to reach Havana and attempt a landing.

Belatedly, Miami Center advised other aircraft to switch their transmissions to different frequencies.

"WE HAVE AN EMERGENCY IN PROGRESS," said the controller.

Haas repeated: "We need a patch to the president."

"Roger—we're trying, Billy Bob. Please continue on this frequency," Norvell requested.

A commercial airliner cut in. "Eastern 587 at three-one-zero."

Then there was another brief exchange between Atlanta and Flight 49.

"Southern 49—your call signal is rather poor and scratchy. Can you climb for better reception if you want to talk to the president?" Norvell appealed.

"We can hear all right here. We're just gonna make a little circle," Haas answered.

"I know that, Billy," Norvell said, "but if you could climb north we could hear you better; and you'd be able to talk to the president if we can get him."

Haas had descended from ten thousand feet and was circling at an altitude of 7,920 feet at 250 knots.

Communications between Atlanta and the hijacked aircraft were troublesome and filled with static.

Norvell repeated his request that the stricken aircraft climb to a higher altitude. Unaware of the inability to pressurize the aircraft interior, he asked dejectedly, "Billy Bob—will they let you fly north for better reception?"

"We're staying around here. We're not coming north," Haas persisted.

"OK, Billy Bob," Norvell agreed. "I heard you good that time. We're trying."

"We're going to circle right here. I don't know for how long. Get President Nixon on the phone," the captain urged.

"Billy Bob, we're doing our best," said Norvell. "Can we have ten minutes more? At the present time we have contacted the White House, and we are trying to reach the president."

"Put the president on," Haas instructed.

"Southern 49—did you copy? We're in contact with the White House, and we're trying to reach the president," Norvell repeated.

"They just want to hear from the president," Haas reminded.

A long, black official limousine screeched to a halt at the White House entrance. Its lone passenger hurried up the steps and across the portico, disappearing inside.

Shortly, a new voice came on the radio.

"Southern 49—do you read me?"

It was the voice of the aeronautical radio operator in Miami.

"We have the White House on the phone. The person calling Southern 49—would you identify yourself, please?"

"The Secretary of Transportation, John Volpe, at the request of the president," said the cabinet member.

The operator repeated, "Southern 49—we have the White House on the phone. Do you read me on this frequency?"

There was no response.

The hijackers didn't want to talk to a member of the president's cabinet. And it was clear to them that the president wouldn't talk to them.

Time had run out. Captain Haas turned on a heading for Havana.

The most grueling and demanding test of the entire thirty-hour ordeal was still ahead.

Donna began the briefing of passengers. Frightened at the prospects of what could happen, the senior flight attendant tried to conceal her inner fear as she spoke.

"Ladies and gentlemen, we will be landing in Havana in about thirty minutes. I'm sure you are aware that the tires on the aircraft have been deflated. So we don't know exactly what's going to happen. But we want you to be prepared to evacuate this aircraft rapidly when we tell you to do so."

Jackson, Moore, and Cale were no longer concerned with guarding the cockpit and cabin. They stood at the front of the passenger compartment, listening to Donna.

"Now the first thing I want you to do," she continued, "is to make sure that we have men seated next to the window exits."

Halberstadt and Witucki moved to the window exit seats on the right side of the cabin. Jackson and Moore went down the aisle and sat by the other window exit. They wanted to be among the first to get out of the aircraft.

Donna continued. "Now you men look at the window exits. They are removed by pulling up on the top handle, down on the bottom handle. The entire panel comes inward. Once it has been removed, slide it under your seat to get it out of the way.

"Karen is going to go through the motions demonstrating the proper way to go out the exit. You will step through with your left foot first. With that foot on the wing, bend down, taking your head and upper part of your body out the window. Next, place your right foot out on the wing. It's all to be done in one continuous movement. You will not find it difficult. Do each of you understand that? It is very important that you do."

There were no questions from the hostages.

"All right; when you drop from the wing to the ground, drop from the trailing—I repeat, trailing—edge, not the forward edge. It will be only a short distance."

"Although the cabin will likely be without lights when we land, the exit signs have independent power sources and will be illuminated.

"We are anticipating that the landing will be made with the wheels down. Therefore, there will be inflatable slides in use at the forward cabin doors.

"When we are on the ground and the aircraft has stopped, Karen and I will direct you out of the various exits. However, we want you ladies and children to anticipate sliding down the evacuation slides forward in the cabin. Each of you must be prepared to respond quickly to our instructions."

As a safeguard against puncturing the inflatable slides, the hostages were told to remove all sharp objects from their pockets and to remove eyeglasses, false teeth, neckties, and neckerchiefs.

Donna concluded the briefing. "Before we land, place your seat in an upright position. Place a pillow in your lap. Make sure your seat belt is fastened. Then, with your head resting on the pillow, lock your arms together under your legs at the knees. Remain seated until the aircraft has come to a complete halt."

Donna's briefing had transmitted fear to the hijackers. They had not given much thought to the danger facing everybody until now.

Lou Moore left his seat and returned to the cockpit.

"Captain—are you sure you can get us down on the ground OK?" he asked meekly.

It was the first time since the hijacking was initiated that Haas had been addressed as "Captain" by the trio. He fought back the temptation to turn his wrath on the gunman.

"Listen, Lou—you get back there—take your seat—and do exactly what the stewardesses tell you to do," Haas said.

Moore started to leave.

"Two more things, Lou," the captain said. "You all make sure those grenades are where they won't explode when we impact. And ask Frank Morkill to come up here."

The hijackers became even more frightened at the prospects of their grenades and ammunition exploding. They surrendered the ammunition to Karen.

The terror created by the gunmen had finally turned on themselves.

Donna reported to the captain. "We've done all we know to do, Billy Bob. But we're not going to make it, are we?"

Tears filled her eyes as the captain cupped her chin in his right hand. Firmly, he pressed his thumb into her cheek as he spoke. "Listen—you'll live to be old and gray and have many grandchildren."

She didn't believe him, but she knew him to be the kind of man who would display nothing but confidence. She couldn't imagine how they would survive a landing without tires. Besides, the captain was almost exhausted, and the copilot could pass out any second.

Donna was fearful of another danger as well. She was concerned that if the landing did not rip the aircraft apart, Henry Jackson might stand up and start shooting when the cabin doors were opened.

The flight attendant went to Jackson and said, "Nobody knows what's going to happen when we land. We may catch fire. We may explode. But we're going to be down in a crash position. The minute we land, if you want us to stay down, we will; I don't want you getting up shooting anybody. If you want all of these people to get off alive, Karen and I are going to open the doors. The windows will be open already, and we're going to get the people off. I mean to do what's necessary to save everybody's life."

Jackson looked up, replying, "Do what's necessary. There'll be no more shooting."

12
El Hombre

Frank Morkill forgot about the splitting headache that had pained him since the takeoff from Orlando. He was just grateful that he had been called back to the cockpit. His spirits soared with the expectations that he would be able to atone for the opportunity he blamed himself for having missed hours earlier in Havana. He didn't know why he was being called forward by the captain, but he had responded immediately when Lou Moore walked through the cabin, asking for the guy who spoke Spanish.

Groggy and somewhat wobbly afoot, Morkill hesitated in the narrow entry to the cockpit. Slumped in the seat to his right was the wounded and bleeding copilot. Johnson was doing the best he could to perform his duties. Captain Haas encouraged him so he would remain conscious.

"Hang in there, buddy—one more landing to go, and it'll all be over," the captain reminded.

Morkill asked, "Where are we?"

"Those are the lights of Havana up ahead," Haas advised.

Incredulously, Morkill inquired, "We are returning to Cuba?"

"That's right, Frank," Haas confirmed, "and I need your help."

"Gladly; I'm at your service," Morkill offered.

"Fold down that jump seat and sit down. Then I'd like for you to get on the radio and establish contact with the tower," Haas requested.

Morkill sat down. Taking the microphone from behind the copilot's seat, he began speaking in Spanish.

"José Martí—José Martí—this is Southern 49."

Instantly came the response.

"This is Havana tower, Southern 49. We have you in sight. Do you see the tower? Do you see the airport?"

Harold Johnson answered. "We have visual contact with the airport."

"And do you see the aircraft on the right?" asked the operator.

"Roger," acknowledged Johnson.

The tower operator advised Southern 49 to fly a circular holding pattern, avoiding the airspace over populous Havana. Assigning a flight level of two thousand feet, the operator inquired about the fuel stage aboard the stricken airliner.

Translating Captain Haas' report, Morkill replied, "We have a fuel endurance of less than an hour. We anticipate a landing at 12:15."

It was 11:45 P.M.

Maintaining his voice link with the tower, Morkill reported the conditions aboard.

"The tires on the aircraft have been deflated; there is possible damage to the undercarriage; the copilot has been wounded by gunfire; and the three hijackers are still aboard. They are armed and must be considered dangerous."

As he concluded, Morkill felt the sweaty, bare belly of Henry Jackson pressed against his back. Mel Cale stood behind Jackson, who placed his hands on Morkill's shoulders. The hijacker attempted to say something, but Morkill ignored him while transmitting a request for foam on the runway.

Fright was evident in Jackson's face. The hijacker sweated profusely as he leaned over Morkill's right shoulder.

"Harold—why did you make me do it? Why did you make me do it, Harold?" Jackson asked regretfully.

Quietly, Johnson replied, "I didn't do anything. I didn't do anything. Now, you know I didn't do anything . . . ."

The copilot's weak response trailed off into silence.

Jackson asked once again for a radio link to Premier

Castro. Morkill rejected the request, explaining that the time for the landing attempt was fast approaching and that all efforts had to be concentrated toward that end. The hijacker turned and walked away.

Cale lingered for a moment. The pale look on his face, the noticeable tightening of the nerves in his temples, elicited Morkill's sympathy. Tweaking the hijacker's nose with a crooked finger, Morkill said, "Don't worry—we're gonna make it."

"Southern 49, this is José Marti," said the familiar voice of the tower operator. "We do not have enough foam at this location to cover the runway as requested, but firefighting trucks will be positioned on each side of the runway for immediate use as required when the plane comes to a stop."

"Roger—we understand," said Morkill.

Captain Haas was going about the prelanding functions as calmly and precisely as if everything were normal. During his many years as a pilot, he had been confronted by more than one emergency: engine failures on takeoff, a variety of mechanical malfunctions, and blinding weather conditions. But what he faced at the moment was a unique situation that had never been faced by any other airline pilot. A landing with four flat main-wheel tires had not been contemplated by aircraft designers. Consequently, the outcome of this attempt couldn't be predicted. However, he knew he had to summon all of his flying know-how and skill to keep from killing those aboard. He wasn't sure that the damaged landing gears would even cycle down out of the wheel wells. But he would know that in a few seconds, when he reached over and flipped the lever to lower the gears. His eyes focused on the control panel forward and to his right.

Three small green lights appeared on the panel—an indication that the two main gears and nose gear were down in place. Still, the captain wanted further assurance. Engaging the automatic pilot, Haas asked Morkill to fold up his jump seat.

"I'm going back in the cabin for a moment," said the captain. "I want you to keep an eye on Harold. Don't let him faint and fall over on the controls."

Looks of disbelief spread across the faces of the hostages as Haas appeared in the cabin. Mary Melton was stunned to see that the captain was alive. Alex Halberstadt grinned as he elbowed his seatmate, John Witucki.

"The captain is still alive," Halberstadt said. "We've nothing to worry about. We're home free."

Walking down the aisle, Haas told the hostages, "Hang in there. We're gonna be on the ground shortly."

Stopping two-thirds of the way toward the rear of the cabin, Captain Haas pulled back the carpet at a seam in the aisle. Getting down on his hands and knees, he opened a small compartment door in the floor. With his right hand he reached into the compartment and extended upward a periscope mounted there. Standard equipment on the aircraft, the built-in device was designed to enable observation of the landing gears should panel-light indicators fail. Although the green lights had appeared, Haas wanted to see for himself that the gears were in their proper positions. Peering through the lens of the periscope, the captain could see that the wheel lights were on. Rotating the periscope to the right, his eyes searched for an orange stripe of paint against a black background. But it couldn't be seen. Rotating the device to the left, he looked at the other gear. Again he failed to see the stripe. Recessing the periscope back into its compartment, Haas stood up and wearily returned to the cockpit.

"The gears are down—that much I could see," Haas said, "but I can't tell if they're in a locked position. Frank, tell the tower we'd like to make a couple of low-level passes so they can visually observe the gears."

Morkill relayed the request in Spanish.

"José Martí—this is Southern 49. The captain wishes to advise that the landing-gear indicators are green. However, he is not certain the gears are down in a locked position. Therefore, he requests permission to make two low-level passes of the tower for your observation."

"Si—permission granted, Southern 49," said the operator.

Captain Haas began the descent from two thousand feet while swinging the aircraft about and placing it on a course that would carry the jetliner by the tower. He would make the initial pass as low as possible to enable the operator to observe the left gear.

Approaching the tower, Haas reached forward to the glare-shield panel and switched off the landing lights to avoid blinding the tower personnel.

With the aid of binoculars, the tower operator followed the path of the inbound aircraft. Closer and closer it came. Within seconds it had zoomed by.

"What did you see?" Morkill radioed.

"Southern 49—the gears appear to be in a normal down position," came the reassuring report.

"Thank you, José Marti," said Morkill. "Please stand by while the captain is reversing course for the second pass."

"Roger, Southern 49," acknowledged the tower.

Several minutes later the jetliner made its inbound approach from the opposite direction. Again, the ground observer in the tower followed the path of the aircraft as it roared past the three-story structure while climbing back to an altitude of two thousand feet.

"Southern 49—His Excellency Dr. Castro is here in the tower with me. He wishes to know how low you were. He ducked each time you came by," joked the operator.

Haas, Morkill, and Johnson laughed aloud at the report.

"Tell them we came by at three hundred feet," Haas said.

Morkill repeated the captain's reported altitude.

Once again the tower operator confirmed that the gears appeared normal except for portions of the deflated rubber "gomas"—tires that clung to the wheels.

Morkill radioed the tower. "The captain requests permission now to make an emergency landing. When we get on the ground, we would like some of that coffee and some cigars for which Havana is famous."

"Come on down," said the operator. "I'll have a steaming hot cup of coffee ready for you."

Then he added, "All is ready. Do not worry. It will be a normal landing. Good luck and Godspeed."

The landing would be attempted on runway 23, which the tower said was better suited for disposition of emergency equipment. Runway 23 was the same one the hijacked airliner had landed on earlier in the afternoon. This time the landing would be made from the opposite end of the nearly twelve-thousand-foot newly resurfaced strip.

Morkill cautioned ground authorities that the actions of the hijackers could only be guessed at, once on the ground.

"Frank, get Donna up here for a minute," Haas requested.

Turning toward the cabin, Morkill called the senior flight attendant to the cockpit from her seat at the front of the cabin.

Donna listened as Haas issued final instructions.

"When we have slowed the aircraft to the proper speed, I'll ring the cabin call bell five times in rapid succession. That'll be the signal for removal of the emergency exit windows. Then I'll make a long final approach to the runway. When we are at an altitude of three hundred feet I'll switch on the "No Smoking, Fasten Seat Belts" sign, and everybody is to assume the crash position."

"Yes, sir," Donna replied.

Returning to the cabin, she told the hostages to watch for the signals to assume the crash position and those sitting beside the exit windows to listen for five bells.

Marge Brennan fingered the rosary worn around her neck. She thought she must have rubbed it thin during the past thirty hours. Holding Patrick's hand, she told him everything would be all right.

Captain Haas began turning the jetliner in a circular pattern that would place it in line with the designated landing runway. The disabled craft was approximately ten miles distant from the airport.

Harold Johnson continued using his left hand to accomplish his prelanding procedures.

Seated next to the left window exit, Henry Jackson and Lou Moore clutched at satchels of money in their laps.

Mel Cale was seated next to the exit window across the aisle and beside Halberstadt and Witucki. Pointing to the satchel of money in the younger hijacker's lap, Halberstadt warned that it might interfere with his getting out through the small opening. Cale tossed the bag over his head into an empty seat behind him. Money was not the most important thing to him at the moment. Saving his skin was of greater concern.

Weariness and fear of the landing attempt increased among the hostages as the jetliner's descent continued.

Dick Senft was calm after accepting the inevitability of death. He wished he were leaving his wife—or widow—better provided for. He agonized over petty arguments they had had; he wondered how many times he'd rushed too fast to reprimand his young son, Mark; he thought of neglected friends; he even thought of the times he had shooed the dog out of the house.

Although resigned to the likelihood of a disastrous crash landing, Mary Melton removed her combination eyeglasses and hearing aid. Taking a foam-rubber pillow from its cloth case, she folded the soft cushion around the glasses to prevent their breaking. If she survived the landing, she would find it impossible to get around without the sight and hearing aids.

The darkened cockpit was silent except for the occasional instructions called out by Captain Haas to his copilot. Lined up with the runway, the aircraft was five miles out on the final leg of its approach. Morkill reached down, further tightening his seat belt as the altimeter reading gradually signaled each increment-drop of altitude. He had done all he could to assist the flight crew and now felt helpless. He wished there were more he could do to assist the captain. Morkill had noticed Haas' bloodshot eyes, which suffered from the long period of almost constant flight. The captain's left hand held a firm grip on the control column; his right hand rested on the fuel control levers, making necessary adjustments in the jetliner's forward flight speed.

Down . . .

Down . . .

Down . . .

The altimeter needle revolved in a counterclockwise direction. It passed the one-thousand-foot mark—nine hundred . . . eight hundred . . . seven hundred . . . six hundred . . . five hundred . . . four hundred . . . three hundred . . .

Captain Haas reached overhead and pressed his thumb against a button that rang the cabin call bell five times. Only a dim glow of light shining from the emergency exit signs illuminated the cabin.

The hostages braced themselves in the crash position.

Henry Jackson and Lou Moore struggled without success to remove the window exit at their seat. Across the aisle Mel Cale tugged at his exit panel. Halberstadt and Witucki gave assistance. Neither of the exit windows would budge.

"We can't get the windows open," Jackson shouted.

Captain Haas leveled off in flight. Deviating fifty degrees from his inbound course, he would allow time for a solution to the problem.

For hours during the hijacking Morkill had sat in his cabin seat, mentally rehearsing the removal of the exits. Turning around, he shouted instructions to the pirates.

"Place one hand on the top lever, one hand on the bottom. Pull up on the top, down on the bottom. The whole thing comes in."

The hijackers did as they were told. Nothing happened.

"They still can't get them out, captain," Morkill advised.

"Wait a second," Haas said. "I think we've got a buildup of pressure in here." Laconically, he added, "I think I can take care of that."

Reaching to his left, the captain opened his cockpit window. The rush of air almost knocked Morkill off of his seat. The two cabin window exits popped loose. Airport approach charts in the cockpit, along with loose ten- and twenty-dollar bills, were sucked out of the window. Empty chicken boxes, pieces of paper, and other debris floated around in the whirlwind created in the cabin before Haas could get his window closed.

The exit problem solved, the captain maneuvered back in line with the runway. Distance to the end of the runway was closing rapidly. Wing flaps were extended to slow the aircraft further. Touchdown was seconds away as Haas eased the control column toward his chest. The jetliner flared out in a nearly parallel position with the runway. Thirty tons of metal inched closer and closer to the approach end of the airstrip, which was outlined by two ribbons of light on each side.

At last the moment was at hand. Twenty feet of air space separated the aircraft from the ground. The main landing gears searched for the macadam surface.

Contact.

A jolting impact was quickly followed by a terrifying noise as the metal wheel rims screeched against the asphalt. The forward section of the aircraft pitched over on its nose wheel.

Unable to see or hear, Mary Melton's reaction typified that of the other hostages—the aircraft had surely clipped off a row of telephone poles. She waited to be consumed in the white heat of fire and explosion that would occur at any instant.

Sliding his feet off of the brake pedals, Captain Haas slammed the engine controls into reverse thrust to allow the aircraft to coast to a stop. He feared that the magnesium wheel-hub assembly would burst into flames. A shower of sparks in combination with white puffs of smoke trailed the crippled airliner.

Smoke filled the interior of the cabin as the wheels surrendered to the friction of the pavement and ground to a halt.

The two flight attendants were on their feet, shouting

instructions for the hostages to get out of the aircraft. Rubber chutes deployed automatically from the two forward cabin doors as Donna swung them open.

Jackson, Moore, and Cale didn't hesitate. They were off the aircraft and running for the tall grass at the edge of the runway. Bright lights from dozens of vehicles lit up the airport until it resembled the Orange Bowl stadium on New Year's Eve.

Frank Robinson and Gale Buchanan, in pain, hobbled to get away from the aircraft. They had mistakenly jumped from the higher forward edge of the wing.

Clad in protective asbestos clothing, firemen sprayed foam on the burning wheels.

Sliding down the evacuation chute, Alvin Fortson was about to reach the safety of the ground when his body took an abrupt change of course. The next thing he knew, he was being picked up off of the runway and placed in an ambulance. The elderly man had suffered head injuries and a sprained wrist.

Everybody had gotten out of the cabin with the exception of Donna and Mary Melton. Donna stood at Mrs. Melton's seat, shaking the woman until she raised her head off of the pillow in her lap. Then the flight attendant got her up and led her to the evacuation chute.

Removing a first-aid kit from its place of stowage, Donna then slid down the chute to the ground. Karen had preceded her and was there to grab her when she reached the ground. The two flight attendants had been too busy to think about being scared. But now they stood trembling and crying in each other's embrace. Cuban medical corpsmen led them away.

Jack Eley was running down the runway at top speed when he realized he was far away from the aircraft. He couldn't believe he was alive and touching the ground again.

Bruce Barnes looked back at the aircraft from a distance. For him it was the first day of his second life.

Cuban ground officials politely rounded up the dazed

and scattered passengers while directing them to nearby vehicles that would transport them to the terminal building. The injured were carried by ambulances to the hospital.

Before loading into the vehicles, the hostages were treated to a last look at the three hijackers. A squad of soldiers armed with submachine guns marched the trio out of the tall grass and across the runway toward the terminal facility. Henry Jackson held a bulging sack of money above his head.

Meekly, Jackson pleaded with his captors. "Don't shoot me, baby. Don't shoot me."

Physically and emotionally drained, Captain Haas hadn't moved from his seat. Morkill remained with him. The two men sat without speaking.

Finally, Haas broke the silence. In a barely audible tone of voice, he asked, "How stupid could I get?"

"Sir?" Morkill answered.

"How stupid . . ."

"I don't understand what you're talking about. That was the most brilliant flying I've ever seen," Morkill praised.

"What I mean is this, Frank. I just can't get out of my head what happened at Orlando. Of course, you know everything that took place there. But there's just one thing you don't know."

The captain didn't look at Morkill as he continued.

"You know—during the shooting and everything else when I felt I had lost complete control of what was going on—and I thought I had a certain amount of "gotcha" up to that point—I had been able to control those gunmen a certain amount—not too much. Just enough to keep everybody alive and to keep the thing going there. When they started shooting and screaming and everything, and when I thought the end was fast approaching, I can remember that I thought, *God, I have done all I can. It's your time.* And just that sheer desperation—you know? *I mean—this is it—I have done everything I can, and I can't conclude this thing. I can't bring it off. It's up to you.*

"And to think—here, three hours later, it's all over with. Why didn't I just ask the Lord to do it a little sooner? You know? Since Friday—and finally—you turn it over to God.

"How stupid can you get? You know? You fly around for almost two days, and finally you turn it over to the Lord—and it's all over with in a couple of hours. I mean—how else did we get off the ground at Orlando? You've heard of a wing and a prayer. I—I think—I think nothing but all the prayers of all the people lifted this old airplane off the ground.

"I don't bother—I don't bother God with trivial matters. I have a thing. I don't bother God with everyday problems. But when I have a really big problem, I know where to go. And usually I get immediate results."

Tears welled up in the captain's eyes as Morkill listened.

"I don't mean to get misty-eyed. I'm not modest. But I know who makes heroes and who makes cowards. And I try to pay him back in certain ways.

"I'll never forget what happened at Orlando. Man—I tell you—nobody knows what it feels like till you look into the face of God. And I guarantee you—it's a scary feeling. Man, I looked at him for a long time. I practically saw him right outside that cockpit window when I looked out there, and I told him that—this captain was turning over the command.

"Like I say, it stopped. Right after I said that, Mel came running up here. I said, 'Get Harold back up here. I need him up here. Don't kill him. Don't shoot. Cut out that shooting, and get Harold back to the cockpit.' And when I started that takeoff roll—it was simply to stop the killing. You know? To stop the shooting. Because right after Henry killed somebody, Lou was going to kill somebody. Right after Lou killed somebody, Mel was gonna kill somebody. And then they were just gonna shoot it out right there on the ground. And they were probably gonna start sticking dead people out the window just like they told me they were . . ."

The captain was interrupted by the appearance of a soldier at the entrance to the cockpit. Tapping Morkill on the shoulder, he asked, "Are you the translator?"

Morkill replied that he was.

"El Hombre is requesting that you bring the captain to him. He would like to meet him," explained the officer.

"Yes—thank you. Right away," Morkill agreed.

"C'mon, Captain. Somebody wants to meet you," Morkill said.

Accompanied by the officer, Haas and the translator walked down the aircraft steps to the runway, where they were escorted toward a group of uniformed officials standing around the left main wheel. Emerging from the center of the group was a tall, bearded man wearing neatly pressed fatigues. Haas thought what a fullback he would make.

It was Premier Castro.

Throwing both arms around Haas, the Cuban leader's strength closed on the captain in a bear hug. Thumping him on his back, he said, "It was a job really well done . . . a truly magnificent landing. It is unbelievable—the stress you must have been under for the past thirty hours. I have the greatest admiration for anyone who could stand up to such conditions and finally bring off such an excellent landing under the most dangerous conditions."

Haas replied, "Please accept the gratitude of myself and my crew and the passengers for all of the help and assistance given us during the course of the landing."

Then the captain apologized for having messed up Castro's nice, new runway by landing on it with rims and no tires. The comment drew hearty laughter from Castro and others in the group. He embraced Haas in typical Latin fashion again; there was another round of back thumping.

The Cuban premier reached out to shake Morkill's hand.

"How very fortunate it was," he said, "that there was someone on board who spoke both English and Spanish."

Then, turning back to Haas, Castro gripped the captain's hands, saying, "I notice the palms of your hands are rough and calloused. They are not the hands of a pilot but the hands of a worker."

Haas explained that the callouses were the result of work he'd been doing on his farm in western Tennessee.

"Very good," Castro replied. "I knew you were a worker."

The premier told Haas he wanted to know more about him.

"I have prepared a little celebration for you and the others. I would like for you to join me in the terminal building," said Castro.

"It would be an honor," Haas answered.

The captain would have preferred to stay with his aircraft to inspect the damage and report through the Swiss Embassy to the company. But he couldn't offend Castro by rejecting the warm and genuine hospitality offered.

"Where are my two flight attendants and copilot?" Haas inquired.

An aide to Castro assured him that all were being cared for and that Harold had been taken to a hospital.

"And the hijackers?" Haas asked.

"We have all four in custody," Castro informed.

"But, sir," Morkill advised, "there were only three hijackers."

A black Navy recruit had been rounded up mistakenly as one of the pirates. The confusion was promptly overcome after Morkill gave descriptions of Jackson, Moore, and Cale.

A well-appointed limousine with a driver was provided to carry Haas and Morkill to the terminal building. They were ushered into a ground-floor reception room, where there were about a dozen civilian and military officials gathered. Among them were two officials of the Swiss Embassy. When Castro entered the room, introductions were made again.

Waiters appeared with enormous trays of enormous frozen daiquiris, glasses of wine, and cigars. The waiters moved through the room, passing out the drinks.

Castro lifted a glass in a toast to Haas, his crew, and the passengers, for the happy outcome of what could have been a disastrous episode.

Haas returned the toast, thanking Castro and the Cuban people, along with the airport personnel, for their landing assistance.

The premier told Morkill someone wanted to meet him. A short, rotund little Cuban man walked over to where Morkill stood. Holding a cigar in one hand, and a cup of coffee in the other, the man was introduced as Señor Almaguer, the tower operator. Morkill accepted the coffee and cigar while thanking the man for his helpful assistance during the landing.

Haas walked over to Morkill.

"Is this the tower operator?" he asked.

"Yes," Morkill replied.

Planting a big fat kiss on the top of the man's head, Haas imitated Castro's bear hug. The room filled with boisterous laughter at the display of gratitude. The celebration became more relaxed, with everybody thumping everybody else on the back.

"Come sit down," Castro said as he gestured toward a table.

Seated, the Cuban leader said, "Tell me about yourself."

Haas explained that he was married, lived on a six-acre farm in La Grange, Tennessee, and was the father of three older sons who ranged in age from nineteen to twenty-one, a four-year-old son, and a two-year-old daughter.

"Ah—then you have not spent all of your time flying airplanes," Castro kidded.

Indicating the young man to the premier's left, Haas asked if that were Castro's son.

"No—much too young," Castro answered.

The premier wanted to know about Haas' ethnic background.

"My earliest known ancestor was Johann 'Hans' Haas, who married a young lady named Salome in 1626. They lived in the very small village of Grimmersbach, which is located in the Black Forest between Baden-Baden and Fribourg, in the southern part of Germany. Five generations of Haases lived in Germany until the eighteenth century, when my great-grandfather, Franz Anton, married Helene Kaltenbrown and moved to America. Two generations later I was born to Henry and Blanche Haas in Jackson, Tennessee."

Castro listened attentively as Morkill translated Haas' ancestry to Spanish. The premier nodded approvingly.

An aide approached the Cuban leader. After a brief whispered conversation, Castro stood up. Shaking hands with Haas and Morkill, he graciously excused himself and left the room. At no time during the twenty-minute meeting had the subject of politics or ideologies come up for discussion. Nor did Castro voice an opinion on the FBI tire-shooting incident at Orlando. He had been interested solely in the well-being of the crew and passengers.

While the meeting with Castro was taking place, the passengers were served beer and sandwiches. They were now assembled in a dining room on the second level of the building, where they awaited the captain's arrival for a banquet.

Accompanied by Morkill, Haas was escorted into the dining room. Upon entering the hall, he was greeted by loud applause and cheering. The spontaneous ovation continued as he walked across the room to a table at the front. Demonstrating their appreciation for the captain's courage and skill, the passengers wanted him to know they credited him with their survival. Unaccustomed to such plaudits, Haas waved awkwardly for the passengers to be seated. But the applause continued. He had to choke back the tears that threatend to spill from his eyes. He had done what he had to do and had expected no special recognition. A dedicated airman, he gave no thought to the possibility that he had done any more than any other airline captain would have done under similar circumstances.

Another burst of applause signaled the arrival of Donna and Karen. They have been given calmatives and were more composed than they were immediately after the landing. The two flight attendants were escorted to the captain's table.

The scene in the dining hall was incongruous. Shoeless and disheveled, the men unshaven, the passengers of Southern 49 sat at tables covered with fine linen cloths and adorned with ornate silverware and long-stemmed wine and water glasses. Fresh flowers decorated each table, which accommodated four to six people. White-jacketed waiters poured wine, while others, attired in blue waistcoats and black trousers, served a dinner consisting of steak, vegetables, and potatoes. Havana cigars were in abundance.

During the dinner, three Cuban officials approached Frank Morkill at the captain's table. They reported that the ransom money had been gathered up and that it appeared to be short of the two million dollars which the airline had announced it paid the hijackers. The officials stated that they didn't want to have to subject anyone to an embarrassing search, but that it was their responsibility to account for all of the money. They noted that the bundles of money had been broken open. Upon questioning, the hijackers told authorities they had thrust money upon the passengers and crew.

Morkill announced the problem to the passengers. Each person quickly responded by turning over the money given to them by the gunmen. Morkill held open the breast pocket of his shirt, inviting the official to remove the three hundred dollars he had received. When all of the money had been collected the officials left the room with approximately eight thousand dollars.

It was three o'clock in the morning when the banquet ended, with the passengers being informed that buses were waiting to transport them to the Riviera Hotel in downtown Havana.

Captain Haas and Morkill requested and received permission to return to the aircraft. They wanted to inspect the damage and to gather up the personal effects of the passengers.

As their limousine moved along the runway, they encountered a huge truck dragging the crippled jetliner ingloriously down the strip toward a hangar area, the tire-less metal wheel rims screeching and grinding against the hard surface. The proceeding stopped to enable Haas and Morkill to go aboard.

The interior was in total disarray. A hurricane's full force couldn't have left the cabin more devastated. Seat backs, seat covers, stowage compartments, and overnight cases had undergone the careful scrutiny of a Cuban search party.

Haas and Morkill began gathering up the personal belongings left behind by the passengers. There were shoes, false teeth, eyeglasses, and wallets that had been abandoned in preparation for the emergency evacuation. The articles were placed in large plastic bags. Among the collection were the two shiny walking canes brought aboard by Jackson and Moore. There was Jackson's long leather coat as well. In a pocket of the coat the captain found a notebook in which the pirates had spelled out their hijacking plan. The notations contained references to airport security, plans for dealing with the cockpit and cabin, an airport in the South of France near Basel, Switzerland, and instructions for the opening of a secret Swiss bank account. The pocket of another of the hijackers' coats contained a compass. Haas speculated that the trio's abortive alternate plan called for a landing in France, followed by their crossing into Switzerland.

Carrying two large bags of personal effects from the aircraft, Haas and Morkill left the cabin to survey the exterior of the aircraft.

The two nose tires were intact, although a spent bullet protruded from the outer layer of rubber on one tire.

Shreds of rubber were wrapped around the dented and scored metal wheel rims.

Shining his flashlight into the right-engine nacelle, Haas looked for damage. The engine appeared to be OK. But an inspection of the left engine revealed damage to a number of fan blades in the first compressor stage. The blades had been bent out of shape by the rubber ingested during the takeoff from Orlando. Bullet marks were found on the underside of the aircraft's metal skin, but there was no significant damage to the exterior.

Haas noted the damage to the aircraft for reporting to the company. He and Morkill left the aircraft and returned to the terminal building.

Walking through the lobby, they passed a room filled with officials from the Banco Nacional de Cuba who were counting the ransom money under the eyes of watchful Cuban soldiers.

"Ask them if they'd cash a check for me, Frank," Haas quipped.

The question was met by stony silence when put to one of the guards. Morkill suggested to Haas that it had lost its humor in his translation. The translator tried again with a suggestion of his own. "If we had some dice we could have one whale of a crap game."

"Si, si," laughed the soldier.

Leaving the building, the captain and Morkill climbed aboard a waiting passenger van for the ride to the hotel. Haas dropped off to sleep, his first in forty-eight hours, before the bus could get underway. During the ride into town, Morkill asked the driver of the vehicle what would happen to the hijackers.

"They will be dealt with very severely," he said. "They will be confined to boxes measuring cuatra-por-cuatra-por-cuatra, or four-by-four-by-four feet."

When they arrived at the hotel, it was 5 A.M. on Sunday morning. The sky was beginning to shed its shroud of darkness. A few of the passengers milled about the lobby of the hotel in hopes of receiving their luggage. They had to settle for the personal articles brought by Haas and Morkill in the plastic bags.

With a minimum of difficulty, they registered at the desk. Haas was assigned to room 1810, Morkill to room 1813. Wasting no time, the two men made their way to the elevators and the eighteenth floor. Haas thanked Morkill for everything he had done, stated his plans for soaking in a hot bath, and said good night.

Entering his room, Morkill had been provided with a three-room suite. It was hot, and the air conditioning wouldn't work. Walking out onto the balcony overlooking the sea, he let the cool tropical breeze that swept inward play across his face. Dawn greeted another sunrise. Morkill concluded that it was the most beautiful sunrise he had ever seen, especially since he had concluded hours earlier that he would never see another one. His eyes lingered on the small fishing boats putting out to the open sea. He felt like shouting a wish for their good fortune. He was so jubilant over just being alive that he wanted to share his joy with the whole world. Soon he would hold his wife and children in his arms again. They would plan another trip to Disney World. But he didn't want to see the Orlando airport anytime soon. The memory of what had happened there was seared into his brain. Would he ever forget it? Probably not. *My God,* he thought, *we are lucky to have survived.*

Weariness drove him back into the bedroom. He mused over the spaciousness of his accommodations. Not during all of his business travels could he afford such luxury; and right now he was too tired to appreciate it. Sitting on the edge of his bed, he tugged at the legs of his trousers. It seemed like five minutes passed before he was out of his clothes. He managed a chuckle over his breezy under-wear. His family wouldn't have to identify his remains by locating a corpse in ragged shorts after all.

Stepping into the shower, he alternated the water be-tween hot and cold in an effort to revitalize himself. Fear struck suddenly at his brain as he recalled the captain's plan to soak in the bathtub. He started to get out of the shower, wrap himself in a towel, and run as fast as he could to Haas' room three doors down the corridor. He thought, *What if Haas, having pulled off the most death-defying landing of the decade, falls asleep and drowns in a bathtub in*

Havana? It would be the irony of ironies.

Putting the thought out of his mind, he turned off the shower, toweled dry, and collapsed into bed. Sleep claimed him instantly.

13
Repatriation

Sunday morning, November 12, 1972
Washington, D.C.

Reporters crowd into a conference room at FBI headquarters to question a spokesman, Thomas Bishop, about
the bureau's role in shooting out the tires of the hijacked
jetliner in Orlando.

Bishop: "I'll be happy to answer your questions. What is
   it you want to know?"
Question: "Some agents in Florida are saying that orders
   to shoot at the plane in Orlando came from Washing-
   ton."
Bishop: "The FBI would have no comment on that."
Question: "Did the agents at the scene make the decision
   to shoot?"
Bishop: "The FBI would have no comment on that."
Question: "Was Mr. Gray involved in the decision?"
Bishop: "The FBI would have no comment on that."
Question: "Do you mind if this conversation is recorded
   to get each of your no comments?"
Bishop: "I would mind it very much. I would mind it very
   much. You just go ahead and ask me the question."
Question: "Can you say why they shot at the plane while
   it was moving? There could have been a crash."
Bishop: "Was there a crash?"
Question: "No—but there could have been one. Were
   those risks taken into account?"
Bishop: "The FBI would have no comment on that."
Question: "Will the FBI have any comment on anything?"

Bishop: "What do you want me to tell you about, the weather? You can ask me about the weather."

Question: "Is Mr. Gray available?"

Bishop: "Mr. Gray is in a travel status."

Question: "Where is he going?"

Bishop: "The FBI would have no comment on that."

Question: "Is the FBI investigating the shooting?"

Bishop: "The FBI is investigating the hijacking."

Question: "Is the FBI investigating the shooting by the agents?"

Bishop: "The FBI is investigating the hijacking. It is a federal offense, isn't it?"

Question: "Is Mr. Gray specifically investigating the activities of agents at Orlando?"

Bishop: "The FBI would have no comment on that."

Disgusted with Bishop's evasive answers, reporters gave up and left the room, having learned nothing new. However, it was evident to them that the bureau had charted a course designed to avoid the storm of controversy that was building as a result of the FBI's action at Orlando.

At Miami's international airport, another conference room was filled, this one with Southern Airways management and flight personnel. They waited for the results of negotiations going on between the Swiss Embassy in Havana and the Cuban government for the release of the hijacked aircraft, its flight crew, and its passengers.

George Gross, Frank Wheeler, and Captains Godwin, Shanahan, Pipkin, and Steele were making plans to fly Southern 963 to Havana to bring the weary passengers home. Two of the captains—it had not been decided which ones—would remain in Havana until maintenance personnel could repair the damage to Southern 49. Then they would ferry the aircraft back to the "nearest and most practicable" airport in the United States, presumably Miami International.

Sleep had not come easily for the passengers of the hijacked airliner. The ordeal through which they had come combined with anxieties over getting out of Cuba. Most of the people were up early, taking a stroll around the hotel and its immediate vicinity.

Arthur Tonsmière examined a rack of picture postcards. One card in particular held his attention. It was an exterior scene of the Riviera Hotel. An inscription on the reverse side read: "Gay as the Sunshine." During the pre-Castro era, the financier had visited Havana on a number of occasions. He couldn't sense any of the gaiety that had once prevailed in the "Sin Capital of the Caribbean."

Outside the hotel, Tonsmière studied the buildings, many of which had fallen into a state of disrepair. However, government buildings appeared well kept.

Shabbily dressed, the Cuban people wore stoic looks on their faces. They drove old, dilapidated cars and old motorcycles with sidecars.

The once-fashionable residential dwellings now housed multiple families. Lacking modern appliances, the occupants hung their washing from balconies to be dried by the sun.

Among the few things that had not changed in appearance were the beautiful plants, shrubs, and trees.

A onetime gaudy, sinful playground for the very rich, Havana had become a sun-kissed vacation resort for eastern Europeans, who lolled about the hotel swimming pool with their families. Attempts to engage them in conversation were futile.

Charlotte Watts browsed in the hotel's one store. She wanted to buy a scarf and a comb. Unable to purchase either, she settled for some cheap perfume and a strand of pearls.

Wearing bandages on his head and left wrist, Alvin Fortson assured fellow passengers that he was feeling all right despite the lacerations and sprain. But he had not been impressed with his hospital treatment.

At breakfast, Mary Melton visited and got acquainted

with other passengers. A Cuban reporter mingled with the passengers in the dining room. Engaging Mrs. Melton in conversation, he wanted to know if her home state of Arkansas got much snow during the winter. She explained that it was too far South to receive much of the white stuff. Mixing his inquiries with propaganda, the reporter boasted of how well off the Cuban people were under Castro. Citing examples, he told of free honeymoons provided for newlyweds from rural parts of the country and the government's payment of burial expenses for the Cuban people.

Overcome with nervous exhaustion, Marge Brennan and Alex Halberstadt had no appetite for food. They whiled away the time talking and relaxing in the hotel's cocktail lounge.

The persistent ringing of the telephone commanded Frank Morkill's awareness at 9:30 A.M. The caller had been connected to his room by mistake. During the four hours he had been in bed, he thought, he must have slept with his eyes wide open if he slept at all. Dry, itchy, and burning, his eyeballs felt as though they had been picked up out of the Sahara Desert. His body covered with sweat, Morkill would try to sleep no more. He was too eager to shower, dress, and get downstairs, where he hoped to learn when they would be returning home.

Captain Haas and his translator arrived in the dining room at the same time. Before sitting down, they circulated among the subdued and semiexhausted passengers. Besieged with questions about a homeward flight, Haas could only tell the passengers that efforts were underway to fly them out of Cuba before evening. He advised them to remain in or near the hotel.

After breakfast, Haas and Morkill went upstairs to the room where copilot Johnson had been taken following hospital treatment during the night. Johnson was sedated and drowsy. His arm was in a cast.

"How do you feel?" Haas asked.

"Mentally, I'm OK," Johnson answered, "but there's still a lot of pain in my arm."

"Well, look, buddy," Haas said, "we're hoping to get outa here today and get you some good treatment in the States. You just rest and sleep. We'll call you when the time comes to leave."

"Okay, boss—thanks," Johnson replied.

Returning to the lobby of the hotel, Haas decided to remain there to await word on the departure arrangements.

Morkill wandered freely around the outside of the hotel—along Malecón Boulevard and the sea wall. Stopping now and then, he chatted with people sitting on the wall fishing. As he strolled leisurely along a route that would take him back in the direction of the hotel, Morkill was approached by a man who introduced himself as a Cuban journalist, Pedro Martinez Pirez.

"My newspaper—*Gramma*—would appreciate very much an interview with the aircraft captain," said Pirez.

"I'm on my way back to meet the captain now. If you wish to accompany me, we will see if he is receptive to an interview," Morkill suggested.

"Si—gracias, señor," the reporter replied.

Entering the lobby, Morkill found Haas surrounded by a group of Southern 49 passengers. Introductions were made between the captain and the newspaperman, who stated the purpose of his visit. Haas consented to the interview. The trio walked into the dining room, where they sat at a table.

"What were the hijackers like?" came the first question in Spanish.

"Crazy—they were absolutely crazy," Haas answered.

Then the interview retraced the path of the hijacking, with Haas giving cautious and cryptic answers to each question.

Haas already had his guard up when Morkill leaned over and whispered a warning to the captain that he should anticipate some tricky questions of a political nature regarding the FBI action at Orlando.

Pirez had carefully led up to the shooting incident. Now he was ready to spring the trap.

"Don't you think the federal authorities were guilty of a great deal of neglect," he queried, "perhaps over-demonstrative in their show of force—putting the crew and passengers into imminent danger by firing at the aircraft?"

Hoping Haas would be critical, the journalist sat poised for the answer.

"Well—all is well that ends well," Haas said.

The captain was more than a little irritated by the FBI for what it had done. But he would refrain from voicing his opinion until a later time and in the proper forum.

Continuing, Haas observed, "Had it not been for the shooting, who knows what would have happened to the aircraft and passengers? By the shooting, they had narrowed the hijacking down to one more landing—right here in Cuba."

It was not the answer the reporter had hoped for.

"I would like to say this," Haas concluded. "We are deeply grateful for all the Cubans did to assist us in making a safe landing, and we appreciate the warm hospitality of your premier. It will not be forgotten."

Pirez stood up, thanked the captain, and excused himself.

By noon, word was dispatched to Southern personnel in Miami from its Atlanta headquarters that the State Department had worked out arrangements through Swiss authorities in Havana to return the hijacked aircraft, its crew, and its hostages.

George Gross called Godwin and his flight personnel together for a conference.

"Jim, we have another aircraft en route from Atlanta to Miami with repair parts: a set of brakes, tires, and wheel assemblies for the main nose gears, along with hydraulic lines, fittings, and tools. Headed by engineers Louis Jordan and Ken Masters, five mechanics will be flown with you to Havana to perform the necessary work."

Then Gross advised, "Neither Frank Wheeler nor myself will be going. The Cubans will not permit any management personnel to accompany 963 to Havana. I guess that rules you out as well."

"There's no way anybody else is going to fly that disabled bird out of there," Godwin stated.

Reaching for his wallet, Godwin removed all personal identification except for his airman's certificate.

"Should we encounter any problem in Cuba, my resignation as vice-president may be considered automatic," Godwin volunteered.

"I was hoping that would be your attitude," Gross said. "Another thing, Jim," Gross cautioned. "There is likely to be a sizable bill of charges presented by the Cubans before you leave. Negotiate the best you can."

Godwin selected Guy Steele as his copilot for the flight to Cuba. Godwin, Steele, and the maintenance personnel would remain in Havana, while Shanahan and Pipkin would pilot the return flight of 963 to the States with the hijacked crew and passengers.

Departure from Miami was scheduled for 2 P.M., with arrival at Havana estimated for an hour later.

Landing on schedule at 3 P.M., Captain Godwin taxied slowly past the hijacked airliner en route to the terminal building. Southern 49, with all of its main gears resting on rims, was practically sitting on its tail. Its exit windows and doors remained open.

Turning to his copilot, Godwin said, "Guy, if we can get one tire on each gear, we'll take that bird out of here. What do you say?"

"I'll be ready when you are," Steele agreed.

There would be little time for Godwin and Haas to discuss the mechanical condition of the stricken jetliner. Cuban authorities had agreed that the two captains could meet and talk for only five minutes. No other members of the arriving company personnel would be permitted to talk with Haas and his crew members.

A bus that transported the hostages and crew from downtown Havana to José Marti Airport had arrived at the terminal facility moments before Godwin's aircraft arrived. Television cameras had been set up at the terminal building by the government-operated station. Cuban civilians stood on the balcony of the building, overlooking the ramp.

Haggard and drawn in appearance, Captain Haas waited in the lobby. Frank Morkill was at his side.

The tower operator who had been in charge during the critical emergency landing approached the two men. At first, he just stood in silence. Then Captain Haas stepped forward, kissed him on the top of his head, shook his hand, and said good-bye.

"I'll be in touch," Haas promised.

Castro's security chief, Abrantes, attired in civilian clothes, escorted Captain Godwin from his aircraft to the lobby for the brief meeting with Haas.

Wasting no time with formalities, Godwin said, "Billy Bob, we have only five minutes together, so I'll wait until we have more time to tell you how proud we are of what you have done."

Modestly, Haas grinned and said, "I didn't do anything but get hijacked, Jim."

"What can you tell me about the condition of the aircraft, Billy Bob?" asked Godwin.

"Well, we came in on both engines, although we had high oil-temperature readings. But that was probably due to the lack of oiling. They just wouldn't let us shut the engines down to get oil," Haas said.

"The left engine was trailed by flames when you took off from Orlando. Have you been able to visually inspect the engines?" Godwin inquired.

"Yes—as best I could—I looked at them early this morning. The right engine appeared to be OK. But the left engine first-stage turbine fan blades suffered damage. There are at least two—maybe more—blades that are bent out of shape," Haas reported.

"Do you think they are reparable?" Godwin asked.

"I believe the mechanics will be able to hammer them into a position where they'll not restrict the flow of air,"

Haas suggested.

"What about the landing gears?" Godwin queried.

"The rims are pretty banged up. If you brought spares, the rims should be replaced. The nose gear is frozen in position for some reason—possibly a broken hydraulic line," Haas explained.

"Any other problems?" Godwin asked.

"Yes—I couldn't get the cabin to pressurize after leaving Orlando. That's the reason I didn't take it above ten thousand feet after the shooting. I assumed there had been internal damage to the system as a result of the gunfire. But there are no indications that any of the shots penetrated the skin of the aircraft," Haas said.

"OK, Billy Bob, it looks like they're beginning to load the passengers out there. You'd better get aboard. If all goes well I'll have the sick bird back in Atlanta sometime tomorrow night," Godwin promised.

"Good luck, Jim. Don't take any unnecessary chances," Haas concluded.

Godwin felt forlorn as he watched his old friend walk away. He had complete faith in the ability of the maintenance crew who had flown in with him. But he knew that anything could happen. There could be an indefinite delay before he could get out of Cuba. It was a feeling born largely out of being in alien territory and not being able to communicate in Spanish. Too, he had departed Miami so hurriedly that he was now in Havana with only thirty-five dollars in his pockets.

Haas joined up again with Frank Morkill on the loading ramp.

"I need to go aboard Southern 49 to get my and Harold's flight bags," Haas said.

Morkill translated the request to Señor Abrantes, who was standing nearby. Permission was granted.

While Haas made his way to the crippled jetliner, Morkill waited on the ramp at the bottom of Southern 963's loading steps. A Cuban official asked him to speed up the boarding process.

"Hurry up—up there," Morkill shouted.

From the top of the steps came the reply, "They're searching us."

"Who is—the Cubans?" Morkill asked.

"No—our people," said one of the passengers.

The outbound crew was taking no chances. Mindful of reports that there had been ten hijackers who had taken over the aircraft, since only three had been taken into custody by the Cubans, they were giving everybody a thorough frisking.

Still nervous and tense, the passengers resented the search but willingly submitted. They had looked forward to a relaxed flight back to Miami and the safety of home. But their hopes for a warm and friendly atmosphere aboard with a drink and hors d'oeuvres had been dashed by the cold, official reception.

An ambulance carrying Harold Johnson drove up to the departing airliner. The copilot was removed from the vehicle on a stretcher. However, he wanted to go aboard under his own strength. Donna and Karen ran over to the wounded pilot. Flanked on each side by the two smiling attendants, Johnson walked jauntily across the ramp and up the boarding steps.

Alex Halberstadt assisted Alvin Fortson up the steps.

"Do you plan to fly again, Mr. Fortson?" Halberstadt inquired.

"Nope," answered the old gentleman.

"Why not?" Halberstadt asked.

"Too much fuss," Fortson complained, apparently thinking his first flight typical of all flights.

Captain Haas and Morkill were the last to board the aircraft. Reaching the top of the steps, Haas put down the two flight bags he carried. Turning around toward the terminal building, he waved good-bye to the spectators and ground personnel. Then he entered the jetliner and sat down on the cockpit jump seat.

Haas couldn't believe the nightmare was drawing to a close. Seemingly, he had been out of contact with the

world of reality for weeks. Now that he had an opportunity
to think about what had happened, he didn't want to think
about it. He only wanted to get home to Ann and the
children. But events of the long ordeal intruded on his
thoughts as the jetliner rolled down the runway to become
airborne. There was the haunting sound of the cockpit door
crashing off of its hinges; the shouted order to "Head
north"; the terrified look on Donna's face; the voices that
threatened death constantly; the frustrated attempts to free
the hostages; the unforgettable settling of the aircraft to the
left, then the right, as the tires were shot out; the an-
guished cry of his first officer. That cry would never be
erased from his memory. Haas hoped he would never hear
a sound like that again as long as he lived.

When the Miami-bound jetliner leveled off at its cruising
altitude, Captain Shanahan announced to the passengers
the reason for the searches they had been subjected to.
And he told them, "We hope you will appreciate that the
searches were performed in the interest of your safety."

The whole thing sent Frank Morkill's imagination racing
off in all directions. He could have sworn he'd never seen
the passenger seated in front of him. He mentioned this to
another passenger, who sought to put Frank's mind at ease.
The mystery figure had been seated in the rear of the cabin
during the hijacking, Morkill was told. But Frank had been
to the rear of the compartment several times—to the rest
room and to talk to Cale. Why didn't he recognize the man?

Each time the man stood up—each time he lit a
cigarette—each time he leaned over and looked out the
window, Morkill froze with fright. What was going to happen next? Would he and the other passengers ever return
home to their waiting families? He wanted to yell for the
plane to stop and let him off. No more—no more. He could
take no more. *Am I cracking up?* he wondered. He passed
out.

When Morkill awoke, the jetliner was making its final
approach to Miami International Airport. What a beautiful
sight Miami was as the late afternoon sun played across the

verdant landscape and the multicolored buildings that stretched out to the horizon. He was awfully glad to have reached Miami—to be home at last. He couldn't wait to get off the aircraft.

Once on the ground, the airliner turned off of the runway and proceeded to a remote spot behind a row of hangars. FBI agents waited inside the facility to conduct a passenger debriefing. The remote location had been chosen in an attempt to isolate the passengers from news reporters and cameramen.

When the aircraft had parked, there were police running around everywhere, cordoning off the area. There were ambulances waiting with four stretchers—one each for Fortson, Robinson, Buchanan, and Johnson. The injured would be spared the FBI interrogation. While the debriefing was being conducted, they would be undergoing examination and treatment at nearby Hialeah Hospital. Later the passengers would reboard the aircraft for a flight that would carry them to their original destinations. Alvin Fortson's flight would end at Miami. His son, Calvin, had driven to Miami from Haines City, Florida. He would drive his father back to Haines City. The old man would spend the winter fishing after all.

Led into a large room, the passengers were equaled in number by FBI agents.

A persistent newsman tried to break through police lines. His determination to get to the passengers melted when a stern-faced security guard warned, "You are really bugging me. Get back or you'll cool it in jail."

The routine questioning by federal agents got underway. Each person was shown mug shots of the three hijackers. This was followed by two questions that never varied, "Are these the armed men who were aboard the aircraft?" and "Were you threatened?"

Each person identified Jackson, Moore, and Cale as their abductors. Each person acknowledged that he had been threatened.

When the interrogation was completed, immigration and

customs officials took over to conduct their clearance procedure. The formality was quickly completed.

Halberstadt, Wanklyn, and Morkill were released to proceed to their Miami homes.

The remaining twenty-one passengers returned to the aircraft to retrace the intended route of Southern 49 in reverse. There would be stops in Orlando, Montgomery, Atlanta, and Memphis. The crew would disembark in Atlanta for reunions with their families and further debriefing by company officials.

Dick Senft was among the first to speak out publicly on the ordeal of the hijacking. As soon as Senft arrived at Orlando, a reporter wanted to know if he had learned anything of lasting value from the experience. He answered, "I hope I have learned humility. I hope I have learned something about my future relationships with family and friends. I wish I could say I had learned to curb my anger at the hijackers, my anger at the FBI. I'm sorry, but I didn't. I'm afraid I still feel that both showed a cold disregard for the consequences of their actions in terms of human life."

Military bands marched up and down the ramp at José Marti Airport on Monday morning while the crew of mechanics and engineers worked to make remedial repairs to the hijacked airliner. Artillery pieces were drawn into place and fired. Troops paraded back and forth in precise formation. A huge poster bearing a picture of an Oriental man was hoisted into place on the exterior of the terminal building.

Captain Godwin asked the escort officer assigned to him what all of the pomp and circumstance was about. He was advised that the Defense Minister of Manchuria was scheduled to arrive the next day for an official state visit. The captain also learned that there would be no flights into or out of Havana during the one-day visit by the Chinese dignitary.

Passing the word along to his maintenance chief, Godwin

instructed, "Get some rubber on those gears, and do what you can to the damaged engines. We're flying out of here not later than six o'clock tonight."

While the work was underway, Swiss Embassy officials presented a stack of invoices for the captain's signature. Sandwiches, lemonade, and coffee furnished during the day for the mechanics totaled $115. When he got over the initial shock of those charges, another set of invoices was presented. They were for hotel accommodations for the crews and passengers at the Riviera Hotel, food and champagne for the banquet held Saturday night, breakfast at the hotel, and fuel taken on by the hijacked airliner. The charges also included each of the Havana cigars handed out to the male passengers and came to a grand total of $12,900. Castro's lavish entertaining would be charged to the airline. Godwin signed the invoices without protest. He didn't think he had any leverage with which to negotiate.

"What about the ransom money?" Godwin asked.

The Swiss advised that the Cubans had impounded the funds.

Work on the aircraft continued without letup throughout the afternoon. A few minutes before six o'clock, the exhausted maintenance personnel climbed aboard Southern 49 for the flight out of Cuba. They had replaced all of the main wheels and tires, exchanged the damaged nose tire for a good one, and made the necessary repairs to the engine and pressurization system. The jetliner would require more work—replacement of its engines and a complete refurbishing of its cabin—before it would be recertified as airworthy. But for the time being, Captains Godwin and Steele would take her home.

Taking off from José Marti Airport, the jetliner climbed to a flight level of 35,000 feet. As they were speeding northerly, an FAA air-traffic controller radioed a reminder that the aircraft's ferry permit called for termination of the flight at Miami.

"Negative," Godwin radioed back. "We are nonstop for

Atlanta."

Three hours later, Southern 49 penetrated a fast-moving squall line of thunderstorms southeast of Atlanta. Visibility at Hartsfield International was zero-zero. Godwin and Steele were too close to being home to divert to another airport. They piloted the aircraft in for an instrument landing.

Through the heavy rain and fog, they maneuvered the jetliner along taxiways and into a hangar. Giant doors were closed and bolted behind them.

Southern 49 was home again. The DC-9's wayfaring odyssey had ended.

14
Aftermath

The hurricanelike fury left behind in the wake of Flight 49's odyssey exacted a heavy toll from the lives of those on board.

It would take the passing of months and even years before the trauma of the event would be extricated from their memories.

Today, most of the hijack victims are able to go about their daily pursuits in a reasonably normal fashion. Each of the crew members continues to be numbered among the airline's "finest." The then first officer, Johnson, now wears the insignia of captain. He fully recovered the use of his right arm, although doctors decided against removing the bullet slug put there by Henry Jackson. Captain Johnson's real first name is Harloyd. But press accounts of the hijacking changed it to Harold.

The notoriety Captain Haas received has made difficult the quiet, contented farm life he and his family enjoyed prior to the incident.

Immediately after the piracy, Southern Airways began efforts to recover the ransom money appropriated by the Cuban government. Haas flew several unpublicized missions to Havana, accompanied by airline representatives who appealed for return of the money. Negotiations were conducted under the watchful eyes of the State Department. On August 9, 1975, Premier Castro authorized the return of the two million dollars to Southern. Shortly thereafter came a relaxation of trade barriers erected against Cuba by the United States and other Western Hemisphere nations during the 1962 missile crisis.

Captain Godwin chose to resign his position as a company vice-president in July of 1973 in order to return to the flight line. In November of 1976, medical examination revealed that the captain had developed a disqualifying hearing loss. He requested reconsideration of the FAA denial of his medical certificate renewal. But when the federal air surgeon failed to act upon his request, Godwin decided against further appeal to the National Transportation Safety Board in the belief it might result in an unjustifiable compromise with air safety. Instead, he prematurely ended his flight career at the age of fifty-three and entered retirement.

Alvin Fortson was confined later to a nursing home, where he died after several years. Ironically, the illness suffered by Fortson during the hijacking was diagnosed to have been an emphysema attack. A devout Baptist, he cherished and wore proudly the rosary given to him by Marge Brennan.

Premier Castro dealt personally with the fate of the three hijackers. He sentenced them to life imprisonment in individual cells measuring four-by-four-by-four feet. Castro merits the thanks of the American people for the speedy and appropriate punishment.

Extradition warrants are still outstanding for the trio. However, one shudders to speculate as to what might have been the result of their trial in United States courts. It is possible that the often lenient system of so-called justice would have produced a light sentence and eventually their freedom, to inflict even greater disregard for the rights of society.

Despite the human suffering brought about by the event, there were some positive consequences. The hijacking served as a catalyst for jolting a recalcitrant Ninety-third Congress and the State Department into long-overdue adoption of needed antihijacking measures.

The fallout from the pirating of the jetliner was extensive. Professional organizations within the aviation industry, most notably the Airline Pilots Association, had been waging a long-standing campaign for legislative action. They had met with only moderate success prior to the incident involving Flight 49.

The complacent mood of Congress was reflected in the month of October immediately preceding the piracy. Both the House and Senate had under consideration several pieces of legislation to combat the growing mania. One proposal sought to legalize air-service boycotts and other sanctions against nations that harbored air criminals. Another measure that originated in the Senate would have installed a tough airport-screening program, along with a thirty-five-million-dollar Air Transportation Security Force.

The Senate acted favorably on the legislation. The House chose to play a potentially deadly game of Russian roulette with the lives of the 170,000,000 passengers who annually boarded United States airliners. The lower House gave its support to only the international provisions of the proposals. Thus, the bills became bogged down between Senate and House conferees. That's where the legislative battle stood on November 10, 1972, the date of the hijacking.

The country's leaders had been given plenty of advance notice that the crime of air piracy demanded their attention as well as urgent action.

On a warm July day in 1961 at Chico, California, a Pacific Airlines DC-3 had been about to take off when a gunman tried to hijack the plane. Capt. O. W. Cleal resisted; there was a scuffle; and a bullet pierced the brain of the pilot, blinding him for life.

Cleal was the first American pilot to become a hijacking casualty. How many other pilot and passenger lives would be jeopardized before lawmakers would awaken to the problem?

During the late sixties, the incidence of hijackings had reached an average of twenty-nine a year.

National Airlines pilot Carl Greenwood earned the dubious distinction of having been hijacked on three separate occasions in 1969 and 1970. Each time Greenwood and his passengers ended up in Cuba.

Greenwood's hijackings numbered among 147 attempts that took place over a five-year period. Not all of the attempts succeeded. But an alarmingly high pecentage did succeed.

Pirates ranged from mental patients and henpecked husbands to would-be revolutionaries and at least one government bureaucrat. They could be classified in general as immature, sexually inadequate, demented persons struggling for undeserved recognition in a world that ignored them.

Some were shot. Others were killed. Still others were imprisoned in foreign jails.

Briefly stated, that was the sorry picture that should have served as a constant reminder to the airline industry, legislators, and public that a state of great urgency existed.

Shunning publicity after the hijacking, Captain Haas stated, "The only recognition I want, if I am due any, is to be the last hijacked pilot."

During the next few months Haas tried, without success, to regain a measure of the contentment and solitude that had been his before the incident. But his desire was not to be. Numerous professional and civic organizations wanted to gratefully acknowledge what Captain Haas had done "all in the line of duty." Being the kind of man he was and is, he would have preferred to forget the whole matter with the exception of several important aspects.

Haas was more than willing to devote his utmost energies to the accomplishment of two matters. First, he wanted to help build a fire under the seats of congressmen until they enacted the needed legislation that was stalled in Congress. Second, the captain wanted to impress upon local and federal law-enforcement agencies that no one should ever again forget that the lives and safety of airline passengers rest solely with the man in the left-hand cockpit seat.

The efforts he would make would exact time and money he could ill afford. But he considered the cost inconsequential when viewed against the value of human lives.

Fortunately, he wouldn't be alone in championing the causes. Some dedicated allies would come forward to join the battle.

Among the first was the man who Captain Haas bowed to as his hero of the Flight 49 hijacking, Frank Morkill.

The bravery and willingness of this man to assist the crew under the most frightening of circumstances was an act above and beyond that which could be expected of the average passenger.

The Canadian citizen, now a naturalized citizen of the United States, sat down and composed an eloquently impassioned plea for tighter security to deal with the problem.

Morkill addressed his letter to Captain J. J. O'Donnell, president of the Airline Pilots' Association. It deserves to be recorded as a part of the history-making efforts that urged legislative action. A portion of the text reads as follows:

"Frankly, I find it very hard to believe it was three weeks ago today that we were in the midst of our travels around the southeast and that it has been such a relatively short time since we almost came upon disaster at Orlando's McCoy Airport.

"I realize that this whole episode, from start to finish, was fraught with imminent disaster—and that we shall likely never know just how many times the skill and dedication of the crew averted serious or catastrophic situations during this long flight.

"On the other hand, however, I am in a position to state, without any doubt or hesitation, that I can attribute my own personal survival to two circumstances that can, and must, be clearly set out and documented.

"First, Henry Jackson did not shoot to wound Harold Johnson in the right arm. He shot at him, and might just as easily have killed him. If Harold had been killed, it could have turned into a completely different ball game—the hijackers with a death on their hands, and willing to spill more blood in their frenzied desperation.

"Second, Bill Haas got the aircraft off the ground—an act which immediately converted the situation from one of imminent crisis and certain serious injury or death for some or all of those aboard to that of a situation where, for the first time, the hijackers became totally aware of the fact that their lives now depended on what Bill Haas could do to avert disaster and save their skins, along with everyone else's aboard the airplane.

"I have my own personal views with regard to the controversy surrounding the FBI's actions at Orlando, but the fact of the matter is that they failed in their attempt to keep the aircraft on the ground. It was a direct result of this failure to execute their plan that the two events I have outlined in the previous two paragraphs came into play.

"The reason I bring this matter up at all is that it has not been clearly brought out—at least not to my knowledge— just what the FBI proposed to do with the situation if they had been successful in keeping this plane on the ground. What then? Negotiations? An assault up the back steps and front door, with bullets flying, and FBI agents as well as hijackers, crew, and passengers getting hit and, most probably, killed?

"Naturally, if any number of possible events had taken place at McCoy—even with substantial loss of life—the FBI or whomever would have come up smelling like roses. Even *that* would have seemed better than the alternative of this aircraft falling into the Atlantic on its long journey to Switzerland—or at least that is what we have been led to believe!

"Captain O'Donnell, this whole episode is so bizarre that it really defies proper description and documentation— only bits and pieces can be firmly grasped and discussed. Information concerning all the events surrounding this hijacking is most likely scattered all over the place, including Havana; and it will likely fall to but a few people in official places to know all the details about Flight 49's trip from Birmingham to José Marti.

"This much I know, however; and that is that this skyjacking might have taken place on any of the many airlines I use in my weekly business travels around the southeast. I have made five flights since November 20, and only on Southern have I felt confident that proper measures were being taken to screen passengers and their carryon luggage.

"I have been most attentive to news coming out of the ALPA meetings this week in Las Vegas and have only heard that some action might be taken when and if the next skyjacking takes place. I am quite frankly appalled at what appears to be official and public apathy about this case. It would appear that a veritable blanket has been thrown over this whole episode and that it is considered an unpleasant subject that should not be discussed because it might cause some embarrassment to the airlines industry and to certain nameless federal agencies who goofed and inconvenience to the traveling public as a whole.

"What if the next skyjacking, when it occurs, turns out to be a 747 with 280 passengers and 16 crew members aboard? Bill Haas averted disaster on our trip three weeks ago, but what will happen if the circumstances surrounding the next skyjacking are not as prone to miracles as this last one? What are we talking about the next one for, when we should be shouting about the last skyjacking?

"Personally, I thought there was a very strong possibility that I was about to die on two separate occasions—when Jackson and Moore were yelling and screaming, when they shot Harold—and again when Bill Haas was pulling that airplane off the ground, and we flew into some turbulence shortly after takeoff. I bring this up, Captain, because I certainly did not come through this whole episode to wait and see what actions were going to be taken after the next skyjacking occurs. I want to see some action as a result of Southern 49's skyjacking, which took place a whole three weeks ago!

"Perhaps it has all been for naught—but I trust not. Many, many times during the past three or four years we—among friends and family—have discussed this issue of skyjacking; and the consensus has been that it will take a major disaster to bring about some concrete worldwide action. There were moments on that flight three weeks ago that I thought, *If we were going to buy it, at least we might make our contributions to bringing about action in behalf of safer air travel in the future.* But we did not buy it, and I am now obligated to do all I can to help those who are sincerely interested in action to stop this lunacy—not just in words to pacify an embarrassed airline industry or an inconvenienced flying public.

"The fact of the matter, Captain O'Donnell, is that this very subject does not, as yet, enjoy the priority that common sense demands it have. The whole subject does not command the public or official interest that it should—mainly because there exists an astute effort to 'public relations' the whole matter into the background and hope that the 'next' potential disaster does not occur!"

Another of the hijacked passengers wasted no time in making his voice heard. Gale Buchanan put the imperative need for action on the desk of his Alabama congressman, Bill Nichols. In part he wrote:

"It was my misfortune to be included among those involved in the recent hijacking of Southern Airways Flight 49. Having been involved in the ordeal, I wish to share with you my feelings regarding such an event. I am sure you realize, just as well as I do, that experiencing one hijacking does not make me an authority on the subject. But I do feel that my ideas and impressions might be of some value in helping you in your actions in Washington.

"The experience of a hijacking such as Flight 49 is something neither I nor any of the others will ever forget. A major portion of time was keen fear, but there were several hours of pure, stark terror!

"I will divide my comments into three main areas. First, prevention of hijackings; second, action taken by authorities once a hijacking has occurred; and third, establishing diplomatic relations with Cuba. Insofar as preventing hijacking, we have not done *all* we can do. For example, on Monday after we had returned from Cuba on Sunday, I made two domestic flights. I was not thoroughly checked on either of these flights. In fact, I was not checked until I prepared to board a BOAC flight in New York's Kennedy Airport bound for London. On my return, TWA made a thorough search in London prior to boarding for the United States; but once in the US, I made two domestic flights without a close inspection.

"I have no idea of the security situation in Birmingham prior to the departure of Flight 49, since I had boarded in Memphis. But this is all history. Speaking of history, I like to recall the extent our government has gone to in the past to protect its citizens. A good case in point is the effort made in the decade prior to the Civil War to protect the early settlers and covered-wagon trains that opened up the western United States. In fact, over 50 percent of the United States Army was deployed in the West simply to protect the citizens. I know they were not always successful, but at least tremendous efforts were made. Can we do any less now? I am not saying that this is a job of the United States Army; I am simply using this illustration as an example of the past efforts made by the government of our country to protect its citizens.

"Also, I am trying to point out that any type of surveillance program will cost a considerable amount of money—far more than the airlines can and should be expected to pay. As a frequent air traveler, I feel it is the responsibility of my government to offer the necessary protection against such incidents as the recent hijacking. The airlines have their hands full worrying about keeping the planes mechanically safe, flying, and on a reasonable schedule. Until effective surveillance programs can be put into operation, what we should do is come up with a better set of standing operating procedures for any such incidences in the future."

Buchanan urged the establishment of a system of communications between a hijacked plane and the ground.

"If we had effective means of communication between pilot and control, such incidents as the FBI's opening fire on the plane in Orlando could be averted. In my opinion, shooting the tires from the plane was ill-advised and cannot be justified. What if we had not been able to get airborne? What if we could not have moved the aircraft at all? Was the FBI going to shoot the lock off the door of the aircraft? Just how were they going to get into that plane? I am sure that the hijackers would not have thrown up their hands at the command of the FBI agents outside the plane. If the pilot had not been able to move the aircraft, I feel sure that the passengers and crew would have not survived the shoot-out that surely would have followed. What this all boils down to is that once it is ascertained that a hijacker cannot endanger the lives of others by flying the aircraft himself, then the captain of the aircraft *should be in complete command.*

"Thirdly, I would like to encourage that we try to reach some type of agreements with Cuba. I feel sure that with better relations with all countries, the chances of ending a hijacking successfully (as far as passengers and crew are concerned) would be enhanced. For example, the pilot could communicate the type of reception that might get the hijackers off the plane. Once on the ground, the hijackers could be dealt with far more effectively. In other words, if the right kind of committee had been on hand the first time we landed in Havana, Cuba, the hijackers *might* have been enticed to get off and end the hijack. This is, of course, speculation; but such an operation would have far more opportunity for success if we had better relations with the country involved. Establishing better relations with Cuba is very complicated, I realize. But why not make some efforts? We trade with China, Russia, and other nations with Communist ties.

"Finally, I was quoted in the paper as saying, 'Our pilot, Bill Haas, was the most courageous man I ever knew.' I was quoted absolutely correctly. He is! The remainder of the crew performed in the same fashion. Also, I feel every passenger conducted himself or herself as they wished they had. *No one* lost his head or did anything but what was absolutely correct and proper in such a situation.

"If I have been overly critical of the FBI, it is in the hopes that no one else has to undergo the ordeal those of us on Flight 49 experienced."

Armed with compelling reasons and a new sense of urgency, the forces demanding antihijacking action mounted steadily. By mid-December, 1972—one month after the Southern Airways incident—the movement was going forward on two broad fronts: international and domestic.

In January, 1973, the domestic attack brought desired action that would help put a stop to air piracy where it begins—on the ground.

The Federal Aviation Agency was empowered to implement stringent new measures of security at 531 of the nation's airports.

Armed guards were posted to seal off access to airliners. An elaborate electronic screening process aimed at both passengers and luggage was initiated. Terminal-building security was made as impregnable as possible.

A part of the program involved the special training of flight crews to deal more effectively with hijackers. And an exchange system among hijacked crews of the various airlines came into being to make possible the sharing of lessons learned.

As its advocates expected, the measures proved costly in terms of money, requiring an annual outlay in the neighborhood of $100,000,000. The cost would be borne by the traveling public through a surcharge of sixty-two cents a ticket.

A look at just one phase of the security measures proves their worth. During the program's first year of operation the seizure of weapons from passengers turned up 1600 guns, 1021 explosive devices, 15,731 knives, and over 20,000 other potentially dangerous items, such as firecrackers, starter pistols, pellet guns, cattle prods, toy pistols, blow guns, and machetes.

On the international front, impetus was growing to enlist the cooperation of other nations in the elimination of their territories from the unofficial list of hijacker havens.

February 15, 1973, became the historic day when an agreement was effected between the United States and Cuba, setting forth a five-year agreement that closed the doors of the two countries to all except political refugees. It marked the first agreement of any kind between Washington and Havana in over a decade. Two years later the total embargo imposed against the Castro government in 1962 was relaxed.

The main feature of the hijack pact between the two countries provided for the extradition of anyone who "seizes, removes, appropriates, or diverts from its normal route or activities" any ship or aircraft belonging to either country, and for the prosecution "with a view to severe punishment" of anyone preparing or taking part in a raid against either country.

Although Captain Haas declines modestly to accept any of the credit for the thawing of relations between the United States and Cuba, one State Department official attributed the improved atmosphere to the captain's demonstration of courage and to the conduct of his crew and the passengers aboard Flight 49.

Prime Minister Castro's personal direction of emergency precautions during the final landing at Havana demonstrated the Cuban leader's grave concern for the victims of the hijacking. The hijack pact evidenced his determination to end once and for all the illusion that Cuba meant freedom for those who placed in jeopardy the lives of innocent persons.

Swiss and Czech diplomats, acting on behalf of the United States and Canada, had been able to hammer out an agreement acceptable to the two signatories within the remarkable period of only three months.

The net results of the actions taken may be summed up by pointing out that in 1972 there was the average number of successful hijackings. Flight 49 was the thirtieth. It has become the last successful armed air piracy in the United States!

There have been several other attempts at hijacking since then. They involved drunks, mental patients, persons under the influence of hard drugs, and a group of political dissidents. But these persons were all apprehended.

Would-be hijackers are confronted by almost insurmountable odds, with the probable reward for their efforts being life imprisonment—if they survive the attempt.

In November, 1972, L. Patrick Gray III served as a temporary appointee to succeed the late J. Edgar Hoover as FBI director. Little did Gray realize that the three hijackers who boarded Flight 49 at Birmingham would involve him in a controversy that would contribute to the withdrawal of his nomination.

Gray accepted full responsibility for the orders given to disable the jetliner at Orlando.

The action violated one of maritime tradition's oldest unwritten laws and one actually included among the statutes of most maritime nations. That dictum gives the captain of a seagoing vessel ultimate responsibility for everything that transpires aboard that ship.

The same tradition has extended to the ships of the sky.

Gray's predecessor, Mr. Hoover, wisely recognized that tradition. Such a policy was in effect among the Justice Department, the Federal Aviation Agency, and the Federal Bureau of Investigation. Mr. Gray either failed to acquaint himself with the policy or chose to ignore it altogether. The policy established by Mr. Hoover said: "The captain of an aircraft is by far the most qualified to make an on-the-spot determination as to the dangerousness of a hijacker; and he should be the one to recommend that action be taken to disable an aircraft or to board it in order to apprehend the hijacker. Our experience has shown that without prior knowledge and the complete cooperation of the captain and his crew, any action by outside forces could end in total disaster."

Several months after the hijacking and the tire-shooting at Orlando took place, the United States Senate took up the matter of Gray's nomination to be the FBI's permanent director.

Gray had already become embroiled in other controversies related to the Watergate affair. Under questioning, he was subjected to sharp criticism on a variety of issues. Before leaving the witness stand, Republican Sen. Richard Gurney of Florida sought to ease at least one controversy that swarmed around the embattled nominee. Senator Gurney began the dialogue.

"One other thing, as a matter of local importance, because it involved severe criticism of the FBI at the time. You may recall the incident of the Southern Airways airplane that cavorted around the United States and Cuba and even Canada, once landing in Orlando, Florida, my hometown. Either some of its tires were shot, or an attempt at such was made. It went to a belly landing in Havana at the time it came down. The FBI was criticized for this, and I do not think the true story has ever really come out. Would you spend a few minutes describing that incident?"

Mr. Gray summed up his explanation of the incident for committee members.

"Yes, Senator Gurney, I would.

"I was in Connecticut at my home Friday evening late when I received the first telephone call of the hijacking from my command center headquarters in Washington. I received several more telephone calls throughout that evening. Those were all informative calls in nature, requiring no decision on my part at the time.

"Then, in the early-morning hours, telephone calls were picked up again and through the day. I stayed in contact, going right down into the evening, and into the evening reports began to come in to the effect that our personnel were in touch with the airline company and with the Federal Aviation Agency. By use of a special circuit we are all linked together and also with the White House Situation Room.

"But the information began to come in toward the end of the afternoon that this thing was reaching a very severe stress situation, not only from the standpoint of equipment but also from the perspective of personal fatigue. Further, the oil condition in the engines was becoming rather severe; in fact, the pilot himself, in landing at Key West, stated over the circuit that he would have to have oil or the engines would cease to function.

"Just shortly before 8:00 Southern Airways, with whom we were in constant contact, stated that it was their recommendation that the flight not be permitted to leave Orlando, that the lives of all on board would be seriously jeopardized because of the condition I have previously enumerated if the airliner were permitted to leave Orlando.

"I can recall that after getting the call, I had about twenty minutes. I sat down and wrote out the pros and cons. I knew that our people in Knoxville had, earlier in the day and on a similar-type aircraft, practiced an assault on it on the ground. I knew that if we disabled that aircraft, we had to be prepared immediately to go in and get the people.

"Another factor—we also knew that these men who had hijacked the aircraft wanted to go either to Africa or Switzerland because they were asking for charts. We knew that the aircraft could not go there.

"So I made the decision at 8:00. I called my command post and told them, 'I am ordering that the tires be shot out of this aircraft.' This was the recommended—a recommended procedure, one that had been investigated, checked with the FAA, checked with the airlines. All said, 'Shoot the tires out, and you disable the aircraft.' There are other ways—we could have sprayed CO_2 into the engines, but these particular hijackers were awfully jumpy. They would make the pilot take off even if they saw people out on the ends of the airway there, anywhere near it. They would let no one approach the plane.

"The pilot was not a free agent; there was no way in the world of getting to him. My special agent-in-charge, leading the special agents, got under the aircraft while it was immobile and stationary at Orlando and went to the fuel truck that was parked some fifty feet away from the aircraft (in fact, aft of the starboard beam of the aircraft) to see if there were any headphones he could plug in to tell the pilot. There were no headphones, and he came back and began to shoot out the tires. The agents did shoot them out.

"As they were starting to put their fingers on the button to open the doors to assault the aircraft, that plane took off at full throttle and went down the runway. Now, no one thought that plane would ever get off the ground. Apparently, in hindsight, it was loaded lightly enough so that it generated its own air cushion and was able to get off the ground.

"Since then—well, during the immediate period following that, when I took the full responsibility, which of course is mine—I had a call from a United Airlines pilot who said to me, "You are taking a lot of heat, but if I am ever in the same situation, come and get me."

"I got a letter from a passenger on the plane who related to me that prior to the shooting out of the tires, the attitude of the hijackers had been dictatorial, domineering, arrogant. After the shooting out of the tires, all the hijackers wanted to do was to get back to Cuba, which they had previously decided was not the place for them. Yet they knew they had to get on the ground, and their attitude changed completely, this passenger said.

"I just rode up yesterday—Monday—came back from Florida with a National Airlines captain who, when we ended the flight, came back to talk to me and say, 'I know you have gotten a lot of heat on the Southern Airways situation, but if I am in that situation, come and get me. You have my complete confidence.'

"This is a rough sequence of the events, Senator Gurney. These were the reasons why we did what we did. We were trained to do it. We had taken every possible step to ready ourselves to do this. In fact, our training program with the airline companies has been extensive. We have worked very, very closely with aircraft crews, and we have helped to train them as to how to react to this type of situation."

Senator Gurney said he appreciated the explanation given and that he had asked the question because a lot of people had gotten the idea that the tires were shot out after the plane was in the air and airborne.

"No, sir, it was stationary, not mobile at all," Gray concluded.

Gray's testimony was riddled with inaccuracies. His statement that the airline recommended the tire shooting was never refuted by the company. Few government-regulated enterprises can afford to challenge Washington bureaucrats. However, the fact is that the official with whom Gray conferred expressed a great reluctance to see Gray's proposed plan carried out.

The FBI chief's contention that the aircraft could not have gone to Switzerland was not true. Captain Haas was confident the DC-9 could have flown to Europe along the route he proposed, provided a navigator and overseas charts were put on board in Orlando.

While it is true that the captain was not a completely free agent when Southern 49 landed in Orlando, he was in contact with the control tower, through which the FBI could have ascertained if Haas would have advised armed intervention. His response would have been in the negative, and the unnecessary risk taken with the lives of those aboard could have been avoided.

Gray's claim that the fuel truck was parked fifty feet away from the aircraft, aft of the starboard beam, was a gross misstatement. The truck and its highly explosive supply of fuel was parked at a forty-five-degree angle from the right cockpit window, forward of the aircraft.

The support Gray boasted he had received from the pilot of another airline is not questioned. However, it is the type of judgment demonstrated by Captain Haas throughout the hijacking that spells the difference between good pilots and great pilots.

Appearing before the Subcommittee on Transportation and Aeronautics of the House Interstate and Foreign Commerce Committee, Captain Haas voiced the majority opinion of his contemporaries.

"Mr. Chairman, I would like to touch upon the one aspect of my particular incident that makes it somewhat unique. My hijacking almost ended in total disaster. While it is true that the flight was in jeopardy from the moment those three criminals stepped on board, it is also true to say that the interference from those people on the ground who were trying to help not only compounded the danger facing my crew and passengers, but was the prime cause of the highly dangerous takeoff and landing I was obligated to accomplish. I am an experienced pilot, but, to this day, I am still astonished that the last leg of that frightening trip ended without loss of life.

"As an airline captain, I accept the tasks and responsibilities of my job. My training and the constant honing of my professional skills ensure my passengers a safe flight. As in a hijacking, when other factors outside those normally encountered in my job thrust themselves upon me, my training and professional skills are still the best weapons to overcome those difficulties.

"When the armed assault was launched on my aircraft, I was totally unprepared, as well as completely surprised. I was within an inch of finally negotiating the release of my passengers and an agreement for a relatively safe flight to Switzerland.

"Gentlemen, as the captain, I had been with these criminals for more than twenty-nine hours. I had reached the point of at least some understanding as to their condition and weaknesses. For an outside force to inject themselves, violently and without my knowledge, was in my opinion foolhardy, to say the least.

"As an airline pilot, I have accepted the awesome responsibilities thrust upon me. I am checked over and over again to determine if I am capable of handling those responsibilities. Why is it that in such a situation as I found myself, people not qualified in aviation matters or aerodynamics made life-and-death decisions affecting my life and the lives of my crew and passengers? This I cannot accept.

"I have always believed that the captain's authority is inviolable. That belief enables me to function in my job. When the situation gets as rough and bizarre as in a hijacking, an airline captain has only three things going for him—skill, training, and authority. He must be allowed to remain the master of his vessel. No one is qualified to control the destiny of my flight from anywhere but the flight deck.

"I can see no circumstances where this rule could be violated. The consequences are appalling. In my case, this could very well have led to some Monday-morning quarterback's explanation of what went wrong . . . being read to my widow and children and the relatives of my passengers and fellow crew members."

During the weeks and months that followed the hijacking, Captain Haas received numerous citations and awards, among them the coveted Daedalus Award presented by an organization composed of World War I pilots.

Citing his "judgment, bravery, patience, and fortitude in the face of overwhelming odds," the Airline Pilots Association bestowed upon him its Gold Medal for heroism. The citation that accompanied the medal said the safe termination of the flight against such odds was "unprecedented and deserving of the highest tribute from his fellow pilots."

While Captain Haas acknowledged the special recognition with pride, the award of which he is proudest was presented by Lloyds' of London. It's an antique gold clock that sets on the mantel in the sitting room of his Tennessee home.

The simple inscription on the clock reads: "For devotion

to duty."

Lloyds' had a long-standing tradition of honoring sea captains for staying with their distressed ships despite great odds of survival.

Capt. William R. Haas became the first airline pilot in history to be so honored for saving his aircraft and its passengers.

The insurance underwriters arranged a special banquet in his honor in London for the presentation of the award.

On receiving the unprecedented recognition, Haas addressed the distinguished group who assembled for the occasion.

"Ladies and gentlemen—I appreciate the honor you have bestowed upon me here tonight. In accepting this award I do so on behalf of myself and my crew.

"It has been my misfortune, since arriving in London, to have caught the flu. Of necessity, I shall be brief. I am an airline pilot, not a public speaker. And I haven't had an opportunity to think about something to say to you. But there are a couple of thoughts I would like to leave with you.

"First, I'd like to thank all of those people on the ground and in the air who tried to help us with their support and their prayers. We deeply appreciate their assistance, and I am confident that the safe ending of the hijacking resulted not so much from anything I did, but from all the prayers of all the people everywhere. When I returned home following this incident, there were hundreds of letters and telegrams from people everywhere who got down on their knees and asked God to spare the lives of those of us on board. The reading of those messages was one of the most touching and moving experiences I shall ever know.

"There's been a lot of rhetoric—I think that's what it's called—used to refer to my actions during the hijacking. I have been referred to as an intrepid airman for getting the aircraft off the ground in Orlando and down again in Havana. I had to look up the word in the dictionary to see just what "intrepid" means. Frankly, I had never thought of myself in terms that merit such a description. And I must say in all humility that I don't think of myself in those terms now.

"There's no doubt in my mind that what we experienced was a miracle, from the beginning to the end of that thirty-hour nightmare.

"It was a part of the design of that miracle that most of the passengers I brought out of Memphis got off at Birmingham and only a few boarded there to continue the flight. It meant that with only a few passengers and their baggage, we had a light load aboard, which worked in our favor at Orlando. It was a miracle that the engines performed as they did toward the final hours, when the oil had dwindled low. It was a miracle that my first officer was wounded, not killed. And it was the strength of Almighty God that lifted us skyward when the dark cloak of death sought to enshroud us at Orlando.

"It's just hard for me to describe to you what happened there. I remember when the gunfire started inside the aircraft, somebody hollered, 'They're just blanks.' Well—that may have been what everybody thought until Harold Johnson's arm exploded in their faces and blood splattered all over the place. And when they saw those blanks tearing gaping holes in people—in a person's arm, you know—they realized that they weren't blanks. And Harold was gonna be the first body that those three stuck through the window.

"I tell you—it must've been much easier for those guys out there. I don't see how it could've been, but it must have been much easier for those guys out there on the ground shooting holes in those tires. You can always say—well—you know—you've got orders. I'm a good soldier. And I believe in the military maxim to sacrifice the few to save the many. But—I tell you—when you happen to be among the few, you've got second thoughts about that.

"I don't know—there's no way to describe it. You would have had to be there to know what happened on the ground at Orlando. And—just—just be crying buckets of tears at the sight. 'Cause that's the way it was down there. That is honestly the way it was. I can hardly think about it without getting misty. Man—that was horrible.

"And in Harold's behalf—he was the guy looking down the barrel. He was the guy fixin' to get snuffed out. I don't care what anybody says, everybody on that airplane should have the Congressional Medal of Honor—not counting me—but I mean everybody on there did their part above and beyond the call of duty. Marge—Frank—Alex—every one of them. And Harold—he gets a Purple Heart, too.

"You know, I felt—I don't know what I felt like. I felt like I was just trying to keep everybody alive. I don't know. How else can you say it, you know? It's been drummed into my head over the years of flying: First protect the people, and then you protect that airplane. Then you protect yourself. Seems like kinda an asinine way to look at it. But you never completely forget that you're up there, too. I mean when it comes right down to it—I think a good airline pilot, first of all, even when he sees—like the boy who saw he was gonna crash in that schoolyard out in California. He didn't eject. He controlled the airplane even though it was on fire. He tried to get it out to sea so it wouldn't hit that schoolyard. He didn't even have time to think that he was dying. He just knew that he didn't want to kill those kids.

"And I don't know—maybe that's the kind of stuff airline pilots are made of. I hope I've got some of that in me. I think any human being with any kind of feelings whatsoever for others will think of his own life secondly. I think all airline pilots and maybe all people have the same thing.

"I think all airline pilots are a special breed of people. I think they have to be to go through the type of stuff they go through with. We get adequate compensation. Don't get me wrong. But I think we try to do the job.

"And at least I hope that I can live up to the Airman's Creed."

Epilogue

The Airman's Creed of the Airline Pilots Association reads, in part, as follows:

"An airline pilot will keep uppermost in his mind that the safety, conduct, and well-being of the passengers who entrust their lives to him are his first and greatest responsibility.

"He will never permit external pressures or personal desires to influence his judgment; nor will he knowingly do or permit any member of his crew to do anything that could jeopardize the safety of his airplane or anyone aboard.

"He will remember that an act of omission can be as hazardous as a deliberate act of commission; and he will not permit himself or any member of his crew to neglect any detail that can contribute to the safety of his flight or to perform any operation in a negligent or careless manner.

"Consistent with his primary responsibility for the safety of his airplane and all those aboard, he will at all times endeavor to maneuver his aircraft in such a manner as will contribute to the comfort, peace of mind, and well-being of his passengers and as will instill confidence in him, his crew, and in the airline he represents.

"Once he has discharged his primary responsibility for

the safety and comfort of his passengers, he will remember that they depend on him to do all possible to deliver them to their scheduled destination at the scheduled time.

"If disaster in some form should overtake him, he will not leave his airplane until he has done all within his power to ensure the safety of his passengers and crew."

To that creed the crew of Southern 49 was faithful!